HITLER'S
GRANDS PRIX
IN ENGLAND

HITLER'S GRANDS PRIX IN ENGLAND
Donington 1937 and 1938

Christopher Hilton

FOREWORD BY TOM WHEATCROFT

Haynes Publishing

First published in 1999

A catalogue record for this book is
available from the British Library

ISBN 1 85960 630 X

Library of Congress catalog card no 99-72051

Haynes North America Inc.,
861 Lawrence Drive, Newbury Park,
California 91320, USA.

Published by Haynes Publishing, Sparkford,
Nr Yeovil, Somerset BA22 7JJ, UK.

Tel: 01963 440635 Fax: 01963 440001
Int.tel: +44 1963 440635 Int.fax: +44 1963 440001

E-mail: sales@haynes-manuals.co.uk
Web site: www.haynes.co.uk

Designed and typeset by
G&M, Raunds, Northamptonshire
Printed and bound in Great Britain by J.H. Haynes & Co. Ltd, Sparkford

Contents

Introduction and acknowledgements

POLITICS AND SPORT are by definition incompatible, and they're combustible when mixed. The 1930s proved that: the Winter Olympics in Germany in 1936, when the President of the International Olympic Committee threatened to cancel the Games unless the anti-semitic posters were all taken down *now,* whatever Aldof Hitler decrees; the 1936 Summer Games in Berlin and Hitler's look of utter disgust when Jesse Owens, a negro, won the 100 metres; the World Heavyweight title fight in 1938 between Joe Louis, a negro, and Germany's Max Schmeling which carried racial undertones and overtones. The fight lasted 2 minutes 4 seconds, and in that time Louis knocked Schmeling down four times. They say that some of Schmeling's teeth were found embedded in Louis's glove...

Motor racing, a dangerous but genteel activity in the 1920s and early 1930s, was touched by this, too, and touched hard. The combustible mixture produced two Grand Prix races at Donington Park, in 1937 and 1938, which were just as dramatic, just as sinister and just as full of foreboding. This is the full story of those races.

The origins of the book rest with Maurice Hamilton, a distinguished writer about Formula One, who, in researching his own books *Grand Prix British Winners* (Guinness) and particularly *British Grand Prix* (Crowood), discovered that far more information was available than he could possibly use about these two races.

More, he felt they should be set in their proper political context: Britain and Germany tramping inevitably into the great darkness of the Second World War *as the races were happening*: two mighty German racing teams – and their drivers, who still linger in deed and mythology – echoing round a track laid in the grounds of a genteel English stately home with war likely not just today but *now*. Into this flowed sub plots: a love story, a seam of blind nationalism and a portrait of two cultures. Just this once, stereotypes are true. Nazi Germany asserted its naked and gathering strength while

British amateurs bumbled along wonderfully. The two races and the events surrounding them reflected this with what we can now see was haunting precision.

Swastikas would fly at Donington and a German motorsport chief gave the Nazi salute to the Duke of Kent, who expressed his disgust impeccably. A sub-plot flowed through that, too, because Donington had been used as a prison for captured German soldiers in the First World War.

By coincidence I was into a political study of the history of Berlin so I could (hopefully) cope with the political context easily enough but, that aside, I pay my dues to those who have helped so much: Tom Wheatcroft, Murray Walker, Donald Hamilton-James, Rob Walker, Anthony Powys-Lybbe, Tich Allen, Arthur Tyler, Derek and Billy Wing, Phil Heath, John Dugdale; Liz Raciti, Jaguar Public Relations, New York; Louis Klemantaski, David Tremayne, Don Woodward; Stan Peschel of the Mercedes-Benz Museum, Stuttgart; Mike Evans of Rolls-Royce; Karen Behr of the Library of Foreign Affairs, Bonn; Joan Williamson, librarian at the RAC Club, London; Dave Fern, Press Officer of the Donington racing circuit; Birgit Kubisch in Berlin, Inga and Barbel in England for translations; Chas Rushton of Lookers, Burton-on-Trent; Michael Passmore, Archives, the Automobile Association; Lothar Franz of Auto-Union; Sergio of British Movietone News; John Gillies Shields for hospitality, memories and lending a wealth of printed material; David Hayhoe, co-complier of the *Grand Prix Data Book*; John Surtees; Rob Widdows, Press Officer of the Goodwood Festival of Speed; Kate Scott of the BRDC; Ian Connell, Wilkie Wilkinson and the late Charlie Martin for broaching their racing memories.

Nigel Roebuck, another distinguished Formula One writer, was a constant source of information, feeding me books, video tapes and his own guidance. He also provided the memories of Rene Dreyfus, who drove in the 1938 race. Eoin Young telephoned with a list of people worth contacting. Colin Warrington of Christie's was instrumental in uniting me with original source material. I owe very particular gratitude to Alan Preston for finding and putting me in touch with people who were at the two races. Preston, incidentally, is working on a history of bike and car racing at Donington before the War and so was perfectly placed to know. I owe a deep debt too, to Paul Parker, motor racing historian and author, for reading the manuscript and making so many invaluable suggestions.

I have cast far and wide for material and rather than list all the sources here they appear in the *Notes* section. I've tried to expand these *Notes* to give background information, whether strictly relevant or (sometimes) not. Often what the sources say is contradictory but it is all we have and I have tried to rationalise the contradictions.

A bibliography appears at the end of the book for further reading, as the saying goes, but I pay more dues. The work of Chris Nixon in researching this period is so broad, deep and important that you can't really begin without his books *Racing the Silver Arrows* and *Rosemeyer!* at your elbow. I thank him for permission to quote from them and for help whenever I asked.

Doug Nye is a historian of exacting standards and comprehensive knowledge: you need his work, too and thanks to him for permission to quote as well as providing a lovely anecdote...

The specialist magazines – *The Autocar, The Light Car, Motor Sport*, and *The Motor* – were invaluable for all the obvious reasons. Copyright rests with Haymarket Magazines Limited and I'm indebted to Simon Taylor, Chairman, and Eric Verdon-Roe, Managing Director, for permission to quote. I owe another debt to Verdon-Roe, because he provided me with the diary entries of his namesake. William Boddy, MBE and Founder Editor of *Motor Sport*, has very kindly allowed me to use extracts of his vivid reporting. The passages from *Berlin Diary* by William Shirer are by permission of the William L. Shirer Literary Trust.

Equally invaluable were the national and local newspapers, especially *The Sporting Life,* whose reporter Tommy Wisdom is still remembered with affection. I hope that the quantity of *Notes* captures my debt to all these sources. A word of thanks to the British Newspaper Library in north London, that magnificent mine of the printed word.

Please note that in the 1930s Britain used three units of currency, pounds (£), shillings (s) and pence (d). For those too young to remember, there were 12 pennies to a shilling and 20 shillings to a pound. Random example: £2 17s 4d was two pounds, 17 shillings and fourpence. It confused foreign visitors completely – including the Germans who came to Donington in 1937 and 1938.

In the text I have left the money as it was expressed at the time, for authenticity and because translating it into today's equivalent is meaningless. Another random example: a room then in a three-star hotel cost the equivalent of 35p now.

Every effort has been made to trace the copyright holders of each extract quoted in the text – and illustrations – but it has not always been possible to find them. If inadvertently I have transgressed – sorry.

Incidentally, a goodly selection of video tapes surrounding the events of 1937 and 1938 – on the track and off it – is available as well as original clips from Movietone News. In videos, the *Shell History of Motor Racing* Volume 2, covering 1930 to 1939, is particularly evocative – and so is *Donington Park: The pre-war Years* (Hay Fisher). Overall, however, the videos present a paradox, because they allow you to witness what the reporters at Donington – in a distant hut and without television – could not. A random example: during the 1938 race a spectacular multi-car incident, which happened far out of sight of the Press hut, was wildly mis-reported. I know because I sit here six decades later, my video flicking through the incident frame by frame, and I can see it all so clearly...

Foreword

I FEEL VERY PRIVILEGED to write this foreword for a book delving deeply into a subject which has so many personal associations for me. I was lucky enough to have been taken – at a young and impressionable age on the back of a motorcycle – to the 1935 Grand Prix at Donington Park. It was only 30 miles from my home and until the outbreak of war I cycled the round trip in all weathers to see every race.

In those days, Silkolene Oil sponsored the bridge at Coppice Corner (and I believe the advertising banners from it still exist). If it had not been for the kindness they extended to me – I was almost an 'adopted son'! – I don't believe I would have held the passion for motorsport that I do. My racing car museum is located on the site of the bridge.

Those races of 1937 and 1938, with the powerful and dominant Mercedes and Auto Union cars battling it out, were the years when grand prix racing became forever imprinted on my imagination. The speeds, the sounds and the smells seemed to me genuinely fantastic – they were awesome compared to our more modest cars like the ERAs.

I well remember being invited to the prizegiving at Donington Hall and often think of the massive marquee positioned on the lawn, but I can't help reflecting that if I saw it again today it would be dwarfed by what have become standard-size marquees. Memory plays such tricks. When Tazio Nuvolari won the 1938 race, the trophy also seemed massive (the more so, I suppose, because Nuvolari was so small) but it's those things which stay with you and it's hard for me to realise it was all 60 years ago.

When I look back I judge that motor racing was more exciting then – but don't forget we could literally get closer to the action and so witness at close hand, as it were, the struggles and the physical effort required to drive – with opposite lock – the thunderous Auto Unions, their back ends sliding out. And of course we saw that great British driver Dick Seaman in one of the 'Silver Arrows' – the Mercedes.

We could not be sure whether war was coming, and I remember the day in 1938 when the international situation was so bad that the two German teams made a run for home from Donington. Mercedes were locked in a police station yard for protection in Leicester and the Auto Union convoy rested in the courtyard of an hotel in Market Harborough. I saw both – and as a teenager on a motor bike, watching them, I never dreamt that one day I'd own Donington Park. I am pleased, incidentally, that this book sets out the political background to the races, and those uncertain days we all lived through.

During the war the Park was requisitioned by the Ministry of Defence and became one of the largest vehicle depots in the country. After the war it drifted into dereliction. In 1971 I was 'nosing' around and was told in no uncertain terms that I had no right to be there unless I wanted to buy it! After a week of negotiations I did...

So I embarked on a long battle, and an extensive development programme, to restore the circuit to greatness. Racing finally did begin again and, in 1993 – the 60th anniversary year of the first car race there – I achieved a lifetime's ambition by returning a Grand Prix to Donington. It gave me particular pleasure that it was an heroic race won by Ayrton Senna, a man I knew well, who will be treasured as one of the greatest of all drivers – just like Nuvolari who I'd watched winning so heroically in 1938.

Tom Wheatcroft

Chapter 1

From
a distance

A PATTERN OF SHADOWS fell across the concrete, moving rapidly. The car which cast these shadows was long, lean, damn near monstrously brutal and being worked hard enough to suck tongues of flame from its exhaust.

July 1997, and an ordinary afternoon in a suburb of Stuttgart called Untertürkheim; warm, then a flurry of plump raindrops from bruised cloud, then warm again with enough sunshine leaking through to create the shadows.

The man arm-wrestling this car round the Mercedes test track was David Coulthard, a current Formula One driver and authentic to that breed, fit and of steady nerve. After three laps he slowed and halted. Even at rest, the car's engine gurgled and churned as if it wanted to shriek. Coulthard's eyes seemed enlarged as he said "this is from a different time altogether. I just cannot relate. You have to drive it to appreciate how frightening it is."

Coulthard's run was a few days before the German Grand Prix, up the autobahn at Hockenheim. It was a chance for the assembled Press to experience what this car looked and sounded like, and an opportunity for Coulthard to experience what it really felt like.

In that different time altogether, October 1937, mist hung over the parkland of Donington and, when enough sun had leaked through to burn it off, *this* car and the others like it created the same pattern of shadows as they brought a phlegmatic English crowd to intoxication and almost to fear. Hardened reporters babbled about being shaken and breathless.

This is the story of a sequence of seemingly different political and social events which stretched full through the 1930s and embraced a host of totally different people, from Adolf Hitler to a 14-year-old building worker from Leicester earning 12s 6d a week. The events were drawn across the full width of human experience, from the most momentous to the most humble, and ultimately they found an extraordinary unity in two sporting events. It's also a story of sharpest irony and contrast, not least because it is centred around such an intrinsically genteel place as Donington Hall which, situated in the countryside between Derby, Nottingham and Leicester, ought properly to have been lost in the slumber of centuries.

That is the first of the sharp ironies because, as it would seem, Donington hadn't always been either genteel or slumbering.

The grounds were famous as a deer park and according to one source "before it was enclosed it would have been, with its oaks and river, a wilderness for hunter-gatherers from the earliest times." A "beautiful stone axe head, estimated at 2,000 years old, has been found."[1] The park is mentioned in the Domesday Survey of 1086 and the first house was built there in the 16th century. The present house, the third, dates from 1793 and is exquisitely English with its central courtyard and Gothic facades. The Hall has (inevitably) its own ghost: the sound of a carriage coming over the gravel bringing late arrivals for dinner, but when you look no-one and nothing is ever there.

A family called Hastings owned the Hall for generations until they were "somewhat ruined by the 4th Marquis who died in 1868 and whose fondness for horse racing led to great scandals."[2] The sister of the Marquis married a wealthy entrepreneur who became Lord Donington.

This is typical English country house history, no doubt, but the outbreak of hostilities between Britain and Germany in 1914 brought an irony of its own. The War Office built camps for internees and military prisoners, the Hall immediately comandeered for that. To the expansive sweep of manicured grounds came barbed wire and sentry boxes.

"Stores and furniture were collected to meet the requirements of a camp destined to be the home of hundreds of German officers for several years. Some of the junior prisoners were compelled to serve their fellow officers, but otherwise the choice of study, work or amusement was up to the individual. Virtually no-one chose to be idle. Small carpentry workshops were set up in the basement rooms where the prisoners produced cabinets, window boxes and scenery for the drama group. Language classes took place and English newspapers were read in the drawing room, furnished now with simple wooden tables and chairs, but no carpets, and a large home-made war map showed the up-to-date position on western and eastern fronts."[3]

John Gillies Shields whose family owned and ran the Hall for 50 years, says that the Germans were "officers and frightfully, frightfully correct. Nearly all had their English relations sending the odd case of champagne and hamper from Harrods and so forth. There was quite an uproar about that. They had an orchestra and played tennis."

Inevitably, escape attempts were made.

Two officers dug a tunnel 70 yards long using only a tin shovel and zinc box for removing earth – Shields says they used empty salmon tins. The officers reached the coast but were literally uncovered as stowaways on a Dutch boat. Later the tunnel became a tourist attraction and by another great irony, the German drivers to the 1937 Grand Prix visited it and commented on it as a curious relic from another time altogether.

Three officers put dummies in their beds and hid in a trench they'd dug at the tennis courts – they buried themselves under fresh-mown grass cuttings – and then crawled under the barbed wire. They were soon recaptured.

However an airman, Gunther Pluschow, did escape and a comrade – referred to only as Treffitz – almost did, too. Pluschow described his exploits in a book *My Escape from Donington Hall* and quite unconsciously was depicting the world Adolf Hitler would kill: "We had manufactured for ourselves several huge maps of the theatres of war, which were correct even to the slightest details, and each morning at eleven our 'General Staff Officers' were hard at work moving the little flags. Often the English Colonel himself stood in front of them and thoughtfully shook his head."

Pluschow found captivity brought him close to despair and "for hours I walked up and down in front of different parts of the entanglements ... all the time noting the ways and habits of the different sentries." A plan evolved. Pluschow and Treffitz feigned illness, staying in bed and missing the morning roll call. The Orderly Sergeant came round, found them lying there and reported them present. Late in the afternoon they hid in the grounds while two comrades replaced them in bed. The Orderly Sergeant came round again after evening roll call, noted two sick men still lying there and reported them present again.

Towards midnight Pluschow and Treffitz clambered over the barbed wire and walked to Derby, which they reached at dawn and where they split up. Pluschow took the train for London (via Leicester) hiding behind a newspaper, ate a modest amount in four restaurants so his "ravenous" appetite wouldn't provoke comment, and slept in a garden.

By now the newspapers were reporting the escape – and giving his appearance, including his Chinese tattoo – as well as reporting the capture of Treffitz at Millwall Docks. Pluschow decided he had to get rid of his mackintosh (no doubt the newspapers had given a description of it), checked it into the cloakroom at Blackfriars station and caught a train to Tilbury. There he managed to board a boat and get back to Germany.

He recounted the details of the escape in a quaint, well-mannered sort of way. The brutality of technical warfare was already evident in the trenches scarring northern France, but not its merciless, remorseless cruelty. Hitler, who served with bravery in these same trenches, would bring that.

In 1918, the war over, Donington settled back into slumber.

Germany, defeated, was forced to go to sleep. Hitler and perhaps a majority of the German people felt that their own generals had betrayed them and it was to prove a deadly inheritance to carry into peacetime; worse, Germany was humiliated by the 1919 Treaty of Versailles which limited her armed forces, gave the left bank of the Rhine to Allied occupation and absorbed seven million ethnic Germans into France and Czechoslovakia.

Europe was the least likely of the world's continents for anything like this to endure. There were too many countries packed too tightly with too many entrenched minorities, languages and cultures overlapping. You only had to consider Czechoslovakia. Founded in 1918 and its independence ratified at Versailles, it was a welding of Czechs and Slovaks (who spoke different languages) with a large German minority in the north – called the Sudetenland – and a Hungarian minority in the south, while Poland eyed an area next to the Sudetenland.

It was to this small country that Hitler would visit his wrath, redeeming both the shame of Versailles and reuniting the Sudetenland with Greater Germany; and it was the fate of this small country which would take the second big Donington Grand Prix to so many different levels.

At the Hall, as the slumber settled, there was continuity. Long, long before, Lord Donington had hired a land agent from Scotland – John Gillies Shields – to help run the estate. If the name seems familiar, you'll see why in a moment. Shields was a highly intelligent man who eventually bought the estate himself. He had nice British eccentricity, too. As his grandson says, he instructed in his will that "any members of the family that inherited any part of the Donington estate had to take the name Gillies Shields. So my brothers and cousins are all Gillies Shields." Moreover … "my father was a John, my grandfather was a John, my eldest son is a John and my cousin was a John. Bank accounts get all muddled up." The family managed to keep the Hall a going concern for half a century until it was sold to the British Midland airline.

"It was in 1925 or 1926 that the Hall was for sale. It was going to be sold to a chap who planned to build model housing estates like Welwyn Garden City and God knows what else. My grandfather had promised Lord Donington on his deathbed that he would never allow the estate to be broken up if he could avoid it. My grandfather now got very worried about this because he visualised his beloved oak trees and the deer going – everything he loved going – so he decided to buy it and move in. But his wife wouldn't. She said it was haunted and she was terrified."

A compromise was struck. Grandfather Shields worked at the Hall every day and "furnished it beautifully, each room – linen curtains, silver, everything – but he couldn't afford to do nothing with the Hall" in the sense of letting it stand idle. It had to be made to pay its upkeep. Grandfather talked to Earl Howe, President of the British Racing Drivers' Club, and "various other people and they suggested motor racing. That would require accommodation which, in turn, would make it into a country club. So they had a golf course made and they had tennis courts made and it was what we call today a leisure centre."

The public were admitted and it cost them sixpence.

Another version of how motorsport began here is[4] that a certain Fred Craner, former motor bike rider and subsequently Derby garage owner, was running a team to compete at the Isle of Man TT races and intended to do some practice round a Lincolnshire gravel pit. Craner, a small and rough-hewn man, fell out with the owner – he spent a lifetime falling out with people – and went off to find somewhere of his own. He discovered three possibilities within range of Derby and the most suitable seemed

Donington's broad and largely empty acres. He paid his sixpence like everybody else but, instead of tramping round the Hall admiring the furnishings and the escape tunnel, wandered the grounds weighing up whether a track could be made by linking the various tarmac drives. A gamekeeper apprehended him: "What you doing here?" Craner typically manipulated this by making sure the gamekeeper took him to meet grandfather Shields. Craner explained what he had in mind and soon enough received a reply. "Yes."

It was 1931. Craner acted quickly when he had the yes. He understood the mechanisms of publicity as well as its value.

Tich Allen was a junior reporter in the Loughborough office of the *Nottingham Guardian and Evening Post*. "A message came that there was some sort of an inspection going on at Donington Park with a view to a race track being set up. My senior in the office, the chap I worked under, had a bicycle and he went most places on that but Donington was too far and there was no bus service or anything. I had a motorbike and I was the only one who could get there.

"Craner had invited various notables from the motorbike and car racing worlds. Gillies Shields was there but Fred Craner did all the talking – he was that kind of man – and he showed us these what I must describe as drives. We congregated at what became known as the hairpin – which never was a hairpin really but always known as that – and he showed us these two drives: one went off under an arched stone bridge in the direction of a farm called Coppice and the other disappeared into Holly Wood in the other direction. Craner explained that this was not a complete circuit because there was a length along the back which hadn't yet been made up at all and was, in fact, only a farm track."

This would become Starkey's Straight, linking the drive which went to Coppice and the drive which went to Holly Wood, closing the circle, making a track with a beginning and an end.

On Whit Monday, five weeks after Craner's original visit, the circle had been closed using parts of the drives and farm roads. The resultant track was let to the Derby and District Motor Club of which Craner was, in a time-honoured phrase, the moving force. Originally, it seems, Craner only envisaged motor bike racing but this modest place was already the one which three of the greatest drivers – Tazio Nuvolari, Bernd Rosemeyer and Rudolf Caracciola – would grace.

As is the way of journalism, Allen became the newspaper's reporter at Donington when the racing began and continued when he joined the *Leicester Evening Mail*. It would take him fully to the coming of the Germans but of more immediate concern, he would be covering the first meeting. It was so unexpectedly successful that the only way the men on the gate could take the admission money was in buckets.

The track had rudimentary aspects, partly because of the haste in which it had been put together, partly because money was tight but mostly because it had to follow the character and contours of the land.

It measured 2 miles 327 yards and the start-finish faced the Hall across undulating meadows. From the grid the racing bikes travelled a short surge to a sharp right (Hairpin Bend) then flowed under the arch of the stone bridge to a left, which was in woodland. They went left again, then hard right (McLean's Corner) and along a straight section to another hard right

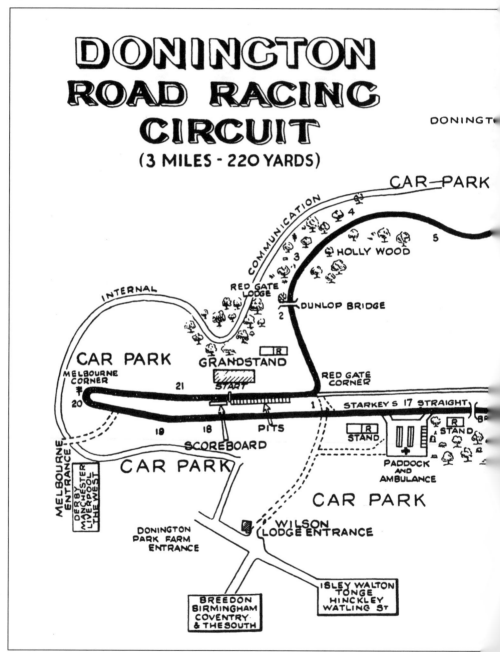

(Coppice Corner). There they found a farmhouse to their left and barns to the right with the track slicing between. It passed through opened five-barred farm gates – an official no-overtaking area! – on to the main straight (Starkey's Straight) which actually wiggled a bit and was almost a mile and a half long. This culminated in a hard right (Starkey's Corner) into more

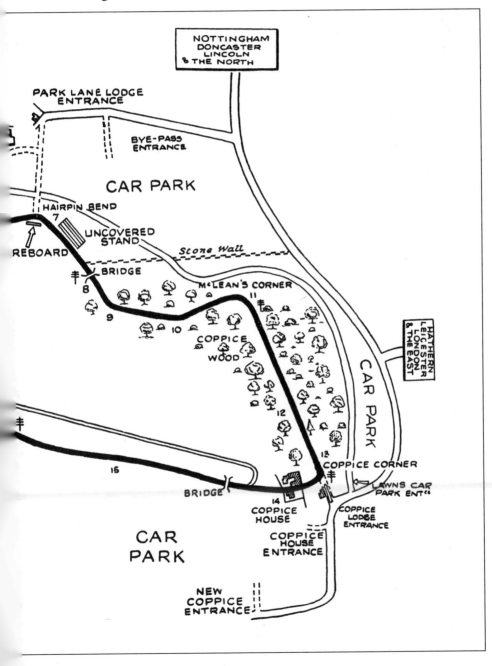

woodland (Redgate Lodge) before a left-right kink fed the bikes through Holly Wood and back to the start-finish.

Craner remained straightforward and prickly in the way self-made men can be. Chas Rushton was an employee at Craner's garage and "when I first met him I immediately took him as a brusque character, but when you got to know him he was a nice bloke. He wasn't tall, he was thick-set and he had a moustache. He was self-made and you could tell that but, to my mind, he always looked after his staff and I got on well with him. He was dynamic. He had a gruff sort of voice. His office was next door to the parts manager's office and I spent a lot of time there. Craner was on the phone day in day out. He swore a lot, swore the whole time. He didn't use filthy language, though."

You can easily imagine the impact such a man had on the Shields, who were traditional in their courtesies and their responsibilities. They didn't behave like Fred Craner and scarcely inhabited the same planet.

The grandson unconsciously charts the chasm. "There was a butler called Blois at the Hall, whose job was to do the silver and welcome guests. That was all he did. Anybody who came to the Hall called him *sir*! They were terrified of him. He wore a powdered wig, everything. When he died he left his possessions to my father. Of course my father couldn't accept that, traced his relatives and Blois's cottage went to them – but it was a lovely gesture from a lovely man. There was a housekeeper called Alice whose husband Tom did the boilers and central heating, and their daughter helped – and so on. It was a family affair. The Whitney girls – there were eight of those, I think, worked there…

"I remember my uncle went to a pub called the Nag's Head in Castle Donington one night looking for a chap – I won't mention his name, his family are still about – who'd been on the gate at a race meeting taking money. Afterwards there was a lot missing. My uncle found him at the pub, got hold of him and turned him upside down, *rattled* him and the notes and coins and God knows what else came tumbling out."

This patrician family had an ambivalent relationship with Craner, as they would have to have.

"Craner knew what he wanted and went out to get it. He didn't care a damn for anybody. He was terribly rude to my grandfather on occasions and they had the most ghastly rows. I think he was a bit frightened of my grandfather, as we all were. Craner would be summoned to the boardroom at the Hall and you had to walk up a long corridor and over a long carpet to get to my grandfather's desk.

"Anyway, Craner was all right really despite having an unscrupulous streak in getting what he wanted. He could swear and be very bad tempered, he could get red in the face, shout and gesticulate. He was fond of me. I don't know why, but perhaps because he had been in the air force during the First War and, I think, seen service in Africa – he could speak a bit of Swahili – and I had been with the King's African Rifles. We'd chat away. He was fond of my grandfather, too, in his own way but he was not a man to cross: very clever, a very swift operator and, I suppose, a very brave man."

That appears to be certain because when the shadows lengthened towards war, and when Czechoslovakia hung suspended between life and death, Fred Craner was extremely *un*intimidated by any suggestions that Herr Hitler's plans to plunge the world into a sea of fire might interfere with his own plans to hold a motor race of 80 laps round the parkland at the track he had built – with victory to the best driver, German or other.

In January 1933, Hitler became Germany's Chancellor, a position he could exploit to take absolute control of the country. Within a month he had committed arson at the Parliament building in Berlin, calling it a communist plot, and forced the country's President to sign a decree suspending basic human rights. Henceforth Hitler decided what human rights were.

That was the end of February, going into March.

The first car race at Donington was on 25 March, an occasion so remote from the politics of Berlin you could barely imagine that, whatever the future brought, events in the latter would exercise a direct bearing on events in the former.

At 11 o'clock that morning Sir George Beaumont announced that the widening and improving of the track, which had been carried out to accommodate racing cars, cost £12,000. In resonant, well-bred tones he wished the whole venture well and withdrew leaving the track to the cars: four of them, MG Midgets and Austins. The winner averaged 56 miles an hour.

Overall it was a day played out to the manners and mannerisms of a solid, entrenched society which seemed so permanent because such a long history had produced it; and which Hitler tried to destroy. He didn't do that, but his war altered the climate it needed for survival and it did not survive in the rigid, structured way that it had always been.

Anyway, the sequence of events which would lead to the extraordinary unity had begun and were accelerated because Grand Prix racing's governing body, the *Association Internationale des Automobile Clubs Reconnus*, took steps to "bring about some uniformity among the racing car builders." Among the new rules they drew up, the most important decreed that cars should not weigh more than 750 kilogrammes – although that didn't include driver, fuel, oil, water and tyres. The races would be over a minimum 500 kilometres (310 miles)[5] and the rules to take effect on 1 January 1934.

Two companies in Germany had decisions to make about whether to build cars and race in this new, properly-regulated formula, Mercedes-Benz and Auto Union. Hitler encouraged both and offered "a prize of 500,000 Reichsmarks [£41,600 then] to the most successful German racing car" under the new rules.[6] "It must be credited to Adolf Hitler that he was quick to see the propoganda value of successful participation by teams of German racing cars in International events."

It was internal and external propoganda because Hitler intuitively understood the impact of power, and – by extension, no doubt – that the gathering strength and technical superiority of his Germany would be well demonstrated by these cars. To do that was not the primary reason they'd eventually come to Donington, but it was what they wielded when they got there: the naked strength.

At Mercedes a great deal of heart-searching still went on before a positive decision was taken, although if Hitler wanted racing cars, who would say he couldn't have racing cars? "Behind locked doors and barbed wire, engineers and draughtsmen set to work at top pressure."[7] They produced a car which had independent suspension and an entirely new engine giving 354 brake horsepower at 5,800 revs – a staggering, stupendous increase over the 200 being developed by such established manufacturers as Maserati and Alfa Romeo.

The car was shown to Hitler in January 1934 and a month later went testing at the Italian circuit of Monza, where it crashed when it was being driven by the aristocratic Manfred von Brauchitsch[8] whose uncle, Field Marshal Walther von Brauchitsch, would become Hitler's Army Commander in Chief and play his part in the death of Czechoslovakia.

Auto Union were more radical. They made a 16-cylinder engine and positioned it behind the driver. The car was unveiled at the Avus circuit on the outskirts of Berlin, a most curious racetrack comprising two parallel straights close together with tight loops at both ends. Hans Stuck, an experienced driver, averaged 134 miles per hour over a run lasting an hour.

Once these cars became reliable, which didn't take long, they completely overwhelmed all opposition. Their power was, as Hitler anticipated, evident everywhere: externally at leafy Monza full of impressionable Italians, wooded Spa in the Ardennes, Brno in troubled Czechoslovakia, the narrow streets of Monaco, the celebrated sand-caked race at Tripoli in Libya and half a dozen other places; internally at the Avus, and the two races run at the mighty Nürburgring circuit – the Eifel Grand Prix and the German Grand Prix itself.

Donington was improved again in 1934 – removing the wiggle from Starkey's Straight Hill and extending the main straight so that it ended in a horseshoe shape, doubling back uphill to a new start-finish area. This increased the length to 2 miles 971 yards but left the feel of it rudimentary. The finishing line was marked by a Belisha beacon, similar to the ones at every pedestrian crossing in Britain, set in the grass at the side of the track.

The drivers, likely products of the Public School system pounding along in their pug-like sit-up-and-beg racing cars, would in time know other battlefields. The cars they drove were like the era, familiar and forgotten, somehow near and far away: Riley, Frazer Nash, Ford, Alvis, Bugatti, MG, Austins, the Cutler Special, Lea Francis, Alta and Singer.

Billy Wing, a bike rider, recaptures the atmosphere. "I remember Earl Howe going round in a Bentley. It was quite a quick car but high – a very ugly looking thing! The Hall was splendid and it had a lovely dining room, all oak panels. Very dignified. After the car meetings there'd be dinners and some of the drivers got out of control. They used to bend the forks and put a vegetable on each prong and once they dashed wine glasses onto the ballroom floor. Horrible. Just like vandalism." Or ripping good fun, if you were a *chap*.

Hitler was tightening his hold on every aspect of German life and felt confident enough to begin his self-appointed mission of restoring the Fatherland to itself. He began with the Saarland, a rich mining area opposite France and under French control since Versailles. He contrived a plebiscite in 1935, some 91 per cent of the population voted to return to the Fatherland and he took possession one rainy day, walking head bared into the town of Saarbrucken surrounded by uniformed officers. His opening foreign policy gambit – defying the Allies and their Versailles – hadn't been a gamble at all. The Allies did nothing.

The *chaps*, meanwhile, contested the Donington Grand Prix. It was called that rather than the British Grand Prix because, legend insists, the RAC didn't think much of Fred Craner (he'd fallen out with them) and Fred Craner didn't think much of the RAC.

Motor racing was popular. A 14-year-old in the building trade, for instance, wanted nothing so much as to be among those attending the race. He was called Tom Wheatcroft and the rate for his job was "10 shillings a week but I got 2s 6d more. I had a boss who must have taken to me. He was very hard on you but fair. At the site I was working on there was a carpenter who said he was going to Donington and did I want to come? It was a big meeting – 2s 6d to get in. He picked me up from home on his AJS motorbike and I went on the back of it – well, we didn't get there, we finished up in Leicester Royal Infirmary. The roads were narrow and he overdid it on a bend – it's 60 feet wide these days! – and off we tumbled into the hedge. Cuts and bruises but nothing broken, either of us."

This did not deter him. He went to a later meeting then returned again and again. Today he owns Donington Park.

The 1935 race, over 125 laps (318 miles) attracted what historian Doug Nye estimates as an "interesting, if not sensational, entry" headed by three well-known Europeans: Italians Giuseppe Farina and Gino Rovere drove Maseratis and a Frenchman, Raymond Sommer, drove an Alfa Romeo. In spite of their presence, and in spite of the fact it was called a Grand Prix, the race wasn't of much international standing. Evidently Rovere found his car "a real handful on this narrow, twisting course" and decided to have a co-driver to help. (Farina would eventually become, in 1950, the first Formula One champion of the modern era.)

The Britons sounded terribly Public School: Earl Howe, the Hon Brian Lewis, 'B' Bira – actually a Siamese prince living in England, 'Buddy' Featherstonhaugh, Freddy Dixon, Charlie Martin, Percy Maclure, Richard Shuttleworth and one of the three Dobson brothers, Austin. Shuttleworth was "the dashing young Bedfordshire squire reknowned as 'Mad Jack' for his reckless driving"[9] and Bira, a Siamese undergraduate at Cambridge whose full name, Prince Birabongse Bhanutej Bhanubandh, had been contracted for obvious reasons. His cousin, Prince Chula Chakrabongse, acted as his team manager.

Farina took pole position but retired with a technical problem and Shuttleworth won in a time of 4 hours 47 minutes 12 seconds from Howe and Martin.

Soon enough Wheatcroft would start spending time at Donington and get to know Craner – "a funny-peculiar man. He was ever so strict. I'd got to know his wife before I knew him because she'd give me cups of tea. They lived in the very same house which today [1998] is the circuit's offices. It was a farmhouse and, inside, ever so dark. Craner had a little office." It contained an old black telephone on his desk, the number of which has survived, Castle Donington 63.

Wheatcroft describes the decor as "outdated brown paint on the architraves [mouldings]. The doors were panelled and had the brown paint on them. When we took over in 1971 the paint was still there. I was in the house, I reckon, half a dozen times and Craner's wife would say 'would you like a little bit of cake?' She had brown home-made cake, always dark brown and it had currants in it. She'd cut the biggest chunk you've ever seen. Craner was frightening when you were young, but as you came to know him you realised he meant half of how he sounded. I remember going to fetch him. His meal would be ready, I'd jump on my motorbike and find him down by the pits or wherever he was."

In February 1936 Hitler launched the "People's Car" – the Volkswagen – and it represented Germany's gathering strength. Ordinary people could afford them and a magnificent autobahn system was being constructed to drive them on. Hitler now ordered the army to enter the Rhineland, in open defiance of Versailles again, to return it to the Fatherland. The Allies did nothing.

The interweaving towards unity – events in Berlin reverberating to Donington – tightened.

This year of 1936 a driver-cum-mechanic, 'Wilkie' Wilkinson, had been at a race at Donington and he still remembers how in those days spectators sat on the edge of the circuit with their feet actually on the track – "they used to lift their feet up as the cars went past!" After the race he went to a local pub, the Turk's Head, which the racing fraternity used as their 'local.' A man he knew as "Dunlop Mac", a famous tyre fitter of the era, came in accompanied by someone he didn't know. This someone had been in the race, evidently spun and his car wasn't performing well, anyway. 'Dunlop Mac' introduced the man to Wilkinson – *meet Billy Cotton the bandleader* – and described Wilkinson as a talented engine tuner. Wilkinson said to Cotton, *never heard of you.*

To which Cotton said – *well, that's a darned good start*!

Cotton was able to hire Wilkinson to work on his car, and do a bit of driving, too. A partnership was born, based on the arrangement that Cotton would pay for the tuning and, if Wilkinson did some of the driving, he'd get a percentage of any winnings. The partnership prospered, though they didn't enter for the Donington Grand Prix in October. The race attracted 24 entries and, Nye writes, "all but one – a Salmson entered by the enigmatic Pablo Curtis – came to the starting line."[10] 'Bira' was among the 24 but most of the 1935 competitors weren't. Instead, such drivers as wealthy Swiss amateur Christian Kautz, Anthony Powys-Lybbe, Ian Connell and T.P. Cholmondeley-Tapper (whose reserve was a Miss Ellison) decorated the grid. Cholmondeley-Tapper was a New Zealander with some Norwegian ancestry and was known as George although his first name was Thomas. They didn't have much of a chance. A handsome Englishman, who'd wanted victory so badly that he wrote to Mercedes asking if they'd lend him one of their mighty racing cars, won it in an Alfa Romeo. He was called Dick Seaman.

He had impeccable credentials – Rugby School then Trinity College, Cambridge – and his father wanted him to be a diplomat, or go to the Bar and possibly stand for Parliament but Seaman had his own ideas about his own life. He wanted to race and could because his mother, a formidable lady, was wealthy enough to subsidise it.

Mercedes had replied to his request for a racing car by politely pointing out that they neither loaned nor sold them, but after Donington they telegrammed to say they were trying out new drivers at the Nürburgring and invited him. Whether Seaman's mother was anti-German is not known but she didn't approve of him doing this and advised him against it. Seaman had his own thoughts about this, too.

The tests were run under the supervision of Alfred Neubauer, the rotund and fabled Mercedes Team Manager who habitually wore suits, collars and ties and a Homburg hat at the races. He wielded the hat as other teams wielded pit boards, to give instructions to drivers. He did this, however, in a theatrical way, using the Homburg as bullfighters use capes.

Seaman wasn't spectacularly faster than the others at the Nürburgring but he made a favourable impression with his consistency which, Mercedes reasoned, also made him a safe driver. Neubauer promised him a decision later. He was in with a chance. [11]

Auto Union realised what was happening and wanted Seaman to test for them but he became "exasperated" because they wouldn't be specific – they also offered Cholmondeley-Tapper a test in 1936 but he preferred to go skiing! Mercedes tested him again, this time at Monza, and despite pleading from Auto Union he signed a provisional contract with Mercedes. No immediate public announcement was made because, as Mercedes explained to Seaman, Hitler's personal permission had to be obtained before a foreigner could drive in a German team. [12] Hitler gave permission.

Seaman would now be measured against the Nuvolaris, the Rosemeyers and the Caracciolas as he joined the immense struggle between Mercedes and Auto Union, whose battle-lines were clear for 1937. Mercedes fielded Caracciola, von Brauchitsch, Hermann Lang, Seaman and Kautz. Auto Union fielded Rosemeyer, Stuck, Rudolf Hasse and Ernst von Delius. (Nuvolari was with Alfa Romeo.)

Seaman rented a chalet at the tiny Bavarian hamlet of Ambach on the

Starnberger lake south of Munich and used it as a base between races. He wrote to his friend George Monkhouse: "The garden runs right down to the water where there is a boathouse. If one tires of the wide open spaces Munich is only 25 miles away."[13]

An Englishman driving for a German team in the Nazi era brought difficulties and disadvantages – some subtle, some blatant – but the mental processes of Fred Craner, entrepreneur, saw only advantages.

He'd already tried to lure the two German teams to the 1935 race and increased the prize money as an inducement, with the winner getting £400 – a considerable sum, as the programme for the race proved. It carried advertisements for the Austin 7 Ruby at £112 and the new De Luxe Ford Touring Car at £135. No doubt to Craner's intense displeasure, he'd had to pay the £400 to Shuttleworth when the Germans didn't come. (Craner rectified the situation in 1936 when Seaman won with Hans Ruesch who, after the war, wrote a couple of fictional motor racing books. With no hope of German entries, Craner lowered the first prize to £250.)

In February 1937 Craner wrote to Mercedes, again asking if they'd compete but he received a non-committal reply. Seaman "stepped in to help the negotiations, although it is not clear whether this was simply a personal thing or whether the team had asked him to."[14] There is also a suggestion that Seaman negotiated on behalf of Mercedes, who looked for a "considerable" sum in starting money.[15]

A few weeks later Mercedes tested at Monza again and Seaman crashed. Rudolf Uhlenhaut, the team's Technical Director, wasn't there but Seaman described the accident to him afterwards, explaining how he had "disappeared into the bushes and crawled out to find the engine lying in the road. He was lucky to get away with only a fractured kneecap and had to have his leg in plaster for a short while. He said that the crash was entirely his fault and that was quite remarkable – he would always tell you exactly what had happened and blame himself if necessary. Other drivers had a tendency to blame the car for everything, but he was very honest in that way."[16]

The season had already begun, with two races in South Africa in January which Mercedes didn't enter. In May, Lang won Tripoli from Rosemeyer and won the Avus from von Delius – a perfect start for Mercedes, who didn't enter the Rio de Janeiro Grand Prix which Carlo Pintacuda, a Scuderia Ferrari regular, won in an Alfa Romeo from Stuck's Auto Union. Rosemeyer won the Eifel Grand Prix at the Nürburgring from Caracciola. That was 13 June.

The shadows lengthened. By now the Spanish Civil War between the Republicans and General Franco's Nationalists had intensified. The Germans were supporting Franco and the German Air Force bombed the undefended town of Guernica, the spiritual home of the Basques, on a market day in what has been described as "a calculated act of terror."[17] It was the first glimpse of a hell which would become familiar and the first mass making of civilians into 'legitimate' military targets.

That month Seaman continued his attempt to get Mercedes to Donington. He wrote to Craner pointing out that "in the past, whenever a foreign driver has come to race in England, some stupid misunderstanding seems to have arisen, usually over some petty and unnecessary regulation. I ask you to run the whole meeting as simple and straightforward as possible. I do hope you will not think it a cheek my writing to you like this, but I honestly do want to see the continental competitors leave England this year waiting to come back again."

Craner responded typically by pointing out that "as you are no doubt aware, from my point [of view] the less restrictions there are, the better for me. You may rest assured that the regulations for the October Grand Prix will have as few restrictions as the RAC will permit."

The world was more casual then. This summer, a bike rider called Billy Wing had hired Donington, as anybody could. His son Derek remembers "dad and another rider had booked the course for practising and B. Bira turned up with his outfit – his entourage – and said to Craner *get these people off the course, I want to practice.* Craner said *well, these people have booked it and they can have it. You'll have to come back another day.* This was just typical of Fred Craner."

"Another time my father took me to have a look at the Bira pit on a race day. All the mechanics wore light blue overalls, and the tools – immaculate tools – were wrapped in cloths which all had powder blue on them somewhere. Ever the porcelain on the plugs was powder blue, which was extraordinary. The car was blue. Bira was small, not a very imposing figure at all."

Billy Wing explains that hiring Donington cost ten shillings. "Craner would let you have the afternoon for that."

At a completely different level, Nuvolari in the Alfa Romeo won the Milan Grand Prix from Farina (in another Alfa) then Rosemeyer beat Seaman for the Vanderbilt Cup in New York. Hasse won the Belgian Grand Prix at Spa from Stuck. That was 11 July.

Two weeks later Seaman drove in the German Grand Prix at the Nürburgring; and The Ring could be a brooding place hemmed by darkening trees. Wilkie Wilkinson was there, too, looking after the Alfa Romeo of Kenneth Evans. "Seaman did all the interpreting for us," Wilkinson says. "Seaman was a charming chap, no *side* [old expression for lack of self-importance] whatsoever. I was introduced to the German drivers but I can't say I knew them."

From the third row of the grid Seaman made a slow start and was tenth. By lap 5 he was up to fourth but, since the circuit measured 22 kilometres, that is not as dramatic as it sounds.

By then Lang "had lost the lead to Rosemeyer, who in turn had lost it to Caracciola when his snaking, sliding Auto Union slammed into a bank with a rear wheel, and damaged the hubcap. Parts of this fell off on lap 4 … and on that lap, too, a tyre burst. Rosemeyer made for his pit, raging as the mechanics struggled with the damaged hub, and his hard-won lead dissolved as the minutes passed – 3 minutes 33.1 seconds elapsed before he got going again, ripping the seat of his overalls as he took a flying leap into the cockpit."[18]

Von Delius in the Auto Union lay behind Seaman and naturally his pit signalled for him to go faster, catch and overtake the Mercedes. By lap 6 von Delius was closing and on the long, long start-finish straight drew level, forced the Auto Union just ahead. Both cars crossed the slight hump of a bridge at around 170 miles an hour and von Delius landed "slightly askew". The car swerved into a hedge, clipped that and was thrown into Seaman's path. Helplessly Seaman struck it with such force that the Auto Union was flung off the track. It "went end over end through the outside hedge, flattened a wire fence and careered down the slope to end up on the far side of the main Coblenz road outside the course."[19] Von Delius did not survive.

Somehow Seaman managed to slow the Mercedes and it struck an iron post. Then it, too, hit the hedge and he was pitched out, landing on – and badly cutting – his face. His nose and left thumb were broken but, because the Mercedes was on the track and a great danger to the next cars coming along, he and some soldiers managed to push it to safety. Then he was taken to hospital at Adenau, the small town just outside the circuit. After a couple of days he wrote to his mother because some reports insinuated that von Delius had crashed into him deliberately and, he wanted to assure her, "no driver in his senses would do it."[20]

Seaman wrote again to his mother, now assuring her that he had plenty of visitors. At first they'd been from Mercedes but then his hospital room became "a kind of shrine for British pilgrims. Many British tourists, either on walking or charabanc tours, went to visit him and brought him good cheer."[21]

On 1 August, Buchenwald, a concentration camp in the Harz mountains, was opened. In time it would acquire a particular notoriety, even among concentration camps, because the commandant's wife, Frau Ilse Koch, had her lamp shades made out of prisoners' skin. Tattooed skins were particularly favoured. The darkness would get no darker than this, because it could not.

From hospital on 8 August, Seaman wrote a letter to Craner in his spidery but very legible handwriting

Krankenhaus,
Adenau
8/8/37

F. Craner Esq.,
Coppice Farm
Castle Donington,
Derby

Dear Craner,
I have been asked by Herr Neubauer, Mercedes racing manager, to get in touch with you regarding the possibility of our running in the Donington

GP. Mercedes would like to participate in this race, if at all possible, and would like to know what the prize money is going to be, as naturally the financial side is of great importance in an expedition of this sort. Would it not be possible for you to offer more substantial prizes than last year? Would it not be possible for you to revert to the 1935 prize of £500 for the winner? [Actually £400]

I really do not feel they could be persuaded to come for anything less.

What are you prepared to do in the way of starting money? Mercedes do not have the slightest desire to extort exorbitant sums, as they do not expect to make a profit from this alone. They merely wish to have a guaranteed sum to partly cover the great expenses which they incur in competing in a race abroad.

They suggest two cars, for Caracciola and myself – I do ask you to try and make an acceptable offer of starting money as I do feel this is a unique opportunity of getting Mercedes to run in England.

That day von Brauchitsch won the Monaco Grand Prix from Caracciola but Auto Union led Mercedes 4–3 on race victories. Seaman, who had eagerly looked forward to trying to tame Monaco's narrow streets in something as powerful as the Mercedes – he'd missed a 1936 supporting race there in his own car, which wasn't ready – had become reconciled to waiting for news of it to reach the hospital.

Craner responded to Seaman's letter by claiming it was going to be "very difficult to make arrangements for the Mercedes people to participate in the Grand Prix unless we definitely know they are coming." For starting money Craner offered cash and Seaman advised him £400 would be about right. Craner naturally tried to find a way round paying so much by pointing out that the London Motor Show – a major event within the industry – was being held immediately after the Grand Prix and publicity from the race would surely help Mercedes there. Mercedes didn't fall for that.

On 15 August, Rosemeyer won the Coppa Acerbo at Pescara from von Brauchitsch and a week later Caracciola won the Swiss Grand Prix at Berne from Lang.

On 30 August, Craner wrote accepting the starting price and by then Mercedes were already making preparations because, on the day Craner wrote, Max Sailer, the director in charge of the whole racing operation, sent a memo to engineers Uhlenhaut and Krauss.

Donington Park race
Referring to my information of the 25th of this month and with regard to several special regulations for the Donington Park race, I went to the organiser in order to ask him to allow us to paint on the starting number as usual and to spare us the trouble of fastening a vertical plate 23 x 28cm to the front. Therefore you don't have to prepare anything in this respect for the time being.

I ask you, however, to be absolutely sure to make a strap across the bonnet since this is a special English regulation and has become a general English practice.

The rear-view mirror of the correct size we already have. It has to be taken into consideration that we will take with us at least two fire extinguishers per pit.

On 2 September, Mercedes wrote to Craner explaining that they would be bringing their full complement of four cars. A day later an internal memorandum was sent to Neubauer which showed that Mercedes were taking it very seriously. Unfortunately the signature isn't legible but it may well have been from a Herr Naumann in the Berlin office.

> Copy: Press Office Untertürkheim
> 3rd September 1937
> Mr Alfred Neubauer
> Donington Park race

Dear Mr Neubauer!

This very moment I am receiving information from Director Werlin that he himself will go to England to attend the event mentioned above and that, as usual, he intends to invite the English writers, most of whom he knows well [presumably from previous Motor Shows] for 5 o'clock tea at the Dorchester Hotel.

At the same time, since Director Werlin considers it necessary that either I myself or another English-speaking representative of the Press Office will attend the race, I ask you to reserve 2 single rooms for the Press Office. One of them is for Mr Pfeiffle whose journey has already been approved by Dr Kissel. The other one can certainly be reserved without giving names.

I would also appreciate if you would see to seat reservations in an express train or plane – depending on what is necessary – for Mr Pfeiffle and a second man.

> Thank you kindly and
> Heil Hitler!

Dr Wilhelm Kissel was Managing Director of Mercedes-Benz. The Werlin is presumably Jakob Werlin, close friend of Hitler and former Mercedes district manager in Munich who was now a senior-ranking Nazi.[22]

Cumulatively it meant that, if Mercedes were going to Donington, Auto Union were going to Donington, too. Craner had the two strongest motor racing teams on Earth and they would provide something the like of which had never been seen in Britain before. The phlegmatic journalists would soon be babbling about being shaken and breathless.

On 12 September, Caracciola won the Italian Grand Prix at Livorno from

Lang, Rosemeyer third, Seaman fourth. Two races remained, the Czech Grand Prix at Brno and Donington, but they were only a week apart and co-ordinating a racing effort to accommodate both of them was a major task: lorry convoys bearing cars, tyres and spare parts travelled at an agonisingly slow pace, especially once they got beyond the reach of the autobahns. For example, Seaman would have three mechanics on his car in Brno (Haug, Kopp and Claar) and three different mechanics (Abele, Anton Fisher and Werder) at Donington.

On 17 September, Neubauer set out in a four-page memorandum how the journey to Donington was to be achieved. He detailed everything, down to: "Foreign currency is paid in English pounds because of the danger of the French slump in prices. Only as much money as absolutely necessary should be exchanged into francs, and that at public banks. Before the latest slump in the value of the franc, the rate was approximately 132 francs for £1 – equivalent to 10.800 francs for one mark. Now you will probably get more (so don't change too much)."

Neubauer anticipated a problem when the convoy of lorries reached Dunkirk to take the ferry to Dover. "Crude oil" – which the convoy of lorries ran on – "may not be allowed on to the ship so we must budget in such a way that the convoy arrives at Dunkirk with not more than a 30-litre reserve. Instructions have been sent to have crude oil available in Dover, i.e. 600 litres for all 6 lorries."

In retrospect, this memorandum carries the chill of an operation being mounted on military lines. For that reason it remains disturbing, but only in the light of what we know now. *Then* it just seemed like the ultimate way to go motor racing, especially against the *chaps* with their funny little sit-up-and-beg cars of antiquity. The beginning of the memorandum set the tone of chill.

The following applies to the participants in the Donington Park race:

1. Keeping to the route fixed by the French Foreign Ministry via Saarbrucken

The German part of this route has been fixed as follows:
Stuttgart – Pforzheim – Durlach – Karlsruhe – Landau – Pirmasens – Zweibrucken – Saarbrucken. Distance 225km.

The French part of the route leads via
Saarbrucken – Forbach – Metz (there is no stop allowed during this section)

It meant that two timetables were operating simultaneously, one getting everybody to Brno in time to race and the other getting more cars and equipment to Donington.

At midday on Tuesday, 21 September the first convoy left Stuttgart for Donington, halting overnight at Saarbrucken the 225 kilometres away – Saarbrucken which Hitler had entered that wet March day two years earlier.

The convoy consisted of lorries carrying what was described as "material" (spare parts and tyres), the mobile workshop and a private car which would be for the use of Neubauer in England. At Saarbrucken the Mercedes representative (one Gustav Seibert of 20 Rosenstrasse) would have made all the necessary arrangements for accommodation and food; and, passing through customs being a complicated matter in those days, an expert in doing precisely that (Sotrapo based at Kehl) was delegated to meet the convoy at Seibert's office during the evening to discuss how it would be done in the morning.

Thus, while the drivers and cars gathered for the Czech Grand Prix at Brno, the convoy slogged across northern France to Dunkirk from the Wednesday to the Friday evening where it had to be "at the latest".[23] The Mercedes representative there (one Peron Hernu of 31 rue Marechal Petain) would have made all the arrangements.

The second convoy – four lorries carrying the four racing cars and six "private cars" for the use of the team and drivers – set off from Stuttgart at midday on the Thursday for Saarbrucken and the embrace of Herr Seibert's organisational skills, not to mention Sotrapo who "once again" had been "ordered to Saarbrucken to help the team with the French customs and hand over the money to the Customs" [not bribes but duty]. Then it slogged across northern France to be in Dunkirk on the Saturday evening. Four of the "private cars" would go to Croydon Airport for when the drivers who'd been racing at Brno flew in on the Monday.

During this week Charlie Martin – a *chap* – flew to Czechoslovakia to drive in the Brno Grand Prix. To be strictly accurate the meeting consisted of two separate Grands Prix, Brno for the less powerful cars (ERAs, Maseratis and Bugattis) and the Masaryk Grand Prix for the big boys like Merecedes, Auto Union and Alfa Romeo. For ease of reference, this Masaryk race is known historically as the Czech Grand Prix.

"Oh yes, Czechoslovakia was quite a journey in those days," Martin reflected. "It was splendid! I went, I think, British Imperial Airways. Anyhow it was a Dragon plane, one up and one down – two wings each side, one on top of the other. The pilot got lost over Czechoslovakia because cloud came down so they said *we'll land here and stop over*. Mark you, I was the only passenger – the only person stupid enough to go. The plane landed somewhere near Prague and I caught a train to the town. It was quite exciting because I didn't know a single word of Czech or Slovak and I didn't know anybody within a thousand miles of the place. In Prague I went to the cinema to see Ronald Coleman [film star famed for his role in Bulldog Drummond] in something or other and next day I caught the rattler – the local train – to Brno."

The contrast between the two Mercedes convoys moving with such precision across northern France, other Mercedes convoys already in place and functioning at Brno and Martin's hit-or-miss approach is very evocative. His car, an ERA, had been driven down by a couple of mechanics/friends in a Ford V8 lorry. He hoped they'd made it.

Brno was near the western Czech border with Austria and situated north of Vienna. Its circuit was some 29 kilometres (18 miles), which made it the longest which grand prix cars used. Worse, half of it was simply local roads and "very rough, bumpy, hilly."[24]

"When I arrived there," Martin added, "I knew the Germans by sight because Dick Seaman, my great friend, drove for them. And I met my mechanics – they had made it!"

As the Mercedes convoys slogged forward towards England, no doubt the personnel obeyed Neubauer. "It is on no account allowed to take French francs into England. We must budget in such a way that when Dunkirk is reached no French francs are left. It is not until the return journey that money will be changed again."

The first convoy – which set off earlier because the "material" it hauled was much heavier than the racing cars in the second convoy, making its progress slower – reached Dunkirk on the Friday and cleared Customs on the Saturday morning, then parked in the 'free port' area beyond. Neubauer had been concerned about this being carried out on time – it had to be "taken into special consideration because the Customs may close and make our shipping the convoy impossible on the Sunday. While there will be no ferry to England on the Saturday there will be one on the Sunday, leaving Dunkirk at 2.30 and arriving at Dover at 7."

Practice was going on for the races in Brno.

Next day, the Sunday, a Mercedes representative from the London office arrived in Dunkirk to greet the convoys and the Royal Automobile Club offered to help in Dover, through what Neubauer described as "their support centres for travellers in the ports."

In Brno the races were going on. In Martin's word, "I finished second, having led to the last lap when an (expletive) plug cut out and Luigi Villoresi [well-known Italian driver] passed me. I'd had it in the bag." A Czechoslovak, recorded only by his surname Pohl, crashed into the crowd, injuring three.

Caracciola won the other Grand Prix but Lang skidded and his Mercedes broke through a fence killing two spectators and injuring a dozen more. It happened at what Lang would describe[25] as the "12.6 kilometre stone" where there was a "fast right-hand bend in wooded country, the road being flanked by deep ditches. It was surfaced with tarmacadam but there was a 'soft shoulder' of earth and gravel on either side." Some drivers used this and churned stones, gravel and mud on to the tarmac. On lap 5 Lang was into the corner when he realised how much had already been churned. He didn't brake because that risked locking the wheels and completely losing control. He fought the car, it clipped a granite stone and somersaulted "over the ditch, the edge of which was full of spectators." Lang was unaware of the tragedy, wandering around in a haze of concussion, and only discovered the extent of it when he reached hospital.

The magazine *Motor und Sport* noted severely: "Lang's serious accident would not have happened, firstly, if the crowd wouldn't have been able to cross the track during the race and, secondly, if they'd been kept away from the outside of the corners by the erection of wire barriers."

Charlie Martin did not recall these people being killed but said "oh, I suppose they were. It was a pretty difficult course." Martin was being neither callous nor dismissive, it's just that danger was regarded in a different way. Seaman finished fourth in his race and, Martin said, "after it Dick and I spent the evening together in Vienna. We were pretty tired, actually. We had a few jars in a nice *caff*, we watched some Viennese waltzing and that was it. We went to our beds and fell asleep."

The first Mercedes convoy reached Dover and cleared Customs, then went to the Lord Warden Hotel[26] for the night. The second convoy arrived and next morning they all set off for Donington via London, a journey which Neubauer had calculated at 320km.

That was Monday 27 September.

Neubauer and three of his drivers – von Brauchitsch, Lang and Seaman – prepared to board a plane in Vienna for London airport in Croydon. Caracciola refused to fly and set off on the long train journey instead. Lang's wife Lydia had never flown before and was, well, you know, frightened – but she did get on the Lufthansa Junkers 52 which went from Vienna via Munich, Frankfurt and Brussels to Croydon. Perhaps she even enjoyed it.

Chapter 2

Friends –
and enemies

OF THE DRIVERS GATHERING for the Donington Grand Prix, two – Rosemeyer and Caracciola – can be regarded as great in a timeless sense. They take their place quite naturally with those who came after and whose names are more familiar, Juan-Manuel Fangio, Stirling Moss, Jim Clark and Ayrton Senna. No doubt we shall be adding Michael Schumacher to the list soon enough. At Donington in 1937 the teams were:

Mercedes: Caracciola, von Brauchitsch, Lang and Seaman.

Auto Union: Rosemeyer, Müller and Hasse.

Writing in *The Motor*, the columnist 'Grande Vitesse' set out the general background. "Ever since the existing era of Grand Prix racing started in 1934, the German teams have been in a rather odd position. They were coming to racing of a new type and lacked drivers of the first quality. The Scuderia Ferrari, on the other hand, had been racing steadily for years and possessed a perfectly equipped team with a first-rate personnel all ready and willing. Mercedes borrowed Fagioli, Auto Union took Varzi. The former had Caracciola as team leader, the latter Hans Stuck, until then a hill-climb champion with no great experience of road racing. Thus they cast about in their own country for men to race in the teams, and in the past three years several have been called and few chosen, which accounts for the fact that this year both Mercedes and Auto Union have been listing comparatively unknown names in their teams."

Rudolf Caracciola was 36, a crisp, medium-sized man with a full face and dark hair swept back over the crown of the head in a static wave. He always looked dapper – no, classically smart – in a suit, collar and tie and, like Neubauer, Homburg hats suited him.

The name Caracciola sounded Italian but in fact the family had lived in Germany for generations. Rudolf believed "every man can achieve the goal he strives for" and began his lifestory[1] with the perfect illustration of that: himself. "I wanted to become a racing driver from my fourteenth birthday.

My wish seemed a hopeless one. In the middle-class circles in which I was raised, automobile racing was considered the passion of mad, rich people or a special kind of eccentricity, like tightrope walking for instance."

He was born into the hotel business in Remagen on the Rhine and his father intended to send him to university but study didn't interest him and his father died. The family decided he should work in an hotel somewhere to learn the business and then come back to the family hotel in Remagen.

Caracciola yearned to be involved with cars and a compromise was struck. He went "as an apprentice, to Fafnir's, in Aachen" – Fafnir made small cars. "Probably this strange indulgence on the part of the family was based on their assumption that the grimy work in the factory would spoil my appetite for automobiles forever and send me back ruefully to the clean-scrubbed family hearth."

He got in a fight with a Belgian at a night club in Aachen, protecting a friend, but Belgium had jurisdiction over the area as a product of the Versailles Treaty. Rather than risk making complications for his family, Caracciola fled to the other side of Germany and the lovely city of Dresden where he'd be Fafnir's representative.

The rest has the familiarity and inevitability of an ordinary motor racing story.

He noticed a newspaper advertisement for a small car race on the Avus circuit and borrowed one from Fafnir. He won, despite a protest about the size of the car's cylinder head. "When we emerged from the twilight back into the sun where friends were waiting with the hard-earned little barrel of beer, everything was quickly forgotten. Because I was young and I had won." Word spread in Dresden.

A few months later he met Neubauer at a Mercedes test session. Neubauer would remember[2] that everyone was too busy to bother much about the "boyish-looking figure" who'd secured a recommendation from Mercedes' branch in Dresden and wondered "rather irritably what we were expected to do with a complete greenhorn."

The greenhorn proved to be a gifted driver in wet weather, but tragedy stalked his life. His first wife Charly was killed in an avalanche at Arosa in 1933 and that same year he was badly hurt when the Alfa Romeo he was driving during practice for the Monaco Grand Prix crashed, shattering his thigh. It may be that he lived the rest of his life in pain – he died in 1959 of cirrhosis, a disease of the liver, probably caused by drinking unclean water in Triploi in the 1930s. There was no doubt in Neubauer's mind that, in 1937, he was the best driver Mercedes had.

A columnist in *The Motor* explained that Caracciola "lives, dreams and thinks of little but motor racing" and added: "Runs a pet dog in the shape of Maurice, a very decent dachshund." The addition, however innocent, may just have been the dawn of journalistic invasion into people's private lives. The column appeared, you see, under a heading 'Getting Personal' and began: "Everyone seems to like personal items about people these days."

Rene Dreyfus, who'd compete in the 1938 race, described (in

conversation with Nigel Roebuck, circa 1985) how "Rudi was not a genuine aristocrat but in terms of the racing hierarchy he believed himself to be."

Someone once wrote that in some very old people there is a pathos, in others a kind of grandeur. **Manfred von Brauchitsch** who now, as I write these words, is into his 90s, has the grandeur. It is not simply that he has lived a strange, inexplicable life of contradictions, but that he has survived. He seems both strong and frail, talkative and oddly reticent. His second wife insists he tires quickly and everybody wants to interview him all the time, so she holds a protective shield round him.

It's a shame, however understandable. There's a lot to ask him about.

Neubauer sums up von Brauchitsch's early years: "He was a good-looking young man who came of good military stock and would have taken a commission himself but for a motorcycle accident [in 1928]. He had considerable talent as a racing driver ... but he had an ungovernable temper. Fortunately he also had a rich uncle..."[3]

According to historian Chris Nixon[4] part of his recuperation from the accident was spent with a cousin who had a 40-room castle. The cousin's hobby was "motor cars and he owned three, one of which was a super-charged Mercedes."

Von Brauchitsch began to race and, in May 1932, won the Avus Grand Prix which, according to Neubauer, made him "famous overnight". It brought him money of his own for the first time and led to a role in a film, which Neubauer describes as highly successful but other reports suggest was "well received" but not more.

Von Brauchitsch joined the Mercedes team in 1934 and now, in 1937, 'Grande Vitesse' described him as "rather temperamental. A human bullet in a racing car, tempestuous, and nervy at the wheel. An overgrown schoolboy off duty. Tall, broad-shouldered, blonde [sic]", although contemporary photographs show his hair as dark.

To recapture the currents and tensions within a team then is extremely difficult, not least because the decorum of the time precluded public mention of the fact that there were currents and tensions. Death was a legitimate subject, for example, and would be covered in detail but the fact that von Brauchitsch looked down on Lang is reduced to almost complete silence. Lang wrote the story of his life[5] and didn't mention it once while Neubauer did, but only once: "Brauchitsch, who was a snob, seldom lost an opportunity of taunting Lang with his 'proletarian' origin."

The idea of inherited privilege as something quite normal – indeed the norm – on the scale at which it existed is perhaps disconcerting now. There seems to have been an in-born arrogance to von Brauchitsch, who lived a life difficult to comprehend. He was evidently too battle-scarred by motor racing to be called up for active service in the War, married his first wife, was drawn to visiting communist East Germany after the war, tried for treason in the West – and finally went East, where he worked for the Ministry of Sport. His wife committed suicide.

The Motor's thumbnail sketch, circa 1937: "debonair, rather like a film star to look at, is nephew to the German general of that name. Temperamental driver, gets very worked up and drives like a demon. Has had some of the world's worst luck. Liable to go round corners sideways but – here's the point – knows what he's doing." 'Grande Vitesse' said he had "very bright eyes and a face which lights up with enthusiasm. And he is a remarkable driver."

Dreyfus described von Brauchitsch as a "good driver, very fast on his day. A snob, a genuine member of the Prussian aristocracy. I think after the war he had nothing. Now [1985] he is Minister of Sports or whatever in East Germany, where I understand he lives in great splendour for saying all the right things when he is abroad."

Hermann Lang was quite unlike von Brauchitsch. He began his lifestory "I was born on 6 April 1909, in humble surroundings, my birthplace being Bad Cannstatt near Stuttgart." He added: "Father died in 1923. Mother brought us up under great difficulties, but managed it with mysterious maternal tenacity which is often inexplicable to us when grown up, yet taken as self-understood when we are children."[6]

Before Donington, *The Autocar* described Lang as a "first-class example of a successful racing driver who started at the bottom. He is 28 years old and was first trained as a mechanic, took up motorcycle racing and made himself a great reputation in sidecar work. He joined the Mercedes racing and experimental department when they expanded their racing policy in 1933, gradually 'wangled' test drivers, became a spare driver in 1935, and then in 1937 started the season by winning the richest race in the world, the Tripoli Grand Prix. Lang is rather a retiring sort of person, good looking, neat with a Roman nose and very penetrating eyes. He was recently married and his wife" – Lydia – "usually watches from the pits. Lang appears very fast indeed when driving, flinging his car about and looking extremely fierce."

The victory at Tripoli changed everything. "When I was reserve driver Lang, people gave advice and treated me like a schoolboy. Now I had become a person of some importance and my opinions were treated with interest."[7] By an irony among so many we've encountered, Lang had a difficult season after Tripoli.

Neubauer revealed part of the reason when he wrote that "Caracciola and Brauchitsch decided to join forces in preventing Lang, who was almost ten years younger and therefore prepared to take more risks, from snapping up the prizes." Neubauer estimated that the problem began at Leghorn (Livorno), a circuit in Italy. From the start of the race there Caracciola and Lang burst clear of the rest but locked into a "bitter duel" for the lead. "Lang tried to pass but Caracciola refused to make way for him – and jammed his foot on the accelerator, which was most unlike him..."[8]

The Motor's thumbnail sketch of Lang: "used to be a works mechanic and operated in the racing department before he got a wheel and went like a levin flash." Levin? That's lightning...

Dreyfus described Lang as a "simple man, with no great style in a racing car but very, very fast. Having been a mechanic, of course, he knew much more about the cars than the other drivers, which was an advantage. The mechanics worshipped him because he was one of them. By 1939 he was the fastest of all but his best years were lost to the war."

Richard Seaman's career is described in full later in the book so a precis will suffice here. "By rights Dick Seaman should never have been a professional racing driver. Born February 4th, 1913, the son of a wealthy distilleries magnate and financier, he sprang from the story-book world of French governesses, London town houses and yachting holidays in France. During his boyhood his family lived in Weald Hall, a splendid Tudor house that had once been the home of Queen Mary and Queen Elizabeth I…"[9]

The Motor's thumbnail sketch: "first Englishman since Segrave to win a Grand Prix, first Englishman to race for a Continental crack team. Rugby, Cambridge, rowing and all that. Has a fondness for motor boats, sleep, good food, good motorcars and good jests."

Bernd Rosemeyer was arguably Auto Union's only leading driver because the team had not renewed the contract of Achille Varzi, the Italian who could claim greatness but was now a drug addict. It was morphine, introduced by Paul Pietsch's wife Ilse, with whom Varzi was having an affair.

Rosemeyer, like Lang, began on motor bikes and joined the DKW racing team in 1934 – DKW were part of the Auto Union group. That interesting fact did not escape Rosemeyer who reportedly "worried" the Auto Union team management for a drive, and got one at the Avus in 1935. Neubauer saw him around this time and would forever reproach himself for "not spotting the genius in this fair-headed, good-looking young man."

The Autocar pointed out that "he is married to Elly Beinhorn, a well-known pilot in Germany, and they are a much publicised couple in Germany. He has untidy flaxen hair, wears Tyrolean hats, shorts, and is full of fun. He drives until he almost drops."

'Grande Vitesse' said: "At the head of the Auto Union team is that volatile person Bernd Rosemeyer, who always seems full of the joy of spring and has rapidly become the idol of young Germany. Rosemeyer skips about around his cars, leaps to the wheel with a running jump, holds out facetious signals from his pit to Caracciola during practising."

In 1936 Rosemeyer won five grands prix and became European Champion, an astonishing feat in only his second season. Elly would remember[10] that after one of the five – the Eifel Grand Prix at the Nürburgring, run in dense fog – he was given "a remarkable accolade: *Reichsführer* Heinrich Himmler was so impressed that he made Bernd an *Obersturmführer* in the SS – a very great honour at the time. All the German motor clubs were affiliated in some way to either the SS (*Schutzstaffel* – the Blackshirts) or the SA (*Sturmabteilung* – Stormtroopers or Brownshirts) and anyone who raced cars or motorbikes had to join the NSKK (*Nationalsozialistisches Kraftfahrer Korps* or Drivers' Corps.) Bernd was the only driver ever invited to join the SS and, of course, it was not the sort of invitation you could refuse!"

Approaching Donington, at least one experienced journalist felt he was the fastest driver on Earth.

Rosemeyer had Hermann Müller and Rudolf Hasse as team-mates. Neubauer judged Müller a brilliant young driver while *The Autocar* described him as a "short, dark and good-humoured young man, who is not spectacular but is gaining a good reputation. He began as a motorcycle rider, joined the DKW team and drove an Auto Union for the first time last year. He had a nasty crash in the German Grand Prix this July, but escaped completely unhurt."

Hasse was "a tall, bespectacled athlete. He usually manages to finish well up, and won his first big race this year, the Belgian Grand Prix. Hasse is pretty tough and used to be a trials driver. He graduated from the Auto Union school of drivers in 1936."[11]

The Motor's thumbnail sketch: "tallest driver of all, is head man of his local fire brigade, this being his father's idea of giving young Rudolf something serious to do when he isn't frittering his time away motor racing for Auto Union." 'Grande Vitesse' said: "Everybody who has witnessed grand prix racing this year will be quite familiar with the tall, slimly built and bespectacled figure of Hasse ... (he) looks like anything on Earth except a grand prix driver, and bears a strong resemblance to a stage curate."

Chapter 3

The master's last win

THAT SUNDAY EVENING after Brno, as Martin and Seaman journeyed to Vienna for a few beers, reporters and bystanders in Dover were deeply impressed by the Mercedes convoy of six lorries, six private cars and 18 mechanics who lined up on the quay for inspection by the convoy chief, Arnold Wychodil – incidentally, a Sudeten German. One reporter marvelled at how each of the four racing cars had its own lorry and wrote that they'd "sped across Germany and France at 70 mph," an astronomical average speed then.[1] More quietly, the three Auto Union cars arrived at Harwich.

The following morning *The Sporting Life* carried a brief paragraph under a small heading:

MRS K. PETRE
Mrs K. Petre, who was seriously injured while practising for the '500' at Brooklands, was yesterday stated at Weybridge Hospital to be "Still the same." She has been unconscious for eight days.

Petre, an extremely good looking woman, would helplessly play a sad and almost haunting part in events surrounding the Grand Prix because she and Rosemeyer knew each other well and, if things had been different, might have known each other a great deal better...

That Monday, Martin flew back to Croydon, landing at about 7.20 in the evening. His wife was there and so were Tommy Wisdom of *The Sporting Life* and William Boddy of *Motor Sport*, preparing to cover the arrival of the Mercedes contingent – Neubauer, Seaman, Lang, and von Brauchitsch – on the approaching Lufthansa Junkers 52 flight. Professor Robert Eberan-Eberhorst, the Auto Union Development Engineer who sometimes had the prefix von, was on it, too.

Martin lingered at the airport to greet the Germans and especially Seaman. Martin appeared to Boddy as being as excited as a schoolboy and told him Donington had become "the greatest thing that had happened since the Flood." (Although 60 years later Martin couldn't remember saying this he thought that he might well have done.) Martin confided some gossip he'd heard: "Stuck dropped by Auto Union."

Lydia Lang was "quite miserable" at the prospect of her maiden flight and confessed to her husband she had a "fear of flying and its attendant airsickness. However, we had lovely weather and flew comfortably to London. She had overcome her fright most bravely."[2]

The Junkers, due at 7.50, descended into view a few minutes late on a dank, sodden evening and landed, framed by the runway floodlighting. There was no sense of occasion and, as a saddened Boddy bemoaned, no official welcome, just a couple of employees from the Mercedes London office in Park Lane, that same office which "could not or would not" tell Boddy when the team had been due. Boddy had done what a reporter does: get there early and wait. The four Mercedes "private cars" which had journeyed with the second convoy were stationed outside.

Boddy wrote that the two Mercedes employees hadn't "thought to obtain tarmac-passes" so only he and Wisdom went forth towards the Junkers as it taxied in under the floodlights. Lang, emerging, looked fit. Seaman was the last to come down the steps and he looked fit, too, never fitter. Wisdom spoke to him and described how Seaman bore "the scars of his many crashes: a broken nose, a broken finger and a smashed knee." Seaman assured Wisdom he was thoroughly looking forward to Donington.

The evening was light-hearted, graced with humanity and spiced with humour. In the Customs hall a passenger caught the anonymity of the arrival by asking the small, peering crowd "are you here to meet me?" At least the Lufthansa pilots made sure to shake hands and have a brief word with each driver as they left the hall. Neubauer joked with the Customs officials and we might risk imagining that: the rotund figure in the Homburg who didn't speak English, really had 'Nothing to Declare', except two convoys of lorries, four racing cars beyond price, several tons of spares, a mountain of tyres, assorted saloon cars and a couple of dozen people...

The most revealing part was when everyone had passed through Customs and milled outside the hall. Von Brauchitsch, full of life, did a little dance in the rain before getting into one of the private cars. Eberan-Eberhorst made everyone laugh by seizing the 'L' plate from a parked MG and threatening to put it on Rosemeyer's car when they got to Donington. Neubauer "called to his drivers as to children to bring their luggage forward – he calls them by their surnames, very clearly" – and then "coatless and ignoring the heavy rain," didn't get into his car until he had made sure the others, plus luggage, were in theirs.[3]

These cars, all black and chromium, moved off from Croydon in the familiar convoy formation through the maze of south London – Streatham and over Clapham Common – towards the Dorchester. Boddy reported that they spread out at first but discipline prevailed and they assumed a "most imposing line-ahead formation. No cheering crowds lined the route..."

The only interest shown was when they had to halt at traffic lights and people's gazes concentrated on the bizarre and unexpected sight of cars with German registration plates in a convoy. Pre television, the drivers would certainly not have been recognised. Pre mass media coverage, nobody emerging from a fish 'n' chip shop down Streatham High Street on a rainy Monday evening would have known Hermann Lang from Manfred von Brauchitsch, or probably have heard of either.

The convoy proceeded smoothly and had only one alarm, when a driver forgot to be on the left (something he may never have encountered before) and rounded a traffic island on the wrong side along Purley Way. This gave the driver of a bus edging out from a side road a *moment.*

It was Lang's first visit to England and he recorded how, threading through mile after mile of the maze, London "seemed enormous to us".[4]

Rosemeyer, meanwhile, returned to Berlin from Brno. He and Elly had driven down to the Czech race despite the fact that she was heavily pregnant. He'd fly from Berlin to London on the morrow, the Tuesday.

Benito Mussolini, the Fascist leader of Italy, was in Berlin cementing the Italian-German Axis...

On the Tuesday, a dozen Auto Union mechanics left Zwickau by car for Leipzig airport. Ludwig Sebastian, who'd be looking after Rosemeyer's car, recorded how at "8 o'clock on the dot the Junkers 52 moved on to the runway. The machine shot forward at full speed, rose elegantly from the ground and, before I really realised it, the airport seemed to me nothing more than a child's toy. We headed for London directly and approached the city of millions in marvellous weather. I will never forget the impression this labyrinth of houses made on me from 2,200 metres."[5]

Drivers Hasse and Müller, with team manager Dr Karl Feuereissen, were on a Sabena Junkers due at 2.20.

The mechanics landed at 1pm and a welcome committee of sorts was there: a Herr Hermann of Auto Union Sales Limited, a Fleet Street photographer evidently unaware of whether these mechanics were drivers or not, the *Evening News* motoring correspondent, a *Motor Sport* photographer – and William Boddy.

The mechanics created confusion in the Customs hall and it took some time for all their luggage to be piled into the lorry outside. Then they waited for the Sabena flight to come in and it was late, not arriving until 2.55. Boddy had the knack of creating portraits with words. Hasse, he'd write, looked "for all the world like a student, with neat overcoat, soft hat, horn-rim spectacles and stubby black shoes." Hasse confided some gossip which in fact was hard news: Varzi wasn't coming. Varzi, an Italian, joined Auto Union in 1935, had an affair with the wife of fellow driver Paul Pietsch and was now a morphine addict – as we have seen. Of him Rene Dreyfus would say: "He was very nearly the equal of Tazio Nuvolari and sometimes better. He was an aloof man. I don't want to talk too much about him and Pietsch's wife and everything that came afterwards, which people know about. The tragedy of the man was that he destroyed himself. Before that, his precision in a racing car was extraordinary."

In the Customs hall something inadvertent (perhaps) happened to Hasse's hat – it was "bashed in"[6] – and that lightened the mood. It became lighter when the *Motor Sport* photographer asked Hasse, Müller and Feuereissen to pose for a photograph, they demanded money and, Boddy recounts, were "vastly amused when we told them we had no English money."

The whole Auto Union contingent set off in an Imperial Airways coach which evidently didn't have enough seats for them all because the "surplus" passengers travelled in a car which an employee from the Auto Union London office had driven down. *This* convoy just had time for a little snack and "off we raced to Middle England"[7] by train.

Rosemeyer flew from Berlin that afternoon in a Dutch Air Lines Douglas and came alone because of Elly's pregnancy. Before he left she packed his evening dress and "told him to phone Kay Petre once he got there and take her out to dinner, as he had enjoyed her company so much in South Africa."[8] (Neubauer gives a different version of this. Elly, he wrote[9] had "sent a telegram to Kay Petre asking her to meet her husband. Bernd Rosemeyer looked so delighted that his wife, as she later admitted, felt a stab of jealousy.")

According to Elly, Rosemeyer wasn't "at all keen" to race at Donington. The car had lost the last three races to Mercedes and been beaten 7–5 across the season. He felt there was "no point in risking his reputation by driving an inferior car on his first visit to England" but competed out of obligation to the team.[10]

Rosemeyer was airborn as the diligent Boddy trekked from Croydon to Victoria station where the Continental boat train came in, bringing Caracciola and his wife. Caracciola "in heavy coat and soft hat, walked lame and seemed tired, though he posed several times for the cameras. He brought so much luggage it overflowed from his big Mercedes-Benz luggage container onto the back seat."

Rosemeyer arrived at Croydon at 9.50 in, Boddy felt, "rather a dour mood and a truly wonderful hat." Kay Petre, of course, was not there to meet him and he spent the night in London because it was too late to reach the Midlands now.

(Neubauer claimed that Rosemeyer "found her in a London hospital, swathed in bandages and still unconscious" and further claimed that, because Rosemeyer did not ring Elly that evening as he had arranged, Elly "began to have some very uncharitable thoughts. The call finally came through about one o'clock in the morning." Something approximating to this did happen but, as we shall see, not until after the Grand Prix.)[11]

At Donington, the Mercedes mechanics began preparing the cars, which the *Derby Evening Telegraph* thought worth a three-picture spread on the front page headed:

GERMAN CHALLENGE. The caption read:
Scenes of activity at Donington Park today where the German Mercedes-Benz and Auto-Union cars are being prepared for the International

Grand Prix race on Saturday. The work area was the farm buildings opposite Coppice Farm at the far end of the long straight and in these buildings the cars were housed. They could be taken to the pits along an inner road.

The circuit had been altered again by extending the extension. Starkey's Corner was gone, creating one of the greatest spectacles in grand prix racing. Cars went along the main straight but continued into the extension, which was a long descending incline, then a right-right at the bottom round a tight horseshoe. It was christened Melbourne Corner, because it was in the direction of the village of Melbourne. From the exit to the horseshoe, the cars were onto a long climb back up. Where they rejoined the old track, there was a sort of hump and, at the speeds the Mercedes and Auto Unions would be reaching, the hump became a launching pad, all four wheels airborne. This was christened Melbourne Rise and those who witnessed what happened there still speak of it.

Seaman could certainly be diplomatic and when a reporter asked him about the extension he said it allowed greater speeds to be reached. He praised Melbourne Corner and noted with pleasure that when the new section of track had been laid there it had been given width. That made it, he concluded, easier to negotiate than the old Starkey's.

The timetable and regulations for the race meeting are so thorough that they have a Germanic feel to them. Although it was surely Craner who drew them up, Neubauer would have heartily approved, and quite probably did.

INTERNATIONAL DONINGTON
GRAND PRIX.
SATURDAY OCTOBER 2nd 1937

INSTRUCTIONS TO COMPETITORS

PRACTISING
The hours for practising are as follows: Wednesday and Thursday September 29th and 30th and Friday October 1st from 10.30am to 12.30pm and 2.30pm to 4.30pm.

All practising will be controlled from the PITS. Each competitor will use the pit allotted to him for the Races. Competitors must enter the course via the Paddock or through Wilson Lodge entrance. Those garaged at Coppice House Garages must leave Coppice House by 10am and 2pm and be driven to the pits at the beginning of each practising period.

In no circumstances will cars be allowed to practice from Coppice Garages, neither will any car be allowed to leave or enter Coppice House from the course during the practising periods. A breach of this regulation, which is made solely in the interest of competitors' own safety, may result in a fine up to £5, or exclusion from the race, at the discretion of the Stewards.

A competitor may leave the course during Official practice by going straight on at RED GATE CORNER up the inner circuit, but will not be able to rejoin during that practice period.

No driver may commence practice unless his car is equipped with the numbers required by the Regulations, excepting the front, when the number may be painted on the front of the car so that it can be plainly read by the timekeepers.

DRIVERS should pay particular attention to the Flag signals which for the practising periods are as follows:

YELLOW FLAG – Take care, Danger Ahead!

BLUE FLAG – Keep to the right.

BLACK FLAG – over Competitor's number – Competitor must stop immediately, and must not proceed until instructed to do so by an official.

RED FLAG – Stop instantly.

WHITE FLAG – Practice concluded. No competitor to begin a fresh lap.

The Stewards may exlude from the Race any driver or spare driver who, in their opinion, has not taken sufficient advantage of the practices to make himself fully acquainted with the course, or by his driving during practices is judged to possess insufficient skill to take part in the Race itself, or has driven in a dangerous or inconsiderate manner.

That Tuesday night in Berlin, on the site of the 1936 Olympic Games, Hitler and Mussolini spoke to a million-strong crowd. When the enormous bell used at the Olympics began to toll, floodlights came on giving that atmosphere which the Nazis valued so much: the strength of the million, the mystery of darkness, the hope of the sudden light all creating an inevitability of communal – but never individual – power. Hitler and Mussolini spoke passionately about their missions of peace...

Sebastian and the other Auto Union mechanics arrived at Derby station at 10pm and were driven to Donington Hall, where they'd be staying.

The Mercedes drivers stayed at the Black Boy Hotel in Nottingham, which Lang described as "a typically English hotel, full of nooks and crannies internally and externally. So much so, that we had a job finding our way about in it. Interestingly enough there were five bars in the hotel, all of which had a different purpose. One, for instance, was barred to ladies."[12]

The Black Boy stood amidst an arcade of shops. It had a massive central tower flanked by timbered gables and a Bavarian balcony with wooden balustrades which made it looked distinctly un-English. It offered 95 bedrooms, and a single room cost from 7s to 9s. Dinner varied from 3s 6d to 5s 6d. The prices represented the standard fare of a three star hotel.

Martin stayed in an hotel at Ashby-de-la-Zouch, probably The Royal which proclaimed it was "entirely modernised and under new management". It offered a new dining room, H&C in bedrooms [hot and cold water] and new bars. These were Martin's problem. "All the drunks were downstairs making an (expletive) row – Tommy Wisdom, Charles Brackenbury [Martin's mechanic] and so on – the usual fun-makers. So there I was trying to get some sleep on the first floor but when they went to town you never heard such a bloody noise in all your life."

Next day, *The Sporting Life* carried a brief medical update:

MRS PETRE: "SLIGHTLY IMPROVED"
Mrs Kay Petre was stated at Weybridge Hospital yesterday to have "slightly improved." She is conscious for longer periods, and seems to recognise people. Her husband, Major H. A. Petre, spends most of the day at his wife's bedside.

Rosemeyer caught the train from St Pancras station at 8.30am and wouldn't be able to practice at Donington until later on in the afternoon. The morning session would start at 10.30 prompt under Craner's decree.

The Mercedes drivers made the 20-minute drive to Donington. Both the Hall and the parkland etched an immediate impression on Lang. "Our mechanics stayed there, and all participants met at an enormous table for lunch. Around the castle [sic] were beautifully kept lawns, and a few hills, dotted here and there with an old oak tree. Large herds of deer could be seen and one could drive up close to them as they were used to the presence of human beings. They lived a quiet, secure existence, as if in a national game reserve."

When practice began, Lang found the track surface less than ideal. He quickly realised that the circuit was too narrow and had too many bends to be really fast. Just as quickly, he discovered Melbourne Rise … "a little hill where fast cars literally took off and flew through the air for a short distance. In particular the chassis suffered here." Despite all this he thought his chances in the race might well be good.[13]

Auto Union were soon adapting their cars because the circuit "made great demands on both drivers and cars." The mechanic Sebastian, also noted that "the 5.2 kilometre track had hairpin bends, short straights and bumps. The rough road surface led to surprisingly high wear of tyres. After ten or twelve practice laps the tyres were already worn down to the white warning lines."[14] This matter of tyre-wear would soon become much more than a talking point: it threatened to reduce any tactics in the race to chaos and could have cost von Brauchitsch his life.

That first morning the Mercedes drivers went out before anyone else and a reporter from the *Derby Evening Telegraph* became the first to babble about being shaken and breathless. The cars, he wrote, "demonstrated their wonderful powers of acceleration in staggering fashion," especially over Melbourne Rise.[15]

Tich Allen, reporting for the *Leicester Evening Mail*, remembers that "the first time I saw the cars I was down at the hairpin and I watched them erupt from Holly Wood. It was a tremendous shock – like at an old-fashioned film of something coming towards you which suddenly blew up in size and nearly hit you in the face. The cars didn't appear to be real. From nowhere they materialised in front of you just like in the cinema.

"It was genuinely quite unbelievable for the first lap or two. They had far more power than they could use and didn't drive in a very smooth way: they tended to go in blips of throttle – you'd hear *baaar-baaarp* – and every time they did that the back wheels, which were really big, spun. Also they were using a strange fuel which made your eyes water.

"One good thing about it, and which made the coverage so much easier, was that – the Germans being so efficient – they gave us all very comprehensive information packs, beautifully prepared. These were wallets containing whole-plate photographs of the drivers, of the cars plus all the cars' technical details and all the drivers' biographical details. These publicity packs ... oh, they were wonderful! They really were. Normally at race meetings you didn't get any help, only a programme – that was all."

The mystery over the whereabouts of Varzi increased as the cars settled into practice. *The Motor* noted cryptically that he didn't arrive so Hasse "was substituted" but *The Motor* doesn't seem to have asked *why* Varzi hadn't arrived. Of more interest to the magazine was that both German teams were running the axles they had used at the Nürburgring and these were too low for Donington. Mercedes were having trouble, too, with their brakes and Auto Union with their carburation. Despite that the laps were coming at an average of 80 miles an hour.

Martin's V8 Ford was still slogging back from Brno with his ERA so he borrowed a 1500 Maserati and would actually set his qualifying time in that. The contrast between this way of going motor racing and their way of going motor racing is another of those aspects which, in retrospect, seem so foreboding.

Von Brauchitsch set fastest time early on at 2 minutes 15.4 seconds (83.2 miles an hour). In 1935 Farina had taken pole with 2 minutes 8.4 seconds but von Brauchitsch was travelling all the way down the extension, slow round Melbourne Corner and all the way back up again, certainly half a mile more. And von Brauchitsch, like the others, had only just begun.[16]

Seaman was second on 2 minutes 16.4 seconds (82.5 mph) and Lang third on 2 minutes 17.4 seconds (81.9 mph). That presented another contrast. Three ERAs were going round and each covered five laps with Earl Howe the fastest of them on 2 minutes 26.2 seconds (76.9 mph). Raymond Mays was 'second' in what already was Another Race on 2 minutes 27.2 seconds (76.4 mph) and Pat Whitehead (no time, but 72.7 mph).

To the non-specialist the difference between von Brauchitsch's fastest lap and that of Howe may not seem a chasm, especially since the ERA was strictly sit-up-and-beg against the full weight of the Germans' onslaught; but those at Donington that Wednesday morning who understood, *knew* the context. The race was over 80 laps and, even if von Brauchitsch made his Mercedes go no faster than he had done in this exploratory period, he would cover each of the 80 laps ten seconds quicker than Howe. That accumulated.

Von Brauchitsch would win by more than 13 *minutes*, which was *six laps*, which was *18 1/2 miles* – which was another world altogether.

Caracciola's Mercedes was ready but that had no immediate relevance because he wasn't due until the afternoon. One of the six "private cars" in the second convoy had been allocated for his use and was at Mercedes in Park Lane awaiting him. He collected it and drove up towards Donington. Many there must have wondered what he would do with all his formidable gifts when he arrived. Eclipse von Brauchitsch? Eclipse Seaman? Eclipse everybody?

Lunch was taken in the Hall and Boddy has a delightful anecdote about this (or a subsequent day). Seaman had left his goggles there and was going to go and get them when Neubauer stopped him. "Ze Seaman stays here, ze mechanic fetches ze goggles." Anyway, after lunch, taken in the Hall, Rosemeyer, Müller and Hasse came out but their Auto Unions sounded a little "bloodshot." Rosemeyer emerged last of the three and did so rather impatiently because the car clearly wasn't performing properly.[17] There was a bizarre explanation. The Auto Union "chemist" had been brought over to blend the fuel ingredients supplied by Shell, had blended 1,500 gallons but got the proportions wrong and, all unknowning, departed for Germany. Shell took this matter in hand and correctly processed a new batch themselves.[18]

It worked. Wisdom went directly into the company of the shaken and breathless. Rosemeyer "frightened the crowd as he shot uphill [over Melbourne Rise], slid sideways past the mechanics standing in front of the pits and disappeared, stones flying from his spinning wheels, with his foot hard down at well over 100 mph. In that fantastic and hair-raising lap the young German had smashed the lap record."[19]

Rosemeyer's time of 2 minutes 14.6 seconds was 0.8 of a second faster than von Brauchitsch. Never mind Earl Howe, who Rosemeyer would have beaten by 16 minutes, von Brauchitsch was now vulnerable on the accumulation. Slower than Rosemeyer by that 0.8, it still translated to more than a *minute* over the 80 laps, and if you've ever stood waiting for a full minute for a racing car to come by you understand how long that really is.

Wisdom, even more breathless than a moment ago, added: "As the cars accelerate at phenomenal speed between the corners, smoke rings the rear wheels and the road is paved with melted rubber."

Practice was bubbling nicely.

(The tyre-wear factor provoked Wisdom to drift into whimsy, which wasn't exactly his usual territory, by recording that Auto Union had brought ten tons of them and at this rate might need all ten. They'd also brought 2 1/2 tons of inner tubes and hundreds of spare wheel rims but he didn't give his opinion on them.)

Caracciola arrived too late to practice. Neubauer was seen to have "some comments to make" when Caracciola told him he'd lost his way.[20] It is, I suppose, comforting to know that even Neubauer's planning was sometimes defeated by the one thing it was designed to guard against, human fallability.[21]

The times this Wednesday: Rosemeyer 2:14.6; von Brauchitsch 2:15.2; Seaman 2:16.4; Lang 2:17.4; Müller 2:20.4; Hasse 2:21.0; Howe 2:26.2; Mays 2:27.2; Dobson 2:29.2; Hyde 2:34.8; and Maclure 2:37.2.

Britain was then a major military-economic power and head of an enormous empire. To recapture the sense of adventure which a first visit must have elicited remains elusive, especially since the presumption must be that few of the personnel of both German teams had visited, or had had reason to visit Britain, before. The exception seems to be Caracciola, who'd competed in Ireland (Phoenix Park, Ards), and spectated at the Brooklands circuit near London in 1936 when he was over for the Motor Show.

Whatever, that made the impact of their cars and drivers on this first day of practice even more enormous; and some of the Germans fully intended to exploit the opportunities which the adventure offered them. That Wednesday evening Ludwig Sebastian went to the "Baseball Ground", Derby's *soccer* stadium, and watched Derby County play a Scottish team. He didn't record the name of the Scots (it was Hearts) but he noted the score. County lost 3–2.

Boddy arrived at the circuit at 8.30 on the Thursday morning for the second day's practise. "The very first thing that we saw was Herr Neubauer and his be-spectacled chief engineer seated at a table in the yard of the barn at Coppice Farm, where Mercedes were stabled, taking careful written notes of the proceedings. There was a typewriter in use at the pits, telephone calls came through from Berlin, both teams retained sump-drawings – presumably for analysis on their return – nearly every mechanic carried his own notebook and used it frequently, and at the end of the day Neubauer lectured a group of mechanics who departed laughing happily."

These glimpses of the German organisation were, Boddy concluded, what "makes such a deep impression on a British onlooker." He set out other impressive glimpses: how nothing was left to chance, how the mechanics worked with calm efficency and attended to every detail, however small – and if one of the mechanics was "entrusted" with a car for a "trial" lap you saw a "look of child-like happiness" on his face.[22]

Neubauer was an obvious and unmissable target for practical jokes and when someone put a firework (a squib, actually) under his "private" Mercedes road car he reverberated with laughter, and so did all the Germans, and so apparently did everyone else.[23]

One German account says: "During practise, the jokers had a very good time. The funniest among them, Charly [sic] Brackenbury, hid a home-made jumping jack under the hood of Neubauer's saloon car, and when Neubauer took the car to go and have breakfast there was a sudden and loud hissing noise accompanied by clouds of smoke and a terrible bang. Neubauer seemed to find it almost as amusing as Caracciola and Rosemeyer, who knew all about it and were watching. Another prank was that somebody attached an 'L' plate to the front of Rosemeyer's Auto Union but unfortunatey he noticed it before he got into the car, and removed it."

The informal nature of the British approach was unconsciously revealed by *The Motor*'s reporter who wrote "Powys-Lybbe not here." Anthony

Powys-Lybbe, who had a moustache, wore glasses and looked positively rakish in his trilby hat, had driven an Alfa Romeo in the Donington race the year before. He was known as a steady driver who won several races in Ireland with an Alfa. The notion that he simply hadn't shown up now – and that the reporter hadn't found out why but dismissed it in those two words – is of its time.[24] The reporter did, however, gather some gossip. "Bira, they say, is to try an Auto Union, as Prince Chula is thinking about buying one for next year."

Out on the track Caracciola was "cunningly"[25] going round varying his line to discover, and remember, where the bumps were. He also approached Melbourne Rise with some caution and visibly leapt less than all the others. Caracciola was in the process of covering most laps and managed a time of 2 minutes 17.6 seconds (81.76 mph). Moreover there are suggestions that Caracciola may have been unwell.

Caracciola's wife Alice was a familiar person in the pit lanes of Europe. Born Alice Hoffmann-Trobeck she was "known for her remarkable ability with languages, and during races she was tops as a timekeeper. With a double chronometer she was unsurpassed, registering all cars, all speeds."[26] On this Thursday, while Caracciola was making mental notes of each bump, Neubauer became embroiled in a good-natured discussion with Alice over who was the more accurate at timing the laps – she or he. They put it to the test and Neubauer won.

Sebastian recorded how Rosemeyer was "not at all satisfied with his brakes. There were parts of the track where the car really took off and Rosemeyer's feet were sore after only a few laps. I had to build in a special air-cooling system."[27] Rosemeyer exploited that in the morning session by producing a lap of 2 minutes 14.2 seconds which lifted the lap record to 83.77 mph.

Wisdom reverted to his normal service. "Time and again Rosemeyer's car left the road and dived through the air. Up the steep hill from Melbourne Corner roared the car, spitting smoke and flames from the short exhaust stacks behind the driver's head. As it breasted the hill it left the road and shot through the air for 20 yards. As it hit the road again the Auto Union slid and snaked and looked as if it would charge the pits. Time and again the smiling Rosemeyer did this, looking as though he were thoroughly enjoying the gamble with death."[28]

Boddy, ever alert and no doubt roaming the pits notebook in hand, observed that Neubauer, having proved his point with Alice Caracciola, was locked into a "long, earnest talk" with von Brauchitsch. About Rosemeyer?

Lang and von Brauchitsch slightly improved their Wednesday times that morning but the tyre-wear worry continued: Müller's Auto Union had stripped a rear after a few serious laps and would do so again in the afternoon.

At lunch in the Hall the Mercedes team ate together in domestic harmony, Seaman sitting next to Neubauer, Caracciola next to Alice and Lang next to Lydia. They all took soft drinks except von Brauchitsch, who preferred milk. The drivers were allowed to smoke. Seaman "derived much amusement" from helping Neubauer, who would have been at a loss with the English language and the impenetrable pounds, shillings and pence, to settle the bill.[29]

In the afternoon Rosemeyer did a lap of 2 minutes 14.6 seconds, von Brauchitsch and Seaman next, both on 2 minutes 14.6 seconds. Boddy was now firmly among the shaken and breathless. If you have not seen the German cars before, he insisted, you will soon be "almost raving with enthusiasm and astonishment. To see them snake down Holly Wood Hill and leap the bump at Hairpin Bend, taking the whole road to corner and somehow fight straight before shooting the narrow stone bridge at Starkey's was – well, a sight worth many, many times the 1s 3d that Mr Craner charged the public to get in. The German mechanics tried hard not to smile when the first British driver came past and someone facetiously suggested that Mr Craner should have constructed cycle-paths for the British competitors." Boddy, writing in *Motor Sport* in June 1999, said that he and John Eason-Gibson were profusely impressed – "in spite of track passes, we climbed back over the fence when we first heard the cars approaching through the woods."

Wisdom remained breathless. "Hard-boiled racing motorists and mechanics who usually do not lift an eyebrow at the thrills of 100 mph duels admitted to me today that they were frightened as they watched the German cars practising."[30]

The airborne leaping has passed into folklore. Charlie Martin, whose ERA had arrived by the Friday – so he'd race that, not the Maserati – said "you didn't get the ERA into the air, oh no, no, no. They wouldn't climb that high. I don't think we ever took off. We did see the Mercedes and Auto Unions taking off, however. We'd be following along behind them and you couldn't miss it. Mind you, you knew they were going to do it so you were waiting for it. I don't think they ever got too sideways when they landed because their drivers would never have been able to hold them if they had."

The times this Thursday: Rosemeyer 2:12.2; von Brauchitsch 2:12.8; Seaman 2:14.6; Lang 2:14.8; Hasse 2:16; Caracciola 2:16.6; Müller 2:16.8; Bira 2:25.0; Hanson 2:27.6; Dobson 2:28.4; Mays 2:31.6; Martin 2:32.8; Whitehead/Peter Walker 2:34.2; Maclure 2:35.2 and Hyde 2:36.2.

Craner had set out very clearly, in another of his Neubaueresque instructions, exactly how scrutineering – making sure the cars conformed to the regulations – would be carried out on the Friday.

INTERNATIONAL DONINGTON
GRAND PRIX
SATURDAY OCTOBER 2ND 1937

INSTRUCTIONS TO COMPETITORS

CAR NO...
The scrutineering of competing cars will take place in the Coppice Garages at Donington Park Friday October 1st.

Competitors will report to the Chief Scrutineer, with their cars at the time at stated at the foot of their instructions.

Cars must be in Racing trim, as laid down in the Regulations and must have:

Numbers painted on either side of the body, and on the front of the car which can be plainly read by the timekeepers and Officials.

After the car has been certified correct and the examination sheet signed, competitors may remove their cars.

Competitors are requested to note particularly that every requirement provided for in the Regulations for the Scrutineering must be strictly adhered to.

Drivers and Spare Drivers must have with them their Competition Licences and Drivers Licences, and MEDICAL CERTIFICATE.

TIME FOR REPORTING: you are requested to report in the PADDOCK at Donington Park at .... on Friday October 1st.

Any car not presented within three hours of the hour named may be excluded from the Race.

On this final day of practice *The Sporting Life* carried a paragraph: "Yesterday's news of Mrs Kay Petre was that she had had a fair night and progress was maintained."

At Donington there was a big increase in the number of spectators. Mercedes' tactic was to get out early and lock up some good times. Lang averaged 83.58 mph, Seaman 82.58 mph, then von Brauchitsch did a lap of 2 minutes 9.4 seconds (86.10 mph) which lifted the lap record again and gave him provisional pole position. On the lap von Brauchitsch had a moment (which Wisdom described as "electrifying"). Powering down the twisting hill from Holly Wood the Mercedes left the track, crossed some grass and, at over a hundred miles an hour, ran along some banking for about forty yards. Von Brauchitsch kept his foot on the accelerator, wrestled the car and got it back on. He continued at full blast. Rosemeyer touched 180 mph but did a 2 minutes 11.8 (85.36 mph).

At the other end of the grid Martin was working all night to get his ERA ready. In the Maserati he'd done a best time of 2 minutes 31.6 seconds which was a much, much greater chasm to von Brauchitsch than the Rosemeyer-Earl Howe chasm of Wednesday. Von Brauchitsch would beat Martin by 29 *minutes,* which was 14 *laps*, which was 43 miles – which was another world again.

After practice Sebastian once more renewed the brake linings on Rosemeyer's car and "would run them in" on the morrow before the race. Grid:

von Brauchitsch	Rosemeyer	Lang	Seaman
(Mercedes)	(Auto Union)	(Mercedes)	(Mercedes)
2:09.4	2:11.4	2:11.2	2:11.2

	Müller	Caracciola	Hasse
	(Auto Union)	(Mercedes)	(Auto Union)
	2:15.2	2:15.2	2:16.0

'B. Bira'	Mays	Howe	Hanson
(Maserati)	(ERA)	(ERA)	(Maserati)
2.25.0	2:26.8	2:26.8	2:27.4

	Dobson	Martin	Whitehead
	(ERA)	(ERA)	(ERA)
	2:28.6	2:31.6	2:32.0

Maclure
(Riley)
2:35.2

Note: There are discrepencies in the various sources for these times and, presumably, they were taken by hand-held stopwatches anyway, with all the variations that that could produce. One German source, for example, gives von Brauchitsch's fastest lap as 2:10.8 and Seaman's as 2:14.6. The fractions were not as important then as they would be now – the 1937 race was long and Donington offered so many places for overtaking that grid positions didn't really matter. I have taken the times above from Doug Nye's *The British Grand Prix 1926–1976* (B.T. Batsford Ltd).

That evening, following Sebastian's lead in maximising the adventure by sampling what was on offer, the Auto Union team went to watch some greyhound racing[31] and the tic-tac of the bookmakers impressed Rosemeyer profoundly. That day, too, according to Boddy: "Herr J. Werlin, Managing Director of the Mercedes-Benz Company in Germany, presided at a tea-party at the Dorchester on the eve of the race … and went up to Donington and back to London the same evening in his type 230." This afternoon tea was the one set out (no pun intended) in the memorandum to Neubauer on 3 September.

Craner had already drawn up and circulated his orders.

INTERNATIONAL DONINGTON
GRAND PRIX
SATURDAY OCTOBER 2nd 1937

INSTRUCTIONS TO COMPETITORS

THE RACE
On the morning of the Race, competitors will assemble in the PADDOCK not later than 11.30am

All spares, fuel, oil, tools and other material required for the Race must be installed in the Pits before 12 noon.

All tenders, lorries, service cars, etc. must be clear of the pits by 12 noon and can be parked on the new road leading from Redgate Corner behind the barriers at the top of the Pits. Please note do not park your tenders just inside but take them to a point behind the notice, so that the

Public can have full view of Redgate Corner from Starkey Hill. PETROL, OIL & TYRE Companies' supply waggons will be permitted to park Lorries behind the Pits, but no other vehicles will be permitted to do so. Service Cars may, if so desired, be returned to the Paddock instead of Parking in the new road.

At 12.30pm competing cars will leave the Paddock led by an Official Car, and will proceed via the new section of the course to the pits, where they will be *Parked in their Starting Order.* The Official car will set the pace, and may not be passed.

At 12.50pm all engines will be stopped.

The race will be started by means of a Union Jack which will be dipped by the Starter, who will be stationed on the Road, opposite the front row of cars. No Mechanics are permitted to be on the road during the Start, the road must be clear save the Drivers and their Team Manager. If a car is started before the Flag is dipped the Car may be excluded or such other appropriate penalty as may be ordered by the stewards.

Retirals. All Cars retiring during the Race must be parked in the Retirement Enclosure at the top end of the pits. On no account will cars be permitted to enter the Paddock or Coppice Garages until the conclusion of the Race.

Finish. As each competitor completes his required distance, a chequered Flag and the competitors number will be displayed at the Pits. He must not stop, but shall complete a further lap, and then pull into the Finishers Enclosure beyond the Pits, where the car will be sealed by the Official Scrutineer if so required.

OUTSIDE ASSISTANCE. Competitors are warned that outside assistance of any description whatsoever may render a car liable to disqualification. Drivers stopping at the pits must pull in to the right of the road and must give clearly the necessary warning of their intention to stop. A Driver pulling out from the Replenishment Depot must satisfy himself that in so doing he is not obstructing the course of an overtaking car.

F.G. CRANER
Clerk of the Course

The admission prices were: All parts except enclosures, 5s (children 2s 6d); covered stand opposite pits, 5s; uncovered stand at Hairpin Corner, 2s 6d; uncovered stand at Starkey Hill, 2s 6d; paddock, 5s; car parking, 2s 6d.[32]

After midnight an RAF officer called Eric Verdon-Roe, eldest son of A.V. Roe – who gave his name to his company, which manufactured aeroplanes – wrote up his diary for the day. He and friends were going to the race and the diary entry seems to capture the spirit as well as the logistics of travel then.

Left home at 16.50 and drove hard to Newbury via Hungerford, arriving 18.00. John in good form. H&O arrived and we were all on our way in the V

8. Paused at Banbury for dinner at Wheatley Hall, decided to stay night, as we were still a long way from Melton Mowbray. Retired 01.00.

Next morning, *The Sporting Life* gave their hospital update: "Last night's bulletin of Mrs Kay Petre stated that she was 'comfortable'."

Interest in the race was so great that it created deep ripples of traffic and locals said there'd never been that many vehicles on Leicestershire's roads at any one time before. It was a misty autumnal morning, the cars ghostly as they came from it in such quantity.

"So bad was the rush at 11 o'clock that a Leicester tramcar took half-an-hour to travel from Victoria Park to the Clock Tower. At the same time there was another hold up in Belgrave-gate and Belgrave-road. Similar traffic jams occurred in many parts of the county, especially in the Loughborough, Coalville, and Ashby-de-la-Zouch districts."[33]

The ripples flowed into Derby. "From an early hour hundreds of cars streamed through the town on their way to the race. Many of them were low, rakish sports models lending an appropriate dash of colour to the scene; others, big saloons carrying full loads of passengers, bore testimony to the irresistible attraction of the event."[34]

The mist lifted and now beautifully pure sunlight cloaked the parkland. Cars were everywhere, in rows in the parking places or crawling towards them. Boddy noted that "Mercedes-Benz models of all ages thundered into the grounds and owners of lesser marques moved their cars that these Mercs might be parked in the front rows." Eventually even the vast car parks were full and cars had to be left at the roadside, drivers and passengers hurrying towards the circuit.

Among them was a specialist motorsport photographer called Louis Klemantaski, whose work endures to this day. He'd stayed at the White Hart Inn at Kegworth, a village some five miles away, set off early and at Donington saw "cars parked everywhere. Every space the whole way round the circuit was full of vehicles and people."

Among them, too, was a 14-year-old in short trousers whose father commentated on motor bike races and, for that reason, wasn't here: so it was mother who'd brought him. He was called Murray Walker. "I had a general interest in grand prix racing although I can't pretend I was as involved then as I am now! In 1937 we went up to Donington with a German – whose name I can't remember but who, unsurprisingly, had a long, black leather coat. He must have been a friend of the family or maybe he was something to do with one of the teams. We drove up in his car.

"We had a great family friend whose name was Joe Woodhouse and he'd been in the army of occupation in Germany after the First World War. He married a German girl, stayed on and got the MG distributorship for the whole of Germany. He retired pretty early and, as a sort of hobby, whenever Auto Union and Mercedes went to English-speaking countries – South Africa for the race there, America for the Vanderbilt Cup – Joe went with them to act as an interpreter. The Woodhouses used to stay with us when they came to England, they were going to Donington, and so I got drawn into the environment as an interested, enthusiastic schoolboy.

"I can remember walking about the track and being absolutely flabberghasted at Melbourne hairpin when the German cars shot over the hill and braked for the hairpin and then shot up again. I walked about the paddock. I don't know if it wasn't difficult for anybody to do that then or whether I had some sort of special privilege which enabled me to do so. I can remember being close to Rosemeyer and the rest of them [and Nuvolari, in 1938]. I got autographs, and I've still got some of them. I don't remember having any difficulty getting close enough to the drivers to ask them for autographs. I was able to mingle freely."

Boddy describes how "community singing occupied the packed mass at the rails, the grandstand filled and Fred Craner's Ford V8 rushed about on divers errands. Programmes sold out and still the crowd poured in"[35] – about 10,000 gathered at the bowl of Melbourne Corner alone (if you see what I mean).

Among the crowd was a 22-year-old called Phil Heath, who'd raced motorbikes at Donington since 1934 and, as a member of the Derby and District Motor Club, was entitled to free admission and parking for all races. "I took advantage of this and because of the traffic I went on my motorbike. You never worried about leaving it – or a car – in the car parks because in those days there was no question of getting anything pinched. It was a gentlemanly occasion in the sense of people behaving themselves, as they did then. No pickpockets, no swearing or anything like that. I'd say the crowd was a good cross-section of national life. I vividly remember getting there just as the big race was starting. I was beside the main straight going down to Starkey's."

On their way to the grid the three Auto Unions came round first and Hasse covered a few laps, then the four Mercedes led by a Lagonda whose driver gave a Hitler salute before withdrawing.

Martin's ERA lined up on the fourth row. "One always got nervous before races like that," he said. "You were surrounded on the grid by all these big German cars and if you'd been hit by one you'd have known about it – or rather you probably wouldn't have known about it. *Keep out the bloody way*, you know, that was the idea."

Like Phil Heath, Arthur Tyler had been a motor bike racer, was a member of the Derby and District Motor Club and "was, shall I say, volunteered to operate the scoreboard." This scoreboard was long and placed on the roof of the pits so Tyler and several others had to climb ladders at the back and stand on the pit roof to operate it. The scoreboard worked in this way: each driver's race number was displayed and beneath it, like a calendar whose pages you progressively tear off, a pad with pages numbered from 1 to 80 – for each lap.

An operator had a small batch of cars to monitor and, every time a member of the batch crossed the line to begin another lap, he tore off the old page – with, say, number 8 denoting the car was on lap 8 – to reveal the number 9 denoting the car was now on lap 9. The operators did this after each lap to the end of the race, unless a car stopped. In that case they left the number alone. It meant, at a glance, spectators in the grandstand and reporters in the Press Box on the other side of the track could see which cars were on the lead lap, which cars were how many laps adrift and which cars had stopped. What it could not do, as Tyler readily concedes, was show which car was leading, because you might have half a dozen cars on the same lap so all their numbers would be the same.

On that grid one of the photographers captured the mood of the moment. Earl Howe, wearing a cheese-cutter cap at a jaunty angle, has intertwined arms with Caracciola who stands in white overalls and a white linen helmet, goggles hoisted to his forehead, and they smile towards the camera – literally comrades in arms.

There were many photographers, among them Klemantaski and the daily press who "didn't normally go to motor races and were news people basically there to witness the accidents which they were all hoping to capture. Well, you know, that's what the daily and Sunday papers wanted."

Seaman's face, a reporter noticed, was badly scarred after his crash at the Nürburgring and he was beseiged by autograph hunters but Caracciola, engulfed by a similar siege – some of whom were extremely persistent – fled to his car, sprang into the cockpit and took refuge there.[36] Presumably even Earl Howe could do nothing to protect him against this fervour of the phlegmatic British who kept proving they weren't phlegmatic.

The grid was a bustle of a place with officials, mechanics, photographers, drivers and dignitaries moving among the cars.

There were bookmakers present, and legend has it that, because they knew nothing about motor racing or the Continental drivers, they assumed the British would win and offered odds accordingly. This obviously didn't happen because a photograph survives of a bookmaker, H. Scotland, standing beside his board which offered these odds:

4	Caracciola	12	A.B. Hyde
5	H. Lang	14	A. Powys-Lybbe
6	M. von Brauchitch [sic]	12	R. Hanson
5	R. Seaman	10	P.N. Whitehead
5	B. Rosemeyer	14	R.E. Tongue
10	H. Müller	14	C.E.C. Martin
10	Raymond Mays	10	A.C. Dobson
10	Earl Howe	12	P. Maclure
10	A.C. Dobson	10	R. Hasse
10	B. Bira		

What these odds did represent was something very generous. You would perhaps have anticipated Lang and Rosemeyer as joint-favourites, with Caracciola, von Brauchitsch and Seaman at short odds *and* the British at much longer odds: 10–1 was ridiculous when viewed across the chasm. These odds were not lost on the Auto Union mechanics who journeyed to the bookmakers and invested heavily on Rosemeyer. The inclusion of Powys-Lybbe remains a curiosity, since he hadn't practised at all and wasn't in the race, but the very fact that he was being quoted does strongly suggest that the bookmakers had not done their homework

Martin had a "nodding acquaintance with the German drivers, apart from Dick, of course. Rosemeyer was outgoing, a smiling chap, very nice. Dick incidentally spent all his time trying to learn the bloody language. In those days you didn't have interpreters everywhere and for people to speak two languages wasn't common. You had millions of people milling around and nobody understanding what the hell was going on!"

Just after midday a blue monoplane with three people in it, flying to Donington for the race, circled the course several times at about 300 feet searching, as it seemed, for a landing place. It veered away and crashed in a field at Breedon-on-the-Hill, a hamlet south of the circuit, bursting into flames. The smoke could be seen a mile away. Villagers rushed to try to rescue the three passengers but it was already hopeless. Their bodies were so badly burned the police could find no marks of identification.

At Donington a truly immense crowd had now assembled from the morning mist for what until this very morning had been a minor and fairly exclusive activity, a motor race. Estimates of this crowd vary between 30,000 and 50,000. One statistic is certain, however: a total of 17 policemen were thought adequate to patrol and control them.[37] BBC Radio broke into their regular programmes to broadcast the start live, something so unusual that it became a news item all of its own.

Tom Wheatcroft had been hanging around and "somebody told me I'd got to move. Someone from Silkolene said 'oh, he's with us' and I was very, very lucky because after that, as a lad, they'd give me tickets. Silkolene Oil was a major company. They had a big marquee in front of the Hall, although it probably wasn't as big as I remember it, and where the Museum is now there was a bridge, the Silkolene Oil bridge." Wheatcroft prepared to watch the race on foot.

In the pits the mechanics of both German teams were unloading great quantities of tyres and preparing their fuel drums, which, "connected to air bottles, refuel the cars through pressure hoses with automatic cut-off valves which shut when the level of the petrol comes up inside the nozzle."[38]

The Press Box, as Tich Allen attests, stood beside the grandstand and was of wood with glass windows "just like a chicken hut, which I am sure it had been. You sat at a counter and there was room for a dozen people, I suppose. The windows did open outwards to get a bit of fresh air but you didn't have them open all the time because the cars were so noisy and people were on the phone to their newspapers dictating their reports. The telephones were in little cubicles – five or six phones, never enough and you had to queue up to get one."

A man who'd been an unpaid official at Donington for years, Donald Hamilton-James, took his place in the time-keepers' hut in front of the grandstand and adjacent to the start-finish line. "You went up about ten steps to it, a wooden hut with a large window. It held three or four people. We only recorded the drivers who were fairly high up in the race and we jotted down their times as they completed their laps. Each time-keeper had certain drivers to record. We had stop-watches." Hamilton-James settled onto one of the tall stools. Paper and pencil were on the shelf in front of him, ready.

As work continued on the grid, Allen – by nature a shy man – was no doubt delighted to see Tommy Wisdom coming along. "Tommy became quite friendly and he had a wonderful ability to remember everybody he'd met. He was also the most approachable of men. The other journalists from London were rather superior towards me, a young chap from a provincial paper nobody had heard of." Klemantaski was on the grid taking pictures with his Leica. "The Continental drivers were almost complete strangers to me. I knew Seaman – just. You spoke to them but they had no idea who you were. Lots of the Germans spoke English. The drivers were very polite. I can't say they were very friendly."

Mechanics changed Rosemeyer's rear wheels and the drivers clambered into their cars except, presumably, Caracciola who'd remained in his cockpit safe from the seige. The crowd in the grandstand could see that the Auto Union and Mercedes steering wheels were fitted *after* their drivers had clambered in (a forerunner of today's detachable steering wheels). Rosemeyer seemed "carefree" as he fitted his. In the Mercedes beside him, von Brauchitsch sat "glowering, looking strung up."[39] The famed and fabled starter of motor races A.V. Ebblewhite, known everywhere as Ebby, held the Union Jack.

Bira wrote of him that he was "seen everywhere on English circuits. He was the time-keeper and a picture of the start would not be complete if one did not see that large but short figure standing by the trackside with a box of stop-watches in one hand and a small Union Jack. His stout curling pipe never left his mouth, and his greyish trilby was hung over his face to shade off his eyes. Sometimes he reminded me of a station-master, standing there without saying a word to anyone, just sending off an express train."

It was two minutes to 1pm.

The Donington Park Press service prepared to put out Official Incident Bulletins throughout the race.

The spectators pressed forward against the railings.

Even static, the silver German cars looked "extremely vicious" and this "dramatic effect" was sharpened by the fact that they were all – the four Mercedes and three Auto Unions – in a bloc on the first two rows while the sit-up-and-beg cars were in a separate bloc behind them.

Ninety seconds to go.

The five ERAs, the two Maseratis and the lone Riley started their engines and "all those engines running together made a fine, exultant noise, but meantime the silence of the silver cars was infinitely more ominous."[40]

Thirty seconds to go.

The Mercedes mechanics applied electric starters to their cars, firing up Seaman's last, and the Auto Unions burst into life. Between them they made a noise so deep and wild it shocked the crowd.

The Light Car tried to distil this moment. "The song of the ERAs has been likened to tearing calico" – a cotton cloth – "but if their note had been audible at all above the competing pandemonium of Mercedes and Auto Union it would have seemed more like the gentle unravelling of a piece of knitting. Each with a 6ft exhaust pipe jutting from their tails, the Auto Unions seemed to shake the very universe."

And the Mercedes were even deeper-throated.

Ebby let the flag fall and the "heavy odour of molten rubber was added to a dozen conflicting smells as spinning wheels tore at the road surface, leaving smoking black streaks in their wake."[41]

Lang made a tremendous start as the cars accelerated, jostling in a shoal, and braked very late for the geometrical left of Red Gate – a corner which acted as a syphon, squeezing the cars from the jostle to a crocodile. Lang would record dryly that "I took the lead from the start."[42]

Caracciola, with "the artistry of long experience, managed to wriggle through to second place."[43] The crocodile stretched, gathering speed, under the arch of trees into Holly Wood, the engines making so much noise that echoes flattened across the parkland like a storm coming.

Von Brauchitsch tucked in behind Caracciola, Seaman pushed hard behind von Brauchitsch, then Rosemeyer, Müller and Hasse with – already – a gap to the chaps, led gamely by Bira's Maserati from the rest who travelled stately behind.

There is a particular, almost primitive, sense of anticipation while you wait for the cars to come round on the opening lap of any race. From nowhere, as it seems, the noise of so many stressed engines grows, sharpens, reaches to you; from nowhere, as it seems, the head of the crocodile bursts into view doing 160 miles an hour – and, on most opening laps, the pursuers are close, trying to hound and harry.

As the noise of the engines grew over there on Starkey's Straight, spectators in the grandstand opposite the pits were unconsciously hauled to their feet in a silent, communal motion. Elsewhere spectators clambered onto the bonnets of parked cars "irrespective of their ownership."[44] The desire to see had become an imperative and a profundity breaking down social fabric.

Those on their feet saw Lang fleeing down Starkey's Straight, the Mercedes bucking at every bump, saw it "shoot" over the brow "in a cloud of dust" on the way down to Melbourne Corner.

One of the Auto Unions must have lost time out in the country before the straight because Heath watched it "proceed to pass sundry ERAs and things like that and even got one wheel on the grass – because the road ahead was a bit full! – but he just kept his foot down. With independent suspension the wheels were doing all sorts of funny things but he went past this bunch and carried on. As the cars passed, you noticed a smell like boot polish. That was the alcohol fuel they were using and it was a very distinct smell, yes, like boot polish.

"When they came up the other side from Melbourne corner they took off and that was fantastic – I mean, nothing else had ever taken off. It was a steep incline. I had a little Ford 8 in those days and on a Sunday you could go to the circuit and just drive round. In the Ford 8 I had to change all the way down to second gear to struggle up the incline. That's how steep it was…"

One reporter wrote how "inoffensive spectators clapped total strangers on the back beseeching them to observe an amazing spectacle"[45] and another noted that Lang didn't seem to be too concerned about conserving his tyres…

The Motor tried to distil this moment. "The powerful brakes went on for Melbourne's 15 mph hairpin and then up the rise they came, leaping clean through the air at the top at over 100 mph – the crowd hugged itself with delight. This was motor racing that they had read about but never quite believed."

Crossing the line it was Lang with Caracciola four seconds behind, then von Brauchitsch, Seaman, Rosemeyer, Müller and Hasse, then a gap to Bira, Martin, Mays, Howe, Whitehead, Dobson, Hanson and Maclure.

Klemantaski remembers the "staggering effect the German cars made and the smell of their special fuel. The impression of speed struck me because they were a good deal larger than the ERAs and when you were close, as I was, it really was a staggering effect when they came by at speed. In those days photographers went wherever they liked – you had to do something extremely foolish for the marshals to say anything to you – so I was actually very close to the cars. You'd cross the track perfectly happily. You just used your sense: you could hear the cars and if you heard them, you didn't cross. In those days, the safety side didn't really come into it. It wasn't frightening to be so close taking photographs because by experience one could see an accident starting long before it got to you and one could take evasive action. You didn't stand in places where you knew you might be wiped away. You used your common sense."

This matter of crossing the recrossing would have consequences, as we shall see.

Tyler explains that "standing on top of the pits we were almost in line with the Melbourne rise and the leading cars came over airborne – but the thing was that there was a slight kink in the track there and they were angling towards the side of the track where the pits were in order to position themselves for the sharp left of Red Gate. They were coming so fast at us that I thought *we'll be lucky if we're still here at the end of it all*. If one of those Germans cars had got loose into the pits it would have been carnage, but somehow people didn't think like that and it was the same with motor cycling."

As Rosemeyer passed his pit he "patted the front" of his car[46], a gesture of reassurance to Sebastian and the other mechanics not to worry about him lying fifth. Sebastian interpretered it like that. "When passing, he gave us signs to show that everything was fine with the car. He was lying in wait behind the Mercedes drivers, driving right tactically."[47]

Tyler and his fellow scoreboard operators faced a fleeting but very real problem. "Because there had been a mass start, for a lap or two they came past us in a mass and you had a job to pick out the cars you were monitoring. You had to scribble what numbers you saw without having time to look down at what you were writing."

Into the second lap von Brauchitsch was going so hard he put wheels off along Starkey's Straight, which dug a cloud of dust, and thrust the Mercedes past Caracciola on the way up to Melbourne Rise.

Rosemeyer was a master and there are characteristics shared by all those who, in their utterly different eras, have mastered the art of winning motor races. They understand that, while the race takes place at high speed in a kind of permanent volatility, the pattern of the race unfolds slowly. At Donington, there would be three hours available for this. Some drivers race in a sublime shriek of speed, wherever it takes them. A few, a precious few, understand how slowly it must be done.

Bernd Rosemeyer was in no hurry.

That is relative, of course. On this second lap he had the rear end of the Auto Union hanging out and sliding – under control – virtually all the way to Coppice Corner. It was awesome to the spectator, comfy for him. Somewhere along the way to Coppice he positioned the Auto Union to overtake Seaman, and did.

It left Seaman in front of Müller, who was charging, driving "sensationally".[48] At Coppice they crashed. The Official Bulletin timed this at 1.11. Seaman may have gone wide because "Müller saw a few square feet of road with vacant possession on the inside"[49] although there are differing accounts of this and a larger question about whether any reporters were at Coppice to see it for themselves.

Seaman was "braking hard and ... was rammed in the tail by Müller. To save himself took to the escape road"[49] – actually a sort of path into the woods.

The Official Bulletin said: "No. 7 [Müller] cut inside No. 4 [Seaman] at Coppice Corner." The Light Car claimed that Müller "made a lightening manoeuvre to overtake. Auto Union and Mercedes connected with a dull thud, the Merc. spun round and Müller went on unhindered into fifth position. Before Seaman could get away again, scowling a dark scowl and sending up a hail of surface chippings from his back wheels, Hasse had gone through to sixth." Seaman's Mercedes was damaged but to what extent wasn't evident.

Rosemeyer was ready now. When he braked hard for Red Gate the whole car "juddered furiously, steering column and wheel shaking, and the engine side panels appearing to flex like so much aeroplane fabric!"[50] Rosemeyer caught and overtook Caracciola at Melbourne Corner – presumably out-braking him going in – giving at lap 5:

Lang	averaging 82.60 mph
von Brauchitsch	at 7$^{1/5}$s
Rosemeyer	at 10$^{3/5}$s
Caracciola	at 16$^{1/5}$s
Müller	at 22$^{1/5}$s
Hasse	at 32$^{4/5}$s[51]

Maclure, running doggedly at the back, was already in danger of being lapped. At 1.16 the Official Bulletin said that Whitehead was "continually broadsiding" at Melbourne Corner while Bira had his Maserati hugging the inside there every time he went round it and was never more than two feet from the verge. Martin and Arthur Dobson steadily pulled away from Mays and Howe, although Boddy was careful to add that "his Lordship was handling the blue ERA splendidly."

Tyler and crew were finding the monitoring a little easier as the field spread and "we did get a check from the time-keepers" – Hamilton-James and the other three – "who were on the opposite side of the track. For the first few laps I should say we were about 97 per cent correct! If we made a mistake we'd get a message across informing us that *so-and-so has done one lap more than you say and you've not torn the old number off.*" Moreover Tyler had now become accustomed to the cars flying from the rise towards him and thought, no doubt, he'd probably survive after all. Hamilton-James clearly remembers the scoreboard operators moving to and fro on the pit rooftop just over there, across the track from where he was sitting.

The power and pace of the German cars was demonstrated at Red Gate where, going in so fast, they slid a little, "hesitated as the spinning rear wheels got a grip" then powered away into Holly Wood with tyres smoking and the engines making a "shattering howl and crash."[52]

Wheatcroft explains that spectators "walked all the way round and you should have heard the echo the cars made because the trees went right up to the edge of the track. Down at Starkey's Bridge you had to put your headlights on even in summer because the trees touched each other in an arch over the track."

By lap 7 Maclure and Hanson had been lapped and by lap 10 the leaders were in amongst all the ERAs. Martin explained that "there was 300 horsepower going the Germans' way which we didn't have. You went rather quietly and kept out of everybody's path. It was simply no good even trying to take any of them on with that kind of discrepancy. What happened was that you got used to them coming at you at such a terrific speed and you had to learn to make allowance for that. There was literally nothing else you could do. If they wanted to pass you going into a corner you more or less had to let them – it was pointless to do anything else because they'd have gone past immediately you came out of the corner."

The Autocar captured the plight of the Britons nicely, writing that Bira led them "driving well, hotly pursued by Charles Martin with his red ERA and Arthur Dobson with another ERA, Raymond Mays' car being out of form because an engine hastily rebuilt two days before was only just run in. And at the tail Percy Maclure strove against desperate odds with the 1.5-litre Riley into which a 1,750 cc engine had been placed at the very last moment."

Von Brauchitsch and Rosemeyer were taking the lengthy loop of Holly Wood in one sustained, immense slide; they were coming downhill to the Hairpin after Holly Wood with the rear of the cars stuck way out but under control – intoxicating the crowd each time they appeared; they were taking the right-hander McLeans at full speed, pitching the cars into elongated slides but again under control. After McLeans they surged down the straight to Coppice Corner and, into that, von Brauchitsch had the Mercedes twitching almost sideways, burning a shroud of smoke from his left rear tyre: so much that even long range photographs show it clearly.

Within this fury Rosemeyer was perfectly composed – cool, as one report put it. He was seen approaching Red Gate at close on 100 miles an hour with one hand off the wheel, no matter that here, like each of the other corners, he had the Auto Union sliding this way and that.

Another report says that the Auto Unions "danced round the corners like peas on a hot plate" and at the pace it was a miracle they didn't fly off the track.[53] Almost unnoticed, Seaman got past Hasse. Lang led by 6.0 seconds on lap 9 but von Brauchitsch began to cut into that, giving at lap 10:

Lang	averaging 82.96 mph
von Brauchitsch	at $3^{2/5}$s
Rosemeyer	at $7^{4/5}$s
Caracciola	at $22^{3/5}$s
Müller	at $32^{4/5}$s
Seaman	at $44^{1/5}$s

The German pit-signal system functioned smoothly. As a Mercedes approached the Rise, Neubauer would already be standing in anticipation on the rim of the track holding a large white-painted board with the relevant information (expressed in numerals) clearly visible on it.

At 1.29 Hanson skidded at Melbourne Corner and his Maserati spilled off onto the grass but he wrestled it back and pressed on. Whitehead had already stopped on the grass at Starkey's with what seemed to be an engine problem, re-started and been into the pits. Now on lap 11 he retired, smoke belching from the engine.

Two laps later the positions at the front tightened. Von Brauchitsch had drawn up to 25 yards from Lang *but* Rosemeyer remorselessly caught von Brauchitsch.

Caracciola circled much further away but, as those in the crowd still capable of rational thought began to realise, he was working to a tactic beyond the sound and the fury.

Now the position at the very front tightened into a tourniquet. On lap 14 a back marker – Bira in the Maserati – travelled down to Melbourne Corner,

Lang closing urgently in a vast lunge but von Brauchitsch – "that slim, red-helmeted figure"[54] – had drawn up to Lang and and was poised, predatory, directly behind him. These three cars, one utterly slower than the other two, were virtually into the mouth of the corner and were held in a timeless arrangement producing a chance common to every motor race: the slower car impedes the leader and creates space for the predator.

Bira moved aside, Lang instinctively checked and that was the chance. Von Brauchitsch saw it and seized it instantaneously, thrusting inside Lang. They came round almost abreast although how von Brauchitsch got round was "a miracle. He must have left the cut-off point to the last possible inch, using his brakes with the utmost violence."[55] As they emerged, von Brauchitsch had the snout of his car ahead by maybe a yard, maybe two.

At that lap 14, even Caracciola in fourth place had lapped all the Britons. At lap 15:

von Brauchitsch	averaging 83.21 mph
Lang	at $3\frac{1}{5}$s
Rosemeyer	at $6\frac{2}{5}$s
Caracciola	at $28\frac{4}{5}$s
Müller	at $44\frac{1}{5}$s
Seaman	at 52s

Lang would record how "when I attacked again" (tried to mount a counter-attack) "I noticed that my car had become unstable." He had a problem with a front wheel and cornering became "very insecure."[56]

At 1.38 Martin pitted to have a portion of the radiator blanketing removed, and resumed after six seconds

By 1.50 Martin was out of it with a broken piston. At lap 20:

von Brauchitsch	averaging 83.36 mph
Lang	at $3\frac{2}{5}$s
Rosemeyer	at 5s
Caracciola	at $31\frac{3}{5}$s
Müller	at $51\frac{4}{5}$s
Seaman	at $60\frac{3}{5}$s

The pit stops among the leaders would alter the shape of the race. Von Brauchitsch made the first of them and the Official Bulletin said: "Changed rear wheels and refuelled. Out in 30 secs." *The Autocar*'s reporter wrote that "both rear wheels were changed by gigantic German mechanics, there was a violent hiss of compressed air as fuel was driven into the tank, and … all three mechanics pushed to restart the engine." To complete a pit stop in that time was regarded not merely as fast but astounding and yet another example of Germanic co-ordination and professionalism.

Eight minutes later, Lang pitted and the Official Bulletin recorded laconically: "Car No. 2 called at Pits to examine rear wheels. Changed rear wheels and refuelled. Removed dead bird from radiator. Out 1m 49s." The mechanics had examined the car's independent suspension because Lang told them it didn't feel right – that problem which made cornering so insecure. The 1m 49s, however, represented a lifetime and cost Lang a place in the top six. Worse, a front shock-absorber had broken and the pit stop revealed it. Lang emerged back on the track to see what he could do.

These two pit stops gave the lead to Rosemeyer.

Neubauer, positioned at the rim of the track, waited for Seaman and signalled that he was eight seconds behind Müller. Seaman responded on the next lap by halving that gap.

By now something else, potentially catastrophic, had begun. As we have seen, the pits were on one side of the track, the time-keepers, grandstand, control building, BBC commentary point, Press Box and Public Address all on the other. The only way to go from one side to the other was across the track, because there was no tunnel (which would later become a standard feature of many circuits) and the two bridges – the Silkolene along Starkey's Straight, the other between Red Gate corner and Holly Wood – were too far away. Therefore people bearing information or instructions would sprint across; but, because of the angle up from Melbourne Corner to the Rise, they couldn't see what was coming and the German cars were coming very quickly indeed. Few of those crossing had the experience of Klemantaski. The *Leicester Mercury* had, in its early edition, already written that "so terrific was the speed of the seven German cars ... that officials forbade even pit attendants to cross the road circuit." The problem had been anticipated but clearly not solved.

Neubauer, sensing tragedy, became "very agitated" about these sprinters and "proclaimed his dismay in every known language."[57]

But the race went on. The people in the crowd who knew how to read a race were realising that Rosemeyer, like Caracciola, was employing a tactic and did not intend to make his pit stop yet. Rosemeyer intended to keep on for another half a dozen laps.

However on lap 25 the Mercedes pit signalled to Caracciola to come in next time round for fuel and tyres but, as he passed, Caracciola shook his head. He'd been nursing his tyres – at the Rise he was in the air for the shortest distance and with the least ferocity – and, if he could manage the race with one pit stop less than the others, that was worth half a minute. At lap 25:

Rosemeyer	averaging 83.27 mph
Caracciola	at 30⁴/5s
von Brauchitsch	at 39³/5s
Müller	at 57³/5s
Seaman	at 1m 6²/5s
Hasse	at 1m 41²/5s

On lap 26, Hanson skidded off at Melbourne Corner again but struggled back, struggled onwards.

A minute later Lang was gone. He came up towards the Rise at a "sedate" speed but the car was in such a condition that it couldn't be cajoled to the pits. He stopped short of them, parked it on the grass and vaulted out of the cockpit. "Since I could not drive without shock-absorbers on the uneven surface, and changing them would have taken too long, I had to retire."[58] The Mercedes mechanics scampered along holding a sheet of tarpaulin and draped it over the car. To shield it from eyes prying into its secrets?

Some eight minutes and three laps later Seaman was gone, too. Parts of the rear suspension could be seen hanging from the Mercedes, a legacy of the ramming from Müller. He parked next to Lang and his car, too, was covered by tarpaulin. He walked the short distance to the Mercedes pits, which happened to be at that end of the pit lane, and clambered onto the roof along from Arthur Tyler and the other scoreboard operators. Using a stop watch, Seaman did some timing.

Still Rosemeyer and Caracciola had not pitted. At 30 laps:

Rosemeyer	averaging 83.18 mph
Caracciola	at 22^1/$_5$s
von Brauchitsch	at 33s
Müller	at 58^2/$_5$s
Hasse	at 1m 51^2/$_5$s
Bira	no time

Rosemeyer did come in, but only when he'd planned to: beyond one third distance. That was lap 32 and Sebastian says the stop was carried out "according to plan". It was quick but in those imprecise days what it really took is uncertain. One source gives 25 seconds, another 29, another 31 and Sebastian suggests 34, adding that it was so quick it "left the English spectators speechless. They had never seen such a thing in England. I remember that we got plenty of applause for our performance."[59]

This stop, however long it did take, gave the lead to Caracciola with von Brauchitsch second over 18 seconds ahead of Rosemeyer, now third. Interestingly neither of the other two Auto Union drivers, Müller and Hasse, had pitted themselves yet. Rosemeyer accelerated, von Brauchitsch responded and on lap 34 set fastest lap at 2 minutes 11^2/$_5$ seconds (85.62 mph). At 35 laps:

Caracciola	averaging 82.78 mph
von Brauchitsch	at 6s
Rosemeyer	at 17^3/$_5$s
Müller	at 1m 22s
Hasse	at 1m 39^4/$_5$s
Bira	at 6m 56^4/$_5$s

The intoxication of the crowd, and its size, threatened a tragedy far more serious than the track crossers. As the German drivers made their pit stops they "complained bitterly"[60] that at certain places the crowd had spilled over on to grass verges and marshals were dispatched urgently to force them back "from the danger zones."

And still Caracciola circled, still he did not pit – but the tactic of forcing an advantage by nursing his tyres had failed. Von Brauchitsch clawed at the distance between them and, after a "brief, fierce duel"[61] took the lead on lap 36.

At that moment Müller pitted, the wheels changed and the refuelling complete in 28 seconds. *The Autocar* noted that "plainly the Auto Union pit work was even better than that of their rivals, and they travelled farther on tyres. Noticeable, too, was the fact that their engines started with an electric starter, saving the seconds necessary to push the Mercedes."

A lap later – it was 2.26pm – Hasse did pit and the Official Bulletin said: "Changed rear wheels, refuelled, driver had a drink. Out in $41^{2/5}$s." In fact Hasse, riven by thirst, snatched the drink but when he was ready to drive away Feuereissen gestured for him to wait – a Mercedes was screaming past.

Earl Howe "overslid at Stone Bridge, struck bank with offside wheels but proceeded" while Hanson pitted "refuelled with 20 gallons. Plugs examined. Away in 3 mins 47 secs."[62] It's hardly necesssary to underline that, compared with both German teams, a stop lasting nearly four minutes was quaint.

The track crossers suddenly came close to the feared tragedy. Two, possibly spectators, were running from the pits over towards the grandstand when Müller breasted the Rise. He braked, the Auto Union lurched but he caught it and "shook his fist" towards the "very frightened people as they scurried for cover."[63] At 40 laps, half distance:

von Brauchitsch	averaging 83.03 mph
Caracciola	at $12^{4/5}$s
Rosemeyer	at $23^{2/5}$s
Müller	at 1m 47s
Hasse	at 3m $5^{2/5}$s
Bira	at 8m $5^{3/5}$s

On that 40th lap Caracciola pitted at last. It was 2.30: he'd been able to nurse the tyres for an hour and a half. He wiped the windscreen himself while Neubauer stooped and spoke briefly to him. While the rear wheels were being changed and the fuel going in, Rosemeyer appeared over the Rise and went by, making Caracciola third. The pit stop lasted 28 seconds.

The hunt was on: Rosemeyer stretching towards von Brauchitsch in what seemed a frenzy. On this same lap – 40 – Rosemeyer equalled fastest lap but – at 2.45 – made a rare misjudgement down towards the Stone Bridge when he pitched the Auto Union into a tremendous broadside. "Going very fast, hit the bank but proceeded."[64] *The Light Car* described crisply how Rosemeyer "flung his car into the corners with an abandon glorious to see."

Von Brauchitsch recorded how he saw Rosemeyer skidding back and forth as he moved through the corners and von Brauchitsch was into the frenzy himself. "I came off the road at some corners and covered spectators with sand and tufts of grass."

By contrast the Britons still proceeded at their own pace and in their own order, although that was disturbed when Dobson pitted on lap 42 because the magneto rotor on his ERA had failed. He negotiated and borrowed one from Martin's long-silenced fellow ERA "No. 10 Magneto Rotor replaced, failed to start, then changed all plugs. Away in 11.5 minutes,"[65] to a round of applause from the grandstand.

Bira pitted and took on 20 gallons of fuel but no new tyres and re-started easily on the crank handle, away in 38 seconds.[66] Boddy noted that "Craner blew vigorously on a whistle to move the German mechanics from in front of the pit-counters but they were conveniently as deaf as drivers!" – which I assume meant Craner was trying to clear a path for Bira to get back out but the Auto Union mechanics nearby continued to go about their business, thank you.

Boddy also noted that "still the October sun shone down on this great scene and flags of various nationalities waved lazily over the busy pits. Howe had a pit stop, the ERAs screen being cleaned, water added and the car refuelled, with bad overflow, and finally push-started which took over a minute, although the wheels were not changed." At 45 laps:

von Brauchitsch	averaging 83.03 mph
Rosemeyer	at 24s
Caracciola	at 1m 6⁴/₅s
Müller	at 1m 59¹/₅s
Hasse	at 3m 54s
Bira	at 9m 15⁴/₅s

Von Brauchitsch squeezed a little time from Rosemeyer, lapped Hasse, whose Auto Union was clearly in some sort of trouble, and on lap 48 he moved past Müller. The decisive moment of the whole race was coming. At 50 laps:

von Brauchitsch	averaging 83.17 mph
Rosemeyer	at 26²/₅s
Caracciola	at 1m 22²/₅s
Müller	at 2m 25⁴/₅s
Hasse	at 4m 56s
Bira	at 11m 17³/₅s

The intensity of the struggle at the front was evident by the smoke billowing from von Brauchitsch's brakes and the way Rosemeyer's Auto Union "flexed appallingly" as he force-force-forced it to reduce the gap; but von Brauchitsch must make another pit stop – soon – and, even if it lasted no more than 30 seconds, that would give the lead to Rosemeyer.

Von Brauchitsch came up the Rise and angled the Mercedes towards his pit, pulled up there. He sat, a prisoner, while the mechanics did their work. The seconds flickered away, flickered away.

As he sat and the mechanics were virtually finished he must have heard the familiar shriek of Rosemeyer's engine echoing up towards the Rise. Did von Brauchitsch turn and watch Rosemeyer leap, land, surge on past him? Did von Brauchitsch make a sign? The moment is lost.

The pit stop had lasted 28 seconds: two seconds too long.

Von Brauchitsch emerged and flung the Mercedes at Red Gate, and now he was a prisoner of motion. He had cold tyres and had to get back up to racing speed then find his rhythm again. The flickering seconds he took doing that pulled Rosemeyer away from him, away from him.

Von Brauchitsch didn't give a damn about that. Von Brauchitsch prepared to smash the gap and win the race.

Mays pitted for fuel but that took 48 seconds and "Engine stopped when restarting,"[67] a euphemism, presumably, for stalling. Nor did it go unnoticed in the Press Box that Mays had taken those 48 seconds only for fuel. Six minutes later Mays pitted again to top up his oil and have the plugs examined. He proceeded and, more or less straight afterwards, the 10,000 at Melbourne Corner watched him stop on the grass, the engine "backfiring badly".[68]

At the front, the hunt went on.

The spectacular section – from Red Gate through Holly Wood to the Hairpin – yielded something approaching the monumental and the majestic. Rosemeyer and von Brauchitsch were at full bore, going to the very rim of the track "clinging within an inch of the edge"[69] and, in desperate moments, over it.

And von Brauchitsch was gaining. He had 25 laps left. He was destroying the gap and he was going to win. At 55 laps:

Rosemeyer	averaging 82.72 mph
von Brauchitsch	at 14$4/5$s
Caracciola	at 1m 6$2/5$s
Müller	at 2m 15s
Hasse	at 5m 16$2/5$s
Bira	at 12m 1$1/5$s

It was not as motor racing is now, on short circuits with gain-and-loss measured in fractions. Donington was more than three miles of bump-bounces and slip-slides through the parkland. The gain-and-loss might be great. As von Brauchitsch crossed the line to begin lap 59, a mechanic in a white coat held up a pit board to him. It bore the letter 2 confirming he was in second place and, under that, *0.13*, meaning in the shorthand of pit boards: *you are 13 seconds behind Rosemeyer*. Von Brauchitsch must have lost time because at 60 laps

Rosemeyer	averaging 83.06 mph
von Brauchitsch	at 20s
Caracciola	at 1m 20s
Müller	at 2m 37⁴/5s
Hasse	at 6m 14s
Bira	at 13m 23³/5s

On that lap von Brauchitsch was doing some 170 miles an hour down to Melbourne and, 20 laps to run, could still win, likely would. The Mercedes moved onto the slope: full bore here. He braked for the corner. Did he lock his brakes? Maybe. The 10,000, spread round the bowl of the corner, watched. With absolutely no warning – nothing at all – the nearside front tyre exploded like a bomb burst and its violence flung shreds of rubber as high as the tops of the surrounding trees.

Von Brauchitsch, thinking clinically as racing drivers do, judged it a consequence of hunting Rosemeyer with the frenzy of putting wheels off onto the dirt.

He braked so hard now that blue smoke churned from the three tyres – each "molten" – which remained. He caught the car, held it steady, brought it round the corner and up the incline to the Rise and the pits.[70] His arrival caught them unprepared because, although the team had signallers spread round the circuit, it happened comparatively close to the pits and, of course, out of sight.

As the car halted, virtually nothing remained of the front left tyre. The race was 2 hours 18 minutes old. A white-coated mechanic pressed the jack under the front of the car, another mechanic stooped and began loosening the wheel nut. Von Brauchitsch lifted his goggles onto his forehead and leant out of the cockpit to observe the wheel being changed. Three photographers scurried towards the stationary car while, over the lip of the pit roof, two men peered down. In the grandstand applause welled.

Where was Caracciola? Closing to take second place?

Arthur Tyler remembers "a very interesting incident. A Mercedes came in for a wheel change and the car had knock-on hubs. One of the mechanics couldn't get the nut on the correct thread to screw it back on again and of course the seconds were ticking by. And seconds seemed like an eternity."

Von Brauchitsch was stationary for 28 seconds. He understood that the race had been taken from him. In the blunt acceptance which many racing drivers learn to accommodate, he'd pay his tribute to the work of the mechanics but say the time lost "could not be made up in the remaining laps."

Tyler adds that "Alfred Neubauer brought this mechanic round the back of the pits just below where I was on the roof and didn't he give him a dressing down? The chap never answered a word. He just stood there. I bet he wanted the ground to swallow him. This brought it home to me that this German motor racing wasn't just pure sport. There was something more at the back of it. *Deutschland uber alles* – very much so."

Tyler concedes that it's all a long time ago and thinks the incident involved the changing of a rear wheel but on the other hand "it could well have been von Brauchitsch. With the depth of the roof you couldn't see over to what was happening underneath and, because we were doing our jobs, we couldn't go to the edge and look down." Wilkie Wilkinson says that "when the tread came off, the Dunlop people went to get it and there was a terrible fuss. They wanted to see the German Continental tyre because they were very interested in its tread. When it flew off they tried to get some, did, and took it away for analysis. The Germans didn't like that at all."

Von Brauchitsch, as it would seem, decided to enjoy himself, "having a marvellous time, laughing like a schoolboy, waving to friends, and when Bira waved him on at Hairpin Corner, von Brauchitsch waved 'thank you' gaily all the way up into the woods."[71]

Rosemeyer had a second pit stop to make and did so on lap 62. It was the final pressure point of the race and, if it went disastrously wrong, of possible consequences to the result. Rosemeyer brought the Auto Union in and the mechanics attacked it with gusto while everybody in the grandstand urged *faster faster faster*. Some 324/5 seconds later Rosemeyer moved away to a tremendous cheer. In dried language, the Official Bulletin reduced this to: "3.20. No. 5 refuelled, changed both rear wheels. Away in 32 secs." At 65 laps:

Rosemeyer	averaging 82.72 mph
von Brauchitsch	at 301/5s
Caracciola	at 424/5s
Müller	at 2m 524/5s
Hasse	at 6m 234/5s
Bira	at 13m 573/10s

Fifteen laps remained, the Donington Grand Prix smoothing itself into legend. Rosemeyer had mastered it and who could know he'd never start another motor race?

Von Brauchitsch kept on forcing as much as he could because, like the British, the Germans didn't give up until it was impossible to go on and the Official Bulletin chugged through whatever incidents came to hand.

"3.34pm Car No. 10 [Dobson] overtook car No. 20 [Maclure] on Melbourne Corner, running right outside him.

"3.35pm Car No. 8 [Mays] officially retired. Reason at present unknown.

"3.37pm Car No. 5. [Rosemeyer] overtook Car No.6 [Hasse] at Melbourne Corner. Car No 6 waved him through.

"3.56pm No. 15 [Hanson] again in at the pits. Took on 15 gallons of fuel. Out again in 30 secs."

On lap 67, Maclure brought his Riley into the pits with a transmission problem which could not be solved and he remained immobile until the end when, in the classical and incomprehensible motor racing way, he'd be classified. Percy Maclure took his modest place in the legend, and remains in it, forever tenth. At 70 laps:

Rosemeyer	averaging 82.81 mph
von Brauchitsch	at 34s
Caracciola	at 54s
Müller	at 54s
Hasse	at 7m 13^1/$_{10}$s
Bira	at 15m 19^1/$_{10}$s

The race was essentially over[72], Rosemeyer maintaining steady and untroubled progress to the chequered flag. Sebastian used the present tense when he recorded how "Bernd drives excellently and does not let himself lead to anything dangerous by the bursts of speed of Caracciola and Brauchitsch. As he passes the pits he gives signs which nobody understands. With one hand, he hits himself in the neck and on the forehead. Our people are helpless – they don't know what this odd sign means, but I do, and I have a lot of fun. Rosemeyer is using the crazy signs [tick-tack] from the dog races we had visited the day before. When he passes again, and his hand – held flat – moves in a circle on his head, I know both driver and car are in excellent condition."

Rosemeyer, however, did not use tick-tack at the instant of victory but, rather, a time-honoured motor racing gesture. "Putting up both arms, he passes the finishing line."[73] As Rosemeyer crossed the line to a tumult of applause the German national anthem was not played – it was the usual custom to play that for a winner at grands prix – and many, Boddy among them, thought this a disgrace. If it was an oversight it was difficult to excuse, if it was deliberate it was impossible to excuse.

Von Brauchitsch remained convinced that "it was only due to the stone" and the resultant puncture which "allowed Rosemeyer to be successful."[74]

Towards the end, some of the bookmakers realised Rosemeyer was going to win and, of course, many of the Auto Union mechanics had backed him at 5–1 and 6–1. Some reports say three, some say six of the eight bookmakers packed their bags and fled but cleverly left their boards so that it wasn't obvious what they were up to.

When Rosemeyer stopped and clambered out he was exhausted. He "limped badly, was very sore, and his overalls, soaked in perspiration from head to foot, had to be taped up at the seat before he could meet Mrs Shields and get his bouquet."[75] Someone took a photograph of the Rosemeyer *derriere* and you can see the tape holding two sides of a tear together. He drank a toast in lemonade because the champagne had been lost.

Von Brauchitsch crossed the line some 38 seconds later, then there were lengthening gaps to Caracciola and Müller. Hasse wouldn't make it for nearly nine minutes.

Rosemeyer said he'd found the circuit "difficult and rather bumpy" and not particularly suited to the Auto Unions so "I was surprised by the average speed we were able to put up. It was a hard-fought race and right up to the end lap speeds were as high as in the beginning. I must congratulate the English drivers who made things as easy as possible for us to pass." (At the time in Germany, the name Rosemeyer was synonymous with speed. Even children riding bicycles fast were apt to be asked: "Who do you think you are? Bernd Rosemeyer?")

An anonymous Auto Union mechanic drove Rosemeyer's car along the inner road to the barn at Coppice, switched off the engine and let it fall silent.

Bira was churning round far behind Hasse and, under the rules, had 15 minutes to complete the 80 laps or he'd be 'flagged off' – a nice way of saying STOP![76] Rather than wait, the crowd's intoxication finally boiled over and, despite appeals from one of the three Public Announcers (a F.L.M. Harris), they rushed forward. The Motor pointed out that "many cars were still racing, the crowd got out of hand and swarmed across the unpoliced track. A bad show."

The Light Car confirmed this. "The half-wits who rushed across the road at the pit area after the first five cars had finished can thank their stars they weren't in Germany, where they have a stern way with such. A sizeable body of bobbies with some knowledge of the dangers of racing could have coped nicely with that situation." The result:

Rosemeyer	3h 1m 2¹/5s (82.86 mph)
von Brauchitsch	3h 1m 40s (82.57 mph)
Caracciola	3h 2m 18⁴/5s (82.28 mph)
Müller	3h 4m ¹/2s (81.16 mph)
Hasse	3h 9m 5s (79.58 mph)
Bira	78 laps in 3h 13m 49³/5s
Earl Howe	77 laps in 3h 14m 47s
Dobson	74 laps in 3h 14m 54⁴/5s
Hanson	72 laps in 3h 14m 54⁴/5s
Maclure	67 laps in 2h 57m 21⁴/5s

Retirements: Whitehead 11 laps, engine; Martin 18 laps, piston; Lang 26 laps, broken damper; Seaman 30 laps, suspension damage; Mays 51 laps, engine.

The Auto Union mechanics, who stood to get at least £50 from the bookmakers, went across to collect and found them gone. Whether the crowd was enraged by this – national honour and so on – or whether members of the crowd had had a bet themselves and come for their winnings is not clear but "by way of revenge, the public smashed up the bookmakers' stands."[77] The crowd also tried to "enlist" the help of the Police but "to no avail." With only 17 policemen in the whole circuit, there simply weren't enough to cope with anything like this.

Klemantaski remembers that "after the race was over one heard that some bookies had welched and I went along to have a look. I took a photograph of all their blackboards lying around and lots of torn up tickets. People were angry, they certainly were." And the race itself? Reporters did not swarm over the drivers wringing opinions and quotes from them. "After a race like that," Tich Allen says, "the journalists were busy trying to get the result sorted out and were busy telephoning, too. We'd each have needed a team of helpers to cover a race of this scale. And anyway the days of 'intrusive' journalism" – the wringing of the quotes and opinions – "was almost totally unknown."

In the background, the immense crowd began to melt away. Soon enough every exit was chocked with cars, the road all the way to Ashby-de-la-Zouche ten miles away solid. Phil Heath had no such problems on his motorbike and thinks he probably stopped somewhere for a drink on his way home to Leicester.

While the cars struggled out Boddy (inevitably) noted something revealing. "Long after it was all over the Mercedes-Benz publicity man and an assistant typed reports in the open in the Press enclosure – our last glimpse of German thoroughness."[78]

Charlie Martin reflected that "there should really have been two races at Donington, because Rosemeyer, in an Auto Union, and an ERA with yours truly on it were not a fair match. What did I do after the race? I dunno. Went home, I expect…"

Tom Wheatcroft had been dazed by anticipating these cars. "You thought *Silver Arrows, what will they be like, what will they be like?* You've got to remember, too, that it was an era of great feats. You had aeroplanes breaking records and the Land Speed Record being broken." Wheatcroft remained dazed after seeing the Silver Arrows, those cars "which bounced: their wheels never seemed to touch the floor. That was the time of Caracciola. I'd think *ah, he's the great man.* I'd seen him walking in the evening when prize giving was on and I thought *you'd need a ladder to talk to him.* Even among his own people I think he was a bit frightening."

That evening, too, the honour of England was restored. The trophies and prizes were presented by Countess Howe at a dinner given by the Derby and District Motor Club at the Friary Hotel, Derby and the Club paid the mechanics what they would have got from the bookmakers. A photograph captures the mood of the dinner: Seaman, Craner, reserve driver Kautz and Dr Peter Glaser (who regularly ministered to both German teams) arrange themselves for the camera, and all four wear suits, collars and ties, all four smile in a subdued, polite, reticent sort of way. You can almost touch the decorum.

And that was the Donington Grand Prix of 1937.

"Naturally," Elly Beinhorn Rosemeyer would remember,[79] "I was expecting Bernd to call me after the race, although I hoped he would be taking Kay Petre out to dinner that evening, so I told him to phone when he got back to the hotel, no matter how late it was." As time went on and no call came Elly became concerned, not least because, when the Rosemeyers had been in South Africa, Petre had mentioned that if Rosemeyer wasn't married to Elly she might have a "little flirtation" with him. Then, very late, Rosemeyer called "with the sad news that Kay had been badly injured in a crash at Brooklands and was in hospital." He had gone to see her, but she was still unconscious, so he had left all the flowers from his winner's bouquet. Happily Kay made a complete recovery in time." She didn't. Her face was disfigured.

From Untertürkheim came a cable:

To the Mercedes-Benz team, Hotel Blackboy, Nottingham/England.
    The Board of Directors thanks you for your performance and congratulates the drivers. Hopefully next time you will be victorious.
                                                     Heil Hitler!

It contrasts nicely with the English way of putting things. When the race finished an old spectator in the grandstand stood up, stretched his stiff legs and said: "Well, I reckon we've had our money's worth." Someone else said in a heavy Midlands accent: "*Ter* think they can make iron and *braas* and *roober* stand up to it, *eeh, well, ah'm dumbfounded.*"

Chapter 4

Life –
and death

THE AFTERMATH WAS PLAYED OUT at differing levels: the polite, the personal and, like an ever-darkening backdrop, the political. This late autumn the different levels of human activity were beginning to come together but were not yet forged into the unity. That would be the story of the next Donington Grand Prix, a year away, when the darkness was gathering moment by moment. Now it was time to be polite and entirely normal before the Germans departed on the Tuesday.

Verdon-Roe described Saturday, 2 October in his diary: *Up at 08.00, breakfast in room 36. We were all installed in the V 8 at 10.00. Made good time to Donington, parked car, had a little to eat and prepared for the race. Watching from the stand on the straight, we were dumbfounded when the Autos + Mercs came round on their first lap. H + I walked round circuit. After race headed south, dining at the Clarendon, Oxford, then to the [New] Forest. A wonderful day. Retired 04.00."*

George Monkhouse, author and friend of Seaman, has written that Uhlenhaut subsequently examined Caracciola's car and found a "piece of rag" inside the supercharger (a "most un-Mercedes-like happening") which might well explain why Caracciola hadn't been faster.

On the Sunday journalist John Dugdale went along to conduct an interview, or rather three simultaneous interviews, for *The Autocar* in his attempt to portray the personalities of motor racing as people rather than names. He had a talk with Caracciola and von Brauchitsch, and started by asking Alice if she minded Rudi racing.

"No. I am very happy for him to race. It is a marvellous … how do you say it? … it is a marvellous career for any man. It requires the greatest courage. The greatest 'obligation'. It brings the greatest satisfaction. It teaches you to be grateful for victory but it also teaches you to grant the other fellow victory, too – to lose fairly. It calls for tremendous will power. I would not have my husband stop racing. Besides that, it is his life. Quite obviously he would not be the same without it."

Rudi said he was pleasantly surprised by Donington, which was wider than he'd been led to expect, and grateful for all the marshals round the circuit waving blue flags – *Keep to the right (faster car behind you!)* – which enabled Mercedes and Auto Union to compete against each other without the sit-up-and-beggars constantly getting in the way.

Von Brauchitsch agreed, although he judged the English crowd "cold, cold but intelligent." It was an odd way of putting it after so much intoxication.

Dugdale quickly found out that something had "shaken them to the very core". They wanted to know why people ran across the track during the race and pointed out that these people simply could not appreciate what speeds the cars were doing. Alice recounted how a man "ran across the track right in front of a car towards our *boxes*," which Dugdale correctly translated as pits. "As he came opposite me I told him quite frankly I thought he was crazy to do it, and all he did was to point to his armlet which said Official."

He explained there was no other way to communicate from one side of the track to the other but then "they told me something which surprised me, that people were crossing the road at the fastest point on the straight. To my question of what speed they were doing there, the two drivers said '260 kph'. That is 162 mph! Whew! Think of that speed coming over the bumps down Starkey's Straight! No wonder they said that the cars seemed more in the air than on the ground."

While Dugdale's interview progressed, Rosemeyer's car was being transported to London by lorry. Next day, the Monday, it would be displayed at the Auto Union Sales Ltd showrooms, 151 Great Portland Street.

There, that Monday, a reception was held to celebrate the victory. Rosemeyer looked impeccable in a natty felt hat; Hermann – manager of the branch – was bespectacled and urgent; Sebsatian looked heavy-faced and serious, hair receding; Eberan-Eberhorst looked positively sporty in a light jacket and white hat with a dark band round it. They spent some time in earnest conversation. Rosemeyer also posed beside a £169 soft-top Auto Union saloon for a widely-used advertisement whose text promised:

The performance is outstanding and 0 – 60 mph in top gear shows the extreme flexibility of the engine. Free-wheel, no-draught ventilation, accessible controls, independent springing, ample accommodation for four adults are only a few of its many features. A trial run will give you a new conception of light car luxury!

That Monday, too, an inquest held at the village dance hall in Breedon-on-the-Hill recorded a verdict of accidental death on the three victims of the Saturday air crash. On the Coroner's desk were two platinum rings found on the dead woman's fingers, a luggage label, several coins and a bunch of keys from which the police had been trying to identify the bodies. A Leicestershire policeman explained how he hadn't seen the plane come down but had seen a column of smoke about a mile away. He ran across the fields towards it and found the body of a woman lying across the debris and a man's body lying parallel with the wing. A third body, that of a man, was under the engine. The policeman saw the bracket of a fire extinguisher between the forearm and upper arm of the second man's body.[1]

That evening the British Racing Drivers' Club held a cocktail party for the German drivers at the Hotel Splendide in Piccadilly. Some 130 people – including John Cobb (who had designs on the World Land Speed Record), Fred Craner and Charlie Martin – attended and Earl Howe welcomed representatives of the German Embassy. The occasion was, *The Autocar* noted, a "most suitable gathering finally to cement the many new friendships which the Germans have formed over here."

It was still possible to write such things quite naturally.

Word emerged that Seaman was staying on in London to drive an exhibition lap in one of the Mercedes at the week-end's Crystal Palace meeting.

Kay Petre had a "better night" but remained semi-conscious.

Ernst Rosemann, who covered the race for *Motor und Sport*, wrote: "I know some men and women who are so good-natured that you can do anything you like to them and they won't mind, but if you have the idea of talking to them about automobile races they'll leave immediately. They're the men who have been through a very exhausting season and the wives who've had to stay at home waiting for them and who, for about half a year, have only seen their husbands when they returned for clean clothes.

"They're the men of German motor racing who in England today have packed their suitcases for the last time and are going home from the last race – and from the last victory. They're the men who are just yearning to sleep long in the morning, go to the theatre, eat in their own houses. They're the men who wish hotel beds and restaurant food in hell. They're the German automobile sport's group!

"How it was in England? Well, very different from the races we have been through in the last weeks before Donington. We were received by a density of motorized traffic that we had not forseen [those queues for the race!]. The friendly men of the Automobile Association and of the Royal Automobile Club greeted every German in a friendly manner, while the organisers of the race anticipated our every wishes and fulfilled them. Mr Craner, the director of the race, looked after us like a hen after its chicks. We were received most cordially, we are honestly glad about the English-German friendship – which was also expressed in toasts – and we liked to be in England.

"Yet the majority of the spectators were so different from those in our country, in Italy, in France … in fact everywhere else. England's sons awaited the big sports event coolly. In the hotels, our racing drivers could move unnoticed like nameless civilians: there were no children waiting for hours for an autograph. It is not in the Englishman's temperament to let any event throw him off balance in his well-ordered life.

"Our racing drivers found it pleasant to be private, 'unmolested' people but maybe they'd have wished for more applause for their excellent performances. However, friendly reactions for us were not completely lacking. As far as the performance of our racing cars was concerned, well, there was nothing else but praise although it was not broadcast effusively."

While Rosemeyer's car was on display, a young man called Denis Jenkinson – who'd become a celebrated journalist with *Motor Sport* – could not resist going along to have a look, especially since he hadn't been able to get to the race. "I was at technical college … not far from Great Portland Street, which was the home of the car trade in those days, and every lunch time for a week I walked up to the Auto Union showrooms and drooled over Dr Porsche's masterpiece. On one glorious occasion there was a group of people behind the car and I recognised my hero, Bernd Rosemeyer. Nervously, I entered the showrooms and asked him for his autograph – not in my Grand Prix scrap-book, unfortunately, because I did not have it with me, but on a page in a note book. With a charming smile, he wrote his name and my joy was unbounded. Although I do not recall it now, I have no doubt that Dr Porsche was in the group of dignitaries in the showrooms, but I was totally star-struck by seeing Bernd Rosemeyer and did not have eyes for anyone else."[2]

The specialist British magazines reflected the continuing interest in the race. *The Motor* admonished that people should "not have run to and fro across the track at the pits during the race, which gave Neubauer hysterics and nearly caused the withdrawal of the Mercedes cars."[3] Nor was that all. "We should not have chosen that announcer for the public address unless he (a) had an enthusiastic voice and a microphone personality; (b) knew something about Grand Prix cars, and (c) could put a little zip into his commentary on the most exciting race we've ever had in this country." There'd been three commentators – Harris of the unsuccessful appeal, R. King Farlow[4] and W.D. Wells – and we'll never know now which was the offender. However, one letter-writer to *The Autocar* was spared this.

"Human nature is long-suffering. Nobody seems to have written to you regarding an old-standing complaint which was not rectified even for the recent G.P. meeting. May I just baldly state that when you are in the grandstand, with cars passing, *you cannot hear the loud speakers.*

Surely grandstand patrons have a right to expect to hear what is going on round the course: the speakers are carefully placed for the benefit of the bookmakers, and a small one a few yards past the stand towards Melbourne.

Why, in heaven's name, cannot a big speaker or two be attached high up on the columns supporting the stand roof, facing directly into the mass of patient seat-holders who, unless there is no car running within half a mile, can barely hear a whisper from the announcer's box?

If journalists sat in the stand, things would soon be altered.

G.T.S. Reekie
Derby

(Many experiments have been made at Donington to achieve the best results, but no loud speaker can reasonably be expected to drown the roar of a racing car at close quarters – Ed.)"

The drivers approached the winter at their personal levels. Lang wanted a holiday because he'd "lost a fair amount of weight. I had built a week-end chalet in the lovely valley of the Rems which had superb views over the county of Wurttemberg [down towards the Swiss frontier]." Lang would spend the winter there getting his weight and his strength back ready for 1938. In particular he'd hardened "the palms of my hands by wielding a pick and spade."[5]

It was still possible to anticipate such things quite naturally.

Seaman did drive a Mercedes (Lang's car) at Crystal Palace in what was described as a demonstration run in the interval between two races. The chaps were there, Maclure, Arthur Dobson, Whitehead, Hanson, Bira, Martin, the Hon P. Aitken and visitors Count Trossi and Count Lurani.

The crowd were "duly thrilled" by the Mercedes – "this low-built yet so powerful-looking silver machine. Driving with extreme care and experiencing wheelspin whenever he accelerated, Seaman made several laps in around 2min 4sec [about the racing pace of an ERA] and was last seen on the roof of the television van answering rather difficult questions on his experiences of this year."[6]

Afterwards, Seaman was able to spend a few days at home for the first time since, astonishingly, the springtime Monza testing. As Chula points out[7] he "made a point of giving his mother as much of his companionship as possible, and, if he went out to dinner in the evening, he would usually try to be in to take tea with her first."

It was still possible to behave like that quite normally.

A day after Seaman drove at Crystal Palace, the British Fascist leader Sir Oswald Mosley was struck by something hurled at him at a rally in Liverpool. Some 8,000 of his followers were heckled and jeered, and mounted police were needed to break it up.

Mercedes naturally wanted their books kept in order and set out what they had won. (RM = Reichsmarks, the German currency):

Donington Grand Prix on 2 October 1937
2nd prize Manfred von Brauchitsch
3rd prize Rudolf Caracciola

2nd prize	£120
3rd prize	£75
Leading after 15 laps:	
von Brau	£25
Leading after 45 laps:	
von Brau	£25

Shared prize for fastest lap:

von Brau	£50	
	£295	@ 12.35 = RM 3.643.25

Starting money

von Brauchitsch	£100	
Rud. Caracciola	£100	
H. Lang	£100	
R. Seaman	£100	
	£400	@ 12.35 = RM 4.940
		RM 8.583.25

In another memorandum the amount of money advanced as expenses was set out: Neubauer £80 6s, Uhlenhaut £64 11s 3d, Caracciola £85, von Brauchitsch £56, Lang £35 but Seaman only £3 – presumably because he could charge travel only from London.

The Mercedes London office wanted to settle their accounts and sent a detailed list to Untertürkheim. It remains a mysterious and slightly bizarre document. For example, on 7 September a Mr Samways took a taxi to Dover which cost 19s 11d, although why he went by taxi we know not. Nor is it clear why on 25 September the London office should pay £602 15s 3d for "customs deposit for tyres Hannover." Two days later Samways went from Dover to Dunkirk at a cost of £13 2s 10d and that same day his "telephone outlay" was 6s. The sum of 10s 6d was paid to J. Iliffs and Sons for photographs. It all came to £1,425 19s 9d, a fortune when you consider, for comparison, that a new Ford 8 cost £117.

A German journalist called C. Rehling wrote an illuminating and, for the era, unusually colourful feature article in the 12 October issue of the Berlin magazine *Reichssportblatt*. It seems worth quoting in full. He'd tried to interview the Rosemeyers in Czechoslovakia, or rather get Bernd Rosemeyer to do an article for the magazine.

"We'll talk about this later. Come and visit us in Berlin. Bye bye," Mrs Elly had said, and the Rosemeyers left in their streamlined limousine. That was in Brunn after the Masaryk race.

Now Bernd must have returned from England. A telephone call from Elly. "Yes, he arrived yesterday night." So I go there, but everything indicates he's leaving again, this time to visit his parents. This has been promised for a long time and Bernd is also invited for hunting in the Emsland.[8]

"Why particularly have I come? Bernd is to write 70 lines for the *Reichssportblatt*."

Mrs Elly laughs: "You'd better tell him yourself and I wish you luck. He has such a heap of correspondence and he never gets through it."

Rosemeyer's eyes widen with astonishment when he learns that he is to write an article.

"Out of the question! ... no secretary ... so many obligations. I suggest you come with me to the Rangsdorf airport[9] – Bigalke[10] is going to make a film there – and we can talk on the way."

So there we are in the splendid limousine of which the Rosemeyers are so pround. Built to the racing driver's own specifications, it has hundreds of useful and nice things and a lot of room for luggage: a car good for long voyages; very fast, marvellous acceleration and stunning road holding!

"How was the Donington Park race?"

"I am very glad that I won this last race of the season but it was a terrible race on an uneven track, a real 'jumping' competition although the car was great again. I didn't have bad luck and I am sure that I'd have won even if von Brauchitsch hadn't had a faulty tyre. In recent days we'd had a lot of bad luck at Auto Union, and that after the year began very well for me. First there was South Africa, then my victory in the Eifel race, then the success in America during the Vanderbuilt Cup – great, the Americans were obsessed – and finally I won the 'Coppa Acerbo'. So I can really be satisfied with 1937, but the races became tougher and tougher and our brakes couldn't keep up with the increase in speeds. As a result, I flew off more often than I would have liked. And finally, the situation arose where I had to face three strong Mercedes racing drivers. Now there is only the week of records on the Frankfurt autobahn left, and that'll be it for half a year.

"And the new cars? Don't they have to be tested soon?"

"I really cannot say anything about this. The chassis will obviously be kept [the same]. I haven't seen so much as a screw from the new engines so far but I look forward to the new race formula. 1938 will not be a question of either Mercedes or Auto Union. France, England and Italy will join in again, and I hope the races will be less dangerous. The fight has become too tough and no single metre is given away. The racing isn't fun anymore."

"How are things going in the Auto Union team?"

"We have always got along well with each other. I am very, very sorry that Hans Stuck won't join in again. He has been a good friend and I am of the opinion that he was a good racing driver. I still find it hard to take that Ernst von Delius is not among us anymore. Hasse and Müller are great guys. We co-operate well and I think we are going to make it next year.

We have arrived at Rangsdorf and I'd the chance of returning to Berlin immediately [a lift, presumably]. One more question. 'How are you and Elly getting along with each other in a plane? Normally, if both partners can drive a car there will be trouble..."

"It's the same when you fly," Rosemeyer says.

Elly breaks in to give the reason. "Bernd often took the opportunity to have a nap when he flew with me but now he has long grown out of being dependent on me as the pilot. In fact, he's very independent."

Rosemeyer says "I am really obsessed with flying. As a result, I've ordered my own plane. Really great, a Klemm KL35 with a cruising speed of 200 kph."

"But this is only", corrects his wife, "because it is not worth flying short distances with my four-seat Messerschmidt. The KL35 is the right machine to romp around." I said we'd "talk about your flying plans when we see each other again on the autobahn in Frankfurt."

That was my visit to the Rosemeyers, at a speed of 150 kph on the road from Berlin to Rangsdorf. But I had my 70 lines.

In mid-October the Duke and Duchess of Windsor made what was described as a goodwill visit to Berlin, where they met Hitler and were generally feted. It expressed the ambivalence of – if I may risk a generalisation – the British upper class to the Nazis, or at least to the German nation.

Perhaps this quandary, which would rise in intensity with each passing month, is best expressed by Gillies Shields (the grandson). I'd asked him how his father viewed the German racing teams coming to Donington in 1937. "He had great admiration for the Germans in many ways. During the First War when the British took over German trenches they were all frightfully clean whilst the French ones were all full of ghastly things. He saw the Germans were very good soldiers, too. After the war he was in the sugar beet industry and he used to go to Germany and in doing so he learnt the language fluently. When he came back from work he'd go straight upstairs to the study and turn on a linguaphone record to perfect his German. He seemed to get on very well with them and when the Second War came he was not very anti-German – but he ran everything round here, like the Home Guard…"

Late in October *The Autocar* was able to report that "Kay Petre is definitely much better. In fact she can be said to be out of danger."

Late that October, too, there was a Speed Week on the Frankfurt-Darmstadt autobahn starting from close by Frankfurt airport. The Nazi government saw the propoganda value of breaking speed records set on roads and *Korpsführer* Adolf Huhnlein, who was in charge of the country's motorsport (as we shall see) organised this Speed Week. It was centred around Mercedes and Auto Union, who, using one ordinary carriageway two lanes wide and made of concrete sections, achieved enormous speeds.

Dugdale reported that "some 15 to 20 kilometres of the autobahn had been cleared of normal traffic. One strip of the two-way road was ceaselessly patrolled by Nazi cars, the other formed the record track. In a parking place opposite the flying field gathered the lorries, racing cars and time-keepers' boxes. Children climbed the tall boundary posts of the aerodrome the better to look down on the busy scene…"[11]

The specially designed Auto Union was wide and smooth and feline (and had a Swastika on the side). Rosemeyer set new records for the kilometre and mile, both at over 252 miles an hour, and a ten-kilometre run at 207mph. Mercedes, however, didn't break any records and sought to have the autobahn closed again in January so that they could have another go. Naturally enough, Auto Union wanted the same facility.

Meanwhile Auto Union fired Stuck because evidently he'd broken his contract in disclosing to Rosemeyer details of what he was being paid – who promptly asked for more.[12] The firing was, of course, dressed up nicely for external consumption. *The Motor* reported that "it is denied" the departure was "on account of any differences between himself and the team managers. He is not as young as he was and finds the full distance of the races a bit of a strain. Appartently ... Stuck has been bitten by the motor-boating bug. Sir Malcolm Campbell's recent world's record at Maggiore has fired him with the desire to build a record-breaking boat himself." (At Lake Maggiore in Switzerland on 2 September, Campbell had raised the record to 129 mph.)

The attractions of the Continent were strong for Seaman. He was learning to ski and would stay in Switzerland "on and off" from late November until the end of February. That period included, however, an operation on his face by a leading British plastic surgeon to repair damage done in the German Grand Prix when, after the crash with von Delius, he'd been flung out onto his face. (At Donington he'd told *The Light Car* he'd be devoting some of his "winter leisure time to having a new nose fitted – the old one looks rather battle-scarred after all his crashes. Plastic surgery has been developed to such an art nowadays that when you place your order for a new nose they produce a kind of catalogue and let you choose any pattern you like.")

In November, Lord Halifax – a senior British politician – visited Berlin and had talks about the Sudetenland. In retrospect everything seems clear. Hitler intended to reunite the German nation into his Reich: first Austria, then the Sudetenland, then invade, conquer and colonise the east – Poland, the Soviet Union – to create living space for what he was also in the process of creating, the master race.

As Seaman and his kind skied in the sunlight of the Alps, the darkness was gathering. It would bring, inevitably, tragedies on more levels than you can bear to think about. Among them would be Seaman marrying a most beautiful young German lady. Seaman's mother never spoke a single word to him ever again; but that was in the future, into the darkness.

Seaman returned to England for Christmas and after it drove back to Switzerland with a couple of his friends. From Davos he went over the Austrian border to St Anton when Charlie Martin and his wife joined him. "Their stay together there undoubtedly did much to cement closer their growing friendship."[13]

Threaded through the people and politics of these months were the record-breakers. In December 1937 a Briton, George Eyston, broke the World Land Speed Record at Bonneville flats, Utah. Driving his Rolls-Royce-powered Thunderbolt he averaged 311 mph over the measured mile. That beat Campbell's 301 mph set at Daytona, the same Campbell who now held the title on the water which had excited Stuck so much.

Mercedes' request for an 'extension' to the Speed Week had been granted. Rosemeyer arrived ready to make an attempt on the flying mile and kilometre records – but earlier that morning Caracciola in a Mercedes had been out and taken the records from him.

Caracciola would remember Rosemeyer "sitting in his car, surrounded by a crowd. I pushed my way through and held out my hand to him. 'Congratulations, Rudi,' he said and smiled, his white teeth flashing. 'Thank you,' I said. I wanted to say something more, too, a lot more. All rivalry was forgotten in that moment. He was my comrade, exposed to the same dangers as I. I saw him sitting there ready to start and I felt a momentary dread. I wanted to tell him that it was perhaps too windy ... my throat tightened – I could not, I must not tell him anything..."[14]

Rosemeyer took it on. He had reached some 430 kph (267 mph) when a fierce gust of wind, funnelled through a gap in the trees which lined the autobahn, plucked the car off line. Two wheels went onto the grass. At such a speed the car was now completely out of control and crashed with immense force. Rosemeyer was found under some trees.

Seaman equated the loss of Rosemeyer with that of Henry Segrave, his boyhood hero. "Sir Henry O'Neale de Hane Segrave, the Baltimore-born son of an Anglo-Irish father and an American mother, was undoubtedly Britain's greatest Grand Prix star of the Golden Age of the World Land Speed Record – the 1920s."[15] Segrave was also, this January of 1938, still the last Briton to win a major grand prix, the French in 1924.

Six days later, heavy politics buried the memory of even Rosemeyer. The date – 4 February – is judged by historian William Shirer as "a major turning in the history of the Third Reich, a milestone on its road to war." On that day Hitler swept aside the conservatives in high office who had been put there to "act as a brake upon Nazi excesses... But in the struggle for control of the foreign and economic policy, and the military power of Germany, they proved to be no match for Hitler." After some hesitation Hitler picked General Walther von Brauchitsch – Manfred's uncle – to command the Army. He "enjoyed a good reputation among the generals but was to prove weak and compliant" at standing up to Hitler.[16]

Seaman wrote to Monkhouse two days after this – Monkhouse was producing a motor racing book of photographs about the 1937 season.

"I think some strong reference to national prestige should be made. This point is always rather laughed at in England, but there is no doubt that it means a lot more than we imagine on the Continent. After all, England is becoming a pretty good joke, especially in the Fascist countries, for her flannel-footed behaviour politically, and we are rather looked upon as a lot of decadent old women. A successful British Grand Prix team would be a very good way of dispelling this idea!"

The darkness gathered.

Hitler ordered the Austrian Chancellor, Kurt von Schuschnigg, to free all the Nazis held in jail and lift the ban on the Austrian Nazi party. Hitler, with nobody to gainsay him, was going to *have* Austria and soon.

That week Seaman was in Berlin for the Motor Show as a member of the Mercedes team. Both they and Auto Union were arranged before the

Chancellory, a heavy stone building in the city centre from whose balcony Hitler watched the torchlight military parades go by.

Hitler inspected the drivers and shook hands with them all. The racing cars then escorted him along a route lined by 20,000 members of the motorcycle corps to the Motor Show. There he made a speech in which he proclaimed that the drivers drove not for the love of their machines but "for the honour of Germany." Chula speculates on how odd and uncomfortable Seaman must have found that.

Seaman, however, wrote to Monkhouse that "unable as I was to understand most of it [the speech] I found him a most electrifying orator. At the end of his 17 minutes' speech, plush curtains at his back swept aside disclosing with a fanfare of brass instruments the main exhibition hall behind. In fact, I doubt if Cecil B. de Mille (of Hollywood fame) could have done it much better himself."[17]

Next day Hitler spoke at the Reichstag – the parliament – giving "a blunt warning that henceforth he regarded the future of the seven million Austrians and the three million Sudeten Germans living in Czechoslovakia as the affair of the Third Reich."[18] Day after day Hitler hammered at Austria, threatening and cajoling, massing troops on the border, promising military occupation and forcing von Schuschnigg to resign. Austria fell at Hitler's feet and on 14 March he made an imperious entry into Vienna.

Czechoslovakia would be next.

While Hitler dealt with Austria, preparations for the fresh motor racing season were going on quite normally just to the south, at Monza. There were new regulations, or rather a new formula, which "laid down a scale of minimum weights commensurate with engine size for capacities from 666cc to 4,500cc with an upper limit of 3,000cc (or 3 litres) for engines with superchargers."[19] Both Mercedes and Auto Union travelled to Monza to test and Auto Union went so far as to "fit 16 exhaust pipes to their new 12-cylinder engine in an attempt to confuse any spies who might be around!"[20]

Seaman was pleased with the new Mercedes and, on 18 March, wrote to his mother that the car was "the goods." To Monkhouse he said it "sounds like half a dozen ERAs. The road holding appears to be even better than last year's cars, and is extremely soft, yet without causing a roll."

Auto Union looked vulnerable, Rosemeyer dead and Stuck gone. They would be fielding Hasse and Müller against the collective might of Caracciola, von Brauchitsch, Lang and Seaman and didn't enter the first race, at Pau on 10 April where, astonishingly, Rene Dreyfus in a Delahaye won with Caracciola and Lang, sharing a car, second. Seaman was reserve ("much to his distaste").[21]

Nor did Auto Union enter the next race, at Tripoli on 15 May, which Mercedes dominated. Lang won from von Brauchitsch and Caracciola but only three cars were entered so Seaman stood by as reserve again. Then he returned to his chalet at Ambach – he'd rented it for the year – and on 20

May wrote to Monkhouse that he now possessed a fast motor boat which was "just what one needs for the lake here. I can bring it alongside the landing stage quite well now."

That same day Hitler issued a highly-secret directive. "It is not my intention to begin to smash Czechoslovakia by military action in the immediate future without provocation … operations preferably will be launched after a period of increasing diplomatic controversies … or by lightning action as a result of a serious incident…"[22]

Hitler then summoned his senior military officers to the Chancellery and said that he had decided to settle the Sudeten question "for once and all." The date for possible military action was given as 1 October. It was the day before the Donington Grand Prix.

By then Dick Seaman was hopelessly in love. On 15 June he'd attended a party at a fashionable Munich restaurant being thrown by Franz-Joseph Popp, co-Founder and President of BMW. Seaman sat next to Popp's daughter Erica who'd remember "we started to chat and I thought he was rather cute and very shy."[23]

They danced a lot and "without any pre-arrangement the floor was soon cleared because most people seemed to have preferred to watch this couple. Erica was then only 18 years of age yet she was already so endowed with such grace and charm that, added to her beauty of face and figure, she was an object of general admiration. Dick Seaman had always been a tall and handsome young man, his dark and neatly brushed hair well matching against Erica's profusion of soft blonde curls. It is true that Dick's face had at first been left with bad scars after his serious accident during the German Grand Prix but in November he had undergone a facial operation which he amusedly called 'having his face lifted' … so that his good looks had been largely restored."[24]

Popp couldn't help noting the nose was "a little off-colour" after the surgery but "that was his fault because he had gone skiing shortly after the operation and the cold had affected the new skin!"[25]

The following day Popp, her family and friends were due to visit Ernst Henne, a world champion motorcycle rider who lived across the lake from Seaman's chalet. Erica invited Seaman and he came across in his speedboat. If it wasn't love then, it would be shortly after.

Hitler was spending time at the Obersalzberg in Berchtesgaden, the Bavarian holiday compound not far from Salzburg – and the opposite side of Bavaria to Ambach. In mid-June he took one of those decisions which, as it proved, would destroy love stories across the Continent and beyond. He would only take action against Czechoslovakia "if I am firmly convinced … that France will not march and that therefore England will not intervene." When he was ready, day after day he'd threaten and cajole, mass troops, promise military occupation just like Austria – but he wouldn't move until he was sure. He had not modified his deadline, that day before Donington.

Auto Union did return for the French Grand Prix at Reims on 3 July but both their cars retired. Von Brauchitsch won from Caracciola and Lang, Seaman reserve again. He did a bit of driving during practice and described the race as "quite one of the stupidest ever." After Lang in third place came Rene Carriere in a Darracq, but ten laps behind.

Seaman returned to Ambach and wrote to Monkhouse that he was becoming "more adept" in his dinghy, feared he might become a sailing convert and had been "surf-board riding behind the motor-boat." He eagerly awaited the arrival of his water skis. He seems to have been silent about his relegation to reserve – a political decision? – and doesn't seem to have mentioned Czechoslovakia, either.

It is easy to miss the *full* magnitude of the background to the German Grand Prix at the Nürburgring. Hitler, brooding and lashing out, had mounted one of his attacks on degenerate art, Viennese Jews were reported to be resorting to suicide as the Nazis introduced their aggressive anti-Sematism there, Italy was mimicking this anti-sematism, Franco was making gains in Spain and – it happened two days before the race – German jews were ordered to wear special identity cards.

The Nürburgring was a massive circuit measuring 22.80 kilometres (14.17 miles) and flowing up, round, down and through the wooded Eifel district in the west of Germany. Constantly flinging corners at the driver, it was a murderous place and many died there. The Grand Prix attracted crowds of 300,000 and they'd savour the race *between* Mercedes and Auto Union but draw a profound satisfaction from the superiority of both over the rest: the Alfa Romeos (there were five), the Maseratis (five) and two Delahayes. The German Grand Prix *here* was definitely not for the ERAs although a Briton, A.B. Hyde, did go. His 3-litre Maserati was "old and ex-Howe, ex-Cholmondeley-Tapper"[26] which is one way of saying it wasn't exactly going to win...

Stuck was back at Auto Union, as a result of high-level government pressure,[27] but the real story was that the team had hired Tazio Nuvolari. Ken Purdy, an American author, wrote this: "It really isn't arguable at all. The men who knew the most about Nuvolari, the motoring journalists of Europe who watched him down the years, were all in essential agreement: the greatest driver of racing cars ever to hold a wheel in his hands."[28]

Erica Popp went to the Nürburgring although racing didn't interest her. Friends took her and they stayed at the Eifeler Hof Hotel at the nearby hamlet of Adenau ("not very fancy, but very nice"). The Mercedes team were staying there, Seaman and all, too. Coincidence. Maybe.

Neubauer records an incident which took place in the hotel, and as we saw in Chapter Two, it's a rarity because it reveals the true tensions within the team. "At the breakfast-table there was a slight scene, which I fortunately missed, but which was reported to me afterwards and had a certain bearing on the race. Brauchitsch, who was a snob, seldom lost an opportunity of taunting Lang with his 'proletarian' origin. That morning he made some sneering remark which brought Lang to his feet in a rage, and it was only Dick Seaman's tact and coolness that prevented a fight."[29] (Lang, as I've recounted, makes no mention of this in his own book.)

The race is simply decribed. Lang led from Nuvolari, who went off the circuit backwards. Lang had problems with oiling plugs, Seaman was behind him but von Brauchitsch moved past them both. That meant Mercedes in the first three positions but Neubauer "felt far from happy. I had been giving signals which meant that a sufficient lead had been established by the Mercedes team for each driver to hold his present position. Brauchitsch had ignored them and passed Seaman."[30]

Seaman tucked in behind von Brauchitsch and you can only guess at these subterranean tensions. Seaman dutifully followed but close enough to unnerve him. Here was the well-bred Englishman – Neubauer describes his driving here as "cool, elegant" and Cyril Posthumus said "smooth, competent" – proving in a German car at the greatest circuit in Germany that he could easily be leading the German Grand Prix from a German *but* that would have meant ignoring team orders. What well-bred Englishman would countenance that or point out that the well-bred von Brauchitsch, whose uncle commanded the German Army, had done?

This "crazy duel" made Neubauer's "hair stand on end."[31]

Von Brauchitsch and Seaman pitted – ten seconds behind – for tyres and fuel, and von Brauchitsch shouted "I've had enough! This damned fellow Seaman's driving me mad sitting on my tail."[32] Neubauer scurried over to Seaman and asked him to back off a bit. Neubauer saw Seaman's hands "tighten on the steering-wheel, then in a low voice he said 'all right, sir.'"

Just a few yards away von Brauchitsch's pit stop went terribly wrong. Spilt petrol ignited and flames engulfed the car. Neubauer claims to have physically hauled von Brauchitsch out and rolled him on the ground to put his flaming overalls out. Fire extinguishers covered the car in foam.

Seaman sat watching.

Neubauer rushed over and asked him why he hadn't gone back out. With what must have been exquisite English irony Seaman said calmly, *I thought I was to let von Brauchitsch keep his lead…*

Neubauer ordered Seaman to return to the race, Seaman obeyed and won from Lang or, strictly speaking, from Caracciola/Lang because Lang had been halted by the plugs and taken over Caracciola's car: Caracciola had food poisoning.

Von Brauchitsch, too, returned to the race after the fire but crashed almost immediately. Neubauer would claim that Korpsführer Huhnlein virtually ordered von Brauchitsch to go back out because the alternative was the Englishman winning, and that was the sort of detail Hitler noticed.

Popp and friends sat in the grandstand opposite the pits and she felt Seaman's victory as "madly exciting".

After the race Neubauer found himself accused, by a Nazi official, of sending von Brauchitsch out in the fire-damaged car, with the implication that he risked von Brauchitsch's life. Neubauer pointed to Huhnlein, or claimed he did.

You need the background to that, need to ask what fear was there in the land? What madness stalked the land and could be visited, on a whim, upon anyone, even a Neubauer? Huhnlein was a career soldier, and who knew what access he had to the most powerful?

The British national anthem was played as well as the German, and Seaman had a huge garland placed round his neck complete with Swastika ribbons. Huhnlein, stiff in uniform, stood beside him, binoculars slung round his neck, medals on his breast. Seaman gave a compromise salute, not Nazi but his arm semi-raised, the palm of the hand open and the hand limp like a flipper. Chula recorded that "the most notable feature of the whole affair was the uncomfortable expression on Dick's face as he had to perform the Nazi salute at the close of the race."[33]

Rene Dreyfus, who finished fifth in a Delahaye, remembered that "I didn't know of anyone who was genuinely a Nazi sympathiser. Certainly Rudi [Caracciola] was not, nor Rosemeyer, but of course they all had to give the Nazi salute – even Dick Seaman, when he won at the Nürburgring..."

Huhnlein presented him with an enormous trophy and, as he was always going to do, embarked on a long speech extolling the virtues of the German motor industry and "referring to Brauchitsch as the real hero of the race and the moral winner, while lastly congratulating Seaman, the actual winner."[34]

John Dugdale, there reporting the race, managed to get near to Seaman while Huhnlein was speaking and offered his congratulations. Seaman thanked him for that and murmured "I only wish it had been a British car" then enquired how Hyde, who'd crashed on lap 15, was.

Huhnlein, who must have been wriggling in his own private agony at the Englishman winning the German Grand Prix at the Nürburgring in a German car, sent a telegram to Hitler:

> *My Führer,*
> *I report: The 11th Grand Prix of Germany for racing cars ended with decisive German victory. From the start the new German racing construction of Mercedes-Benz and Auto Union dominated the field. Storm Leader Manfred von Brauchitsch, leading from the beginning and giving admirable proof of his courage and ability, was deprived of victory by his car catching fire while refuelling. The winner and consequently the gainer of your proud prize, My Führer, was Richard Seaman on a Mercedes, followed by Chief Storm Leader Lang, also on a Mercedes, Hans Stuck and Tazio Nuvolari on Auto Union cars.*
>
> *Heil, My Führer.*

That evening Mercedes held a celebration dinner at the Eifeler Hof. Caracciola realised that von Brauchitsch was not present. "Go and see what the boy is doing," he told Alice.

She "went on tiptoe over to the next room and there the big fellow was, stretched out on the bed and sobbing with anger and disappointment." She sat on the edge of his bed and "ran her hand over his tousled head and I sat down on a chair. We let him give vent to his feelings."[35]

Downstairs Neubauer had drawn up the seating plan in the large dining room. "I noticed that at one end of the table, next to the lovely Erica Popp, was an empty chair. Either Manfred von Brauchitsch was very late or had decided to sleep off the shock to his nerves and his pride. Suddenly Dick Seaman appeared and there was a burst of applause. He walked straight to the end of the table and Erica Popp raised her glass. Then with a gesture of her hand she invited him to take the empty chair. I knew then that these two delightful young people were in love and I was glad."[36]

Popp "sat on Dick's right, which caused a few eyebrows to be raised as he was known to be too involved with racing to have any time for girls!" Erica explained that she shouldn't really have been at the dinner, because she had friends and their three children as house guests at Grainau and ought to have been there with them instead.[37] Seaman pointed out that the next major grand prix – the Swiss at Bern – was not until 21 August, Grainau wasn't far from his chalet and they really should see each other more.

They did.

Chula records that "after her coming to luncheon rather formally at Ambach on the Tuesday after the German Grand Prix, Erica and Dick were soon constantly driving to and from Ambach and Garmisch, exchanging hospitality and getting to know one another better." They swam together and he taught her how to water ski. "Actually this period was exceptionally brief and lasted for only six days, from Tuesday, 26 to Sunday, 31 of July."

Between those two dates Seaman's mother, who had taken up a long standing invitation to visit him, travelled to Munich with a German-speaking companion and arrived on the 28th. Because Seaman was entertaining a large house party[38] she spent time in Munich and reached Ambach on 1 August. This furnishes an authentic glimpse of the times, large house party, mother travelled almost a thousand miles but it was not proper to intrude on her son.

When she did arrive she was enchanted with the view from her room and with Erica Popp but, flinty and straight-seeing as Mrs Seaman undoubtedly was, enchantment did not obscure her perception of reality.

Monkhouse, who was in Bavaria and knew Mrs Seaman had had misgivings about rumours of Seaman's possible Continental girlfriends, decided to take a "bold step" and introduce her to the idea of Erica. During one lunch, Monkhouse blurted out: "Mrs Seaman, we have found a wife for Dick, in fact the only possible wife for Dick."

Mrs Seaman was momentarily taken aback but recovered strongly. "If my son wants a wife he is quite capable of finding one himself."

Seaman said nothing.

Mrs Seaman regained her composure and, according to Monkhouse, "decided it was just a joke."

Moreover, Mrs Seaman had something in common with Winston Churchill. Whatever anybody told her, whatever allowances were made for Hitler and why he was doing what he was doing, she was not deceived. She saw war. The incessant gossip – especially among the Germans she met – that marriage between her son and Erica was inevitable solidified her opinion. She had "nothing but admiration for Erica, both for her looks and capabilities," but understood what it would mean.[39]

The reticence of Seaman in resolving this appears strange (in a fiercely brave racing driver) although only, perhaps, because we don't know more and can never know more. In tackling over-bearing mothers, racing drivers may be as cowed as you or I. And anyway, did he discuss it? On that we hear – silence. We do have a fragment, because evidently Mrs Seaman warned him about the "attentions" of a married German woman who was a keen follower. Seaman explained how he knew about the woman and realised the dangers but took the opportunity to add a question. "What would you say if I were going to marry Erica?"

Mrs Seaman spoke of the darkness coming.

Hitler had begun to apply the tourniquet to Czechoslovakia. On 3 August Chamberlain dispatched a mediator to Czechoslovakia to try to help what was now the Sudetenland Crisis. Hitler tightened the tourniquet. On 15 August, the day after the Coppa Acerbo at the Italian circuit of Pescara which Caracciola won (and Auto Union did not enter), Hitler repeated at a military conference that he would solve the crisis by force. No voice was raised against him.[40]

Mrs Seaman moved into the Alpenhof Hotel in the town of Garmisch. Before leaving for London she held a dinner party and "even danced with a young German officer from another table" but "warded off" the question of Seaman's marriage. Popp describes how, after dinner, everyone went down to the Casino bar and did a popular dance called the Catch. The bandleader threw coloured ping-pong balls and if a couple didn't catch one they had to go off the floor. In the end the couple remaining would be the winners. Popp points out that Seaman, 6ft 3in, caught everything and they won.[41]

Mrs Seaman later wrote to Chula: "What a pity Erica is not an Englishwoman."

Seaman was second to Caracciola at Berne in the Swiss Grand Prix.

Three days later, a member of the German High Command stressed to Hitler the importance of arranging the exact timing of the "incident" to provoke German forces to invade Czechoslovakia, a country France and Britain were bound to defend.

In those days, apart from grands prix and records, there were competitive mountain-climbs. In the week when the death of Czechoslovakia was being arranged, Seaman was at the Grossglockner climb over the border – or rather what had been the border – to Austria. He'd gone there with Erica and during a picnic he proposed to her. She accepted.

Seaman flew back to England to take part in the RAC Tourist Trophy race at Donington where he'd drive a Frazer Nash BMW (and finish 21st). He called to see his mother, who'd heard he was unofficially engaged to Erica and admitted this was "more or less" true.[42] Mrs Seaman knew that Popp's father would be travelling to England for the Donington Grand Prix on 2

October and she would have the matter out with him then. This would not necessarily have been good news for Herr Popp.

Seaman returned to Germany on Sunday, 4 September. He had the Italian Grand Prix at Monza the following Sunday, the last race before Donington, to think about.

These many years later it is extremely difficult to construct a living, breathing portrait of Richard John Seaman covering his contradictions, uncertainties and inner thoughts. The difficulty centres around the era: as we've seen, penetrating personalised journalism was all but unknown. Dugdale, for example, was simply attempting to introduce the drivers as *people* and that was regarded as pioneering.

As Charlie Martin implied, *chaps* didn't bear their souls to other *chaps* or to anybody else. Martin said: "Dick was a nice chap, a good friend of mine and he got this magnificent drive with Mercedes. He was well-spoken but hard as nails. I first met him way back at Brooklands. I suppose we'd raced together since 1934. The atmosphere of racing was Public School-like, it was what you might do instead of playing *rugger* or whatever. It wasn't all that serious, except there was a lot of loot involved as far as Dick was concerned. He got a big 'whack' (slang for money) out of Mercedes but, in the early 1930's, racing was just the sort of thing a chap did. You needed money. I had a little but not much. You did have to have some, and Dick did – he had a mother who looked after him. She was a tough old harridan. Dick had a manager called Tony Birch who did all the negotiating. He was a German-speaking chap but British. It was unusual to have a manager in those days but Dick needed one because so much money was involved."

Ian Connell, who would compete in the Donington race this year of 1938, "didn't know Dick very well at Cambridge because we were in different colleges. I was at Caius and I have a feeling he was at Trinity. [He was.] We used to meet at the Cambridge University Automobile Club. I liked him very much. He had a terrible handshake – sloppy. You know how it is when some people shake hands, terribly limp, and in him that was extraordinary. Dick used to drive me to the circuits and he drove beautifully. Several times I was with him on the roads and he never went too fast, just extremely nicely. He was a well-spoken sort of chap, a gentleman as it were."

Dugdale, who knew Seaman well enough to holiday with him at Ambach, describes him as "very tall and steely-eyed. He had a large nose, like a Spanish conquistador. He was a very determined man who sort of knew his destiny. He was going to be a racing driver and that was it. He wouldn't let anything get in the way of that. Was there a hard side to him? No. He was a man of destiny, going his own way. He was opinionated but usually right! Popp was terribly young, you know, but she loved him very much."

Seaman remains, as he will no doubt always remain, at a great distance from us: a man of his time and, like all men inhibited from expressing themselves by their time, almost a caricature. What fires burned within? What was his anguish of living, driving, loving in Germany then?

We hear – silence.

Erica Popp insists that Seaman was not political, just a racing driver. He had however, discussed any potential political problems with Earl Howe. Popp accepts, naturally, that he "was aware of what was going on in Germany to some extent and disliked the Nazis intensely." She insists that "he was in no way compromised by driving for a German team and there were no political pressures on him from Mercedes or the German government."[43]

Maybe Tom Wheatcroft captures it best. "Seaman looked so tall and smart. You know what it's like when you're young. *Oooh, that's Dick Seaman over there*, the *Dick Seaman*."

We should leave it, and him, there, leave him safe in the memory of his time and forever something of a stranger to us.

Chapter 5

Each
dangerous day

ON FRIDAY, 9 SEPTEMBER 1938 the overnight sleeper from Munich slipped
into Milan's central station, a stone building so imperiously heavy and
immense – broad staircases, porticos – that it might have been a monument.
As the train slowed and nestled alongside one of the long platforms a figure
in racing overalls stood watching it. Seaman had taken part in the qualifying
session for the Italian Grand Prix at nearby Monza – the session began at
5am – and, the instant it was over, didn't change but drove immediately to
Milan to meet the train because Erica was on it. Two friends accompanied
her, a Mercedes director called Dr Wilhelm Haspel and his wife, known as
Bimbo.

Perhaps all three were relieved to shed the weight of Germany for a while
because, this Friday, German radio repeated that Britain had announced she
would fight if Czechoslovakia was invaded.

Seaman, who had travelled to Milan with a couple of his friends, Robert
Fellowes (a famous amateur photographer) and Morris Goodall, was staying
at the Principe de Savoia, one of the best hotels in Milan and, situated in the
Piazza della Repubblica, only a short distance from the railway station. He
drove Erica to the Principe and she remembered that "when we went to the
dining room for lunch many of the other drivers were there and they all did
a double-take – *Seaman with a girl! What's this*? Some of them had seen us
together at the Nürburgring, of course, and now we could tell them of our
engagement."[1]

In these dangerous days background and foreground were interwoven, as
they so often are before a great crisis. Momentous events are unfolding
while mundane everyday life continues under its great imperatives.

Certainly some of the drivers were uneasy about the interweaving and
what it might mean. "The political situation worried all of us. In Italy we
were met with some sympathy, but on the whole with outright hostility. War
seemed inevitable. However ... as yet we were still racing and the drivers of

many nations participated. It was as hot as only Italy can be in autumn," wrote Caracciola.[2]

On the Sunday, the day of the race, a well-known French driver, Louis Chiron (later to be more famous as the starter of grands prix at Monaco) asked Fellowes and Goodall, "what do you think of Dick's engagement to Erica Popp?" They were taken by surprise because he hadn't mentioned it to them.[3] They sought him out, he confessed it was perfectly true and they congratulated him.

During the race "it was hot in the cars, even hotter in mine because a gasket had burned out," Caracciola wrote. "The heat of the exhaust came directly through the openings of the gear and throttle pedals at my feet. In spite of asbestos lining, the throttle burned a hole through the leather sole [and] the asbestos inner sole right to the sole of my foot. Brauchitsch took over from me for a few laps then he had enough. I got in again, pressing down on the red-hot throttle with just the edge of my foot."

Seaman retired after 16 of the 60 laps with engine trouble. He had been fourth. Popp sat in the grandstand "so bored" but when Seaman retired he made his way up and joined her. His heart, she estimated, was not in the race.[4] Nuvolari won for Auto Union, three laps ahead of Farina with the shared drive of Caracciola/von Brauchitsch third.

Evidently Mercedes had been so confident of winning that they'd ordered a "celebration dinner for seventy persons."[5] The party was cancelled but Neubauer then decided he would have one "just the same", and that it was to be a celebration of Dick's engagement. They went to a little place, which was a favourite restaurant of Neubauer, and Fellowes distinctly remembers that altogether 13 persons sat down to dinner. After dinner Dick and Erica, accompanied by Fellowes and Goodall, went to a cabaret, where Dick was in excellent spirits, culminating in his dancing the Lambeth Walk, and receiving a big applause."

Popp remembered the details with a slight difference. Neubauer had gone for a "quiet dinner alone with his wife. It turned into a riotous evening and the crowning glory was our visit to the Ambassador's nightclub afterwards, where Dick and I taught everyone the Lambeth Walk. They all thought it was great and we were *Oi'-ing* all over the place."[6]

Donington was three weeks away.

Before Seaman and Popp left Monza Caracciola suggested Zurich was "the best place to buy diamonds" and on the way back they stopped there so he could buy her an engagement ring.

It must have been the Monday and that night, while the lovers drove on towards Munich, Hitler spoke at Nuremberg, hurling "threats and insults at Prague. But he did not demand that the Sudetens be handed over to him outright. Everyone in Czechoslovakia must have listened to the speech, the streets being deserted from eight to ten. Prague on this day when war and peace have apparently hung in the balance has been dark and dismal, with a cold, biting, soaking rain."[7]

Next day – Tuesday – the juxtaposition between mundane everyday life

David Coulthard experiences the awesome power – and lack of brakes – which the 1937 Mercedes W125 still offered. This picture was taken at the company's test track at Stuttgart before the German Grand Prix in 1997. (Courtesy of Wilhelm/Mercedes-Benz)

If you go down to the woods today. It's 1934, this is what Donington looked like and this is what it felt like: 'Wilkie' Wilkinson (left) and co-driver have broken down and wave to a passing competitor – a driver called Eddie Hall. (Courtesy of 'Wilkie' Wilkinson)

Left *Donington 1937. An aerial drawing of the full circuit, with the new extension down to Melbourne Corner in place. Note that the nearest arrow pointing from the corner is the wrong way!* (Courtesy of Gillies Shields)

Below left *Construction work at Melbourne Corner…*

Above *… and here it is, a magnificent panorama and, with the rise at the top, perhaps one of the most inherently dramatic of any grand prix circuits anywhere, ever. The horseshoe corner still exists although it is isolated in a field now.* (Both courtesy Gillies Shields)

Below *A sign of the times. 'Wilkie' Wilkinson (standing, centre) beside the Alfa Romeo of Kenneth Evans before the 1937 German Grand Prix at the Nürburgring – but helplessly your eye is drawn to the guard and the swastika.* (Courtesy of 'Wilkie' Wilkinson)

Left *The chaps. Dick Seaman (left) with Swiss Hans Ruesch, his co-driver at the 1936 Donington Grand Prix. They are celebrating victory in their Alfa Romeo. This was the race which established Seaman.* (Ludvigsen Library)

Below *The chaps. Andrew Cuddon-Fletcher in his MG before the start of the 1938 Donington Grand Prix. The Duke of Kent and Dick Seaman – hands in pockets – are walking behind the car.* (Ludvigsen Library)

Top right *The chaps. Band leader Billy Cotton, here with Wilkinson at a race in 1937 where they co-drove this MG. Behind Wilkinson is another driver, Peter Whitehead who rests an arm on 'young' Billy Cotton, later to be Managing Director of BBC Television, 1984–88.*

Middle right *Another study of Wilkinson, Cotton and 'young' Billy.* (Both courtesy of 'Wilkie' Wilkinson)

Bottom right *The man who would smash the world of the chaps. Hitler inspects the 1936 Mercedes racing cars at the 1937 Berlin Motor Show in Berlin. Left to right: Hermann Lang, Manfred von Brauchitsch shaking hands, and Rudolf Caracciola.* (Ludvigsen Library)

Above *Hitler shakes hands with Rudi Caracciola (who hated the Nazis). Saluting is team manager, Alfred Neubauer. (Ludvigsen Library)*

Below *The grid for the 1937 Donington Grand Prix. The front row (from right to left): von Brauchitsch, Rosemeyer, Lang, and Seaman.*

Bottom *The start, and the front row has already gone. Hermann Müller is No. 7, Rudolf Hasse No. 6 and Rosemeyer, who struggled to get away, No. 5. (The Derby Evening Telegraph)*

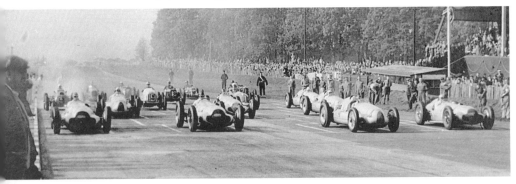

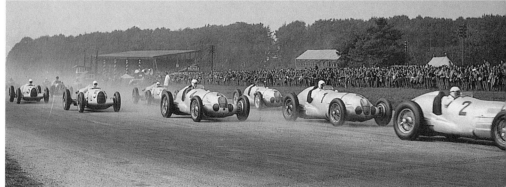

Top *A mirror of the war to come: the start of the 1937 Donington race with the mighty Germans heading off into the distance and the first of the British drivers (Chas Martin, ERA) just appearing.* (Ludvigsen Library)

Above *Into Red Gate Corner: Lang (2) leads from Rudolf Caracciola (1), Seaman (4) third, and Rosemeyer recovering fast.* (Ludvigsen Library)

Right *The decorum of the day. Most men wore jackets, collars and ties even to watch sport. The car is von Brauchitsch's Mercedes.* (LAT)

Above *That magnificent panorama. Seaman followed by Rosemeyer and Müller approaches the rise from Melbourne Corner. The long descent and ascent allowed the crowd to compare the speed difference between the chaps and the Germans.* (Ludvigsen Library)

Below *Müller landing …* (Ludvigsen Library)

Bottom *… and from a different angle. At speed and in cars of such weight it must have been even more frightening than it looked.* (LAT)

Above *Landed.* (Ludvigsen Library)

Below *Manfred von Brauchitsch is airborne in his Mercedes Benz at Melbourne Rise.* (Ludvigsen Library)

Bottom *Von Brauchitsch, airborne again.* (Ludvigsen Library)

Above *As Rosemeyer crosses the line the Auto Union team salute him.* (Courtesy of Archiv Auto Union)

Top left *Rosemeyer into Red Gate – having just overtaken Bira? The photograph, taken at the end of the pit lane, gives a good idea of the width of the track. Note, too, the people standing unprotected directly ahead.* (LAT)

Middle left *Them and us. Rosemeyer gets off line into Red Gate but is still far, far too fast for one of the chaps to do anything about it. This must have been quite a moment for the unprotected people standing there.* (Ludvigsen Library)

Bottom left *Rosemeyer wins the 1937 Donington Grand Prix. Is that Alfred Neubauer (bottom left) watching and ruminating on a race lost?* (Ludvigsen Library)

Below *Seaman and his fiancée Erica Popp at their hotel at Adenau – the village on the far side of the Nürburgring – during the German Grand Prix of 1938. Note the swastika behind them, like something you could never get away from.* (Ludvigsen Library)

Left *Tazio Nuvolari, who many consider the greatest driver of all time, before the German Grand Prix (where the suspension of his Auto Union failed after two laps). Note the Nazi salute behind him while he adopts a compromise position. The tortoise which Nuvolari wore for luck is clearly visible.* (Courtesy of Archiv Auto Union)

Below *Englishman Dick Seaman wins the 1938 German Grand Prix in a Mercedes Benz – and gives this compromise Nazi salute.* (Ludvigsen Library)

Top right *Tuesday, 27 September 1938. Auto Union mechanics pump petrol from one of their cars before leaving Donington in case war broke out immediately.* (The Derby Evening Telegraph)

Bottom right *Wednesday, 28 September 1938. The mechanics load an Auto Union and leave Donington again as Germany mobilised and the Grand Prix was postponed.* (Quadrant)

THE LEICESTER MERCURY, TUESDAY, 27th SEPTEMBER, 1938.

'PHONE TALKS—THEN PLANS CHANGED

GERMANS TOLD TO STAY AFTER LEAVING DONINGTON FOR HOME

WILL TAKE PART IN GRAND PRIX ON SATURDAY

'THERE WILL BE A RACE BUT NO WAR,' THEY SAY

A PARTY of Germans—members of the Mercedes Benz motor racing squad—were stopped by the police in Leicester this morning as they were hurrying to get back to Germany. The Auto Union team, with their mechanics and equipment, were similarly stopped at Market Harborough. Now, with reassurance from Herr Hühnlein, the leader of the German motor sport, following phone calls to Germany, the teams have returned to Donington Park, where they will compete in the Donington Grand Prix on Saturday—the day of the expiration of Hitler's ultimatum to Czechoslovakia.

THE Mercedes convoy consists of about ten lorries, with five racing cars and thousands of pounds worth of equipment, and 27 mechanics, in charge of Herr Arnold Wychodil, a slight, fair-haired, bespectacled Sudeten German.

Following Hitler's speech last night, urgent telegrams were sent to the two German teams who were staying at Donington Hall, and this morning everything was ready for a dash to London and so across the Continent to their headquarters in Germany.

The two firms concerned, however, made a quick change of decision, and all police stations on the route from Donington to London were asked to detain the teams.

Optimistic 'Phone Talks

Thus it came about, that the Mercedes convoy was drawn up at the roadside in Conduit-street and Church-street adjoining the Leicester police station. The cars were ...

Members of the German Mercedes-Benz racing team outside Leicester police station where they were given instructions not to return to Germany, but to stay for the Donington Grand Prix next Saturday.

No Time For Wordy Warfare

CITY COUNCIL DEBATES DROPPED

IN view of the international crisis, the contentious subjects on the agenda of the Leicester City Council business this ...

Herr Arnold Wychodil (right), who is in charge of the party, with three of the team, in cheerful mood after receiving information to return to Donington.

[From Page One]

EX-LEICESTER INFIRMARY

Left *Mercedes and Auto Union returned to compete in the race. It had been scheduled for 1 October but was run three weeks later. In practice Nuvolari could not avoid one of the Donington deers.* (Courtesy of Archiv Auto Union)

Below *He was presented with the stuffed head.* (Ludvigsen Library)

Right *A picture which captures perfectly how rural – and dangerous – Donington remained. In places, the trees formed an arch screening out much daylight. This is Lang in practice.* (Ludvigsen Library)

Below right *Getting ready to go to the grid: Müller's Auto Union on what must be the inner road from the stables…*

... Nuvolari's, with a mechanic at the wheel ...

... and Walter Baumer's Mercedes. It's getting a tow – the rope is being attached to the car in front. The tyres have an elaborate tread pattern. (All Ludvigsen Library)

The 1938 grid: mechanics working on Seaman's car with – probably – Rudolf Uhlenhaut, the Mercedes Technical Director, bending over the nose between the two mechanics in white overalls.

In the background Lang watches the mechanics work on his car (No. 7). The steering wheel has been hung over a side-mirror. In the foreground mechanics work on Hasse's car. Again, note the detachable steering wheel – detached! Hasse is almost obscured by a Derby and District Motor Club official, left.

Hasse standing beside his car (No 2). Baumer is No. 5. The rear of Lang's Mercedes – on pole – can just be glimpsed.

Left to right: Professor Robert Eberan-Eberhorst, Auto Union's Development Engineer; von Brauchitsch; Dr Karl Feuereissen, Team Manager, and Nuvolari. (All Ludvigsen Library)

Above left *Seaman introduces the Duke of Kent to Billy Cotton.* (The Derby Evening Telegraph)

Above right *Moment of tension. The Duke is introduced to Huhnlein who gave the Nazi salute – just before or after this moment.* (The Derby Evening Telegraph)

Below *Nuvolari seized the lead and began to pull away almost immediately. Here he is at the Hairpin followed by Müller and then the four Mercedes, the chaps already falling back. To the right, behind the five-bar gate, is the hut where Mrs Craner took refuge.* (Ludvigsen Library)

Above *Two worlds meet. Müller screams past Arthur Dobson's ERA…*

Below *… Ian Connell tries to keep his ERA behind von Brauchitsch into Red Gate, but won't be able to.* (Both Ludvigsen Library)

Right *The Auto Union of Christian Kautz comes to grief at Melbourne Corner – to be followed by Cuddon-Fletcher's MG.* (Ludvigsen Library)

Müller under pressure from two Mercedes into and out of the Hairpin. Robin Hanson's Alta (No. 14) seems what it was, an irrelevance. (Courtesy of Archiv Auto Union)

There really was a farm gate. Here is von Brauchitsch going past it. (Ludvigsen Library)

Müller holding off Seaman. (Ludvigsen Library)

This is Lang, coming up from Melbourne. (Ludvigsen Library)

Below and right *Both sides of the bridge. Hasse chasing Baumer ... Müller leads a Mercedes, probably Seaman.* (Ludvigsen Library)

Above *A Mercedes, probably von Brauchitsch, passes Percy Maclure's abandoned Riley. Note the graphic 100 yard warning board on the left.* (Ludvigsen Library)

Below *Dick Seaman wrestles the Mercedes at Donington in 1938.* (Ludvigsen Library)

Bottom *Nuvolari accelerates from a pit stop.* (Ludvigsen Library)

The maestro, showing his precision of line. These two photographs were taken on different laps. (Ludvigsen Library)

Victory! (Ludvigsen Library)

Nuvolari prepares to be garlanded. (Ludvigsen Library)

The most popular victor…

... prepares to go up to receive the trophy. Note the cigarette. Dr William Werner, the Auto Union Technical Director, is immediately behind Nuvolari and smiling; Feuereissen next to him. (Both Ludvigsen Library)

A sign of the times. Nuvolari adopts the compromise position again but Dr Carl Hahn (in glasses), Auto Union's Group Sales Director, and Werner, give the Nazi salute. So does Feuereissen, to Nuvolari's right. (Ludvigsen Library)

That's more like it. Even Huhnlein (above and to the right of Nuvolari) is smiling. (Courtesy of Archiv Auto Union)

Darkness, and the war coming. The Auto Union team members pay their respects in 1939 to the memory of Rosemeyer a year after he died in a speed record attempt. Left to right: Hasse, Nuvolari, Kautz, and Müller. (Courtesy of Archiv Auto Union)

June 26, 1939. Seaman receives what would prove to be fatal injuries in the Belgian Grand Prix at Spa when his Mercedes struck a tree. (Ludvigsen Library)

Seaman's funeral. Neubauer with, to his left, von Brauchitsch, Caracciola, and Hasse (hatless, wearing glasses) behind them. (Ludvigsen Library)

Seaman's grave at Putney, London. (Ludvigsen Library)

and momentous events was sharply underscored. Fellowes had passed news to *The Times* of Seaman's engagement and it appeared in that morning's issue.

Amidst reports of shooting in the Sudetenland and the looting of Jewish shops, the Czech government proclaimed martial law in the five Sudeten districts. That evening, Konrad Henlein – leader of the Sudeten German Party and a Hitler acolyte – sent a six-hour ultimatum to the government demanding the cessation of the martial law and the withdrawal of Czech police from the area. The government refused that. "It could not have done otherwise. It has made its choice. It will fight. We wait now for Hitler's move." Shirer wrote,[8] "The tension and confusion this night in the lobby of the Ambassador Hotel, where the diplomats and correspondents gather, has been indescribable. Fascinating to watch the reactions of people suddenly seized by fear."

On the Wednesday, Chamberlain agreed to fly to meet Hitler at the pretty Alpine town of Berchtesgaden the following day. The important point, surely was that – at the age of 69 and never having flown before – Chamberlain was going to Hitler, not the other way round.

On the Thursday, Chamberlain took off from Heston and flew to Munich. He was taken to Berchtesgaden on a special train. When he got there Hitler indulged in an historical harangue which included the words that he was "prepared to risk a world war" rather than let the Sudeten Crisis continue. More pragmatically he said that if the British Government would publicly accept the principle of secession "there would be something to talk about." Chamberlain agreed to put all this to his colleagues and asked Hitler not to do anything drastic until they had had a chance to meet again. Chamberlain flew back to London on the Friday.

Chula writes that "the danger of war was further heightened when it became known that the Prime Minister had found it necessary to fly to Germany in person to have a talk with Herr Hitler. He returned without, at that time, achieving any results. Mrs Seaman was naturally more distressed than ever. From all the accounts given by his friends, Dick himself was deeply worried about the coming war. Erica, owing to her comparative youth and innocence, was oblivious of any danger. Thus in her presence Dick kept his fears to himself."[9]

Seaman telephoned his mother to say that he would be flying to London on the following Monday accompanied by Erica and her father. It would be a chance to discuss the marriage (and in Mrs Seaman's case, discuss why in the present situation there shouldn't be a marriage).

The week-end had to be endured before that. Rumours circulated that Britain and France were asking the Czechs to simply let Hitler have the Sudetenland and that Chamberlain would fly to Germany again – Godesberg, on the Rhine this time – during the coming week.

Over the week-end the *Volkischer Beobachter* newspaper continued its propoganda. *Moscow arming the Czechs (according to secret documents just found) ... the Czech rulers want to destroy all Germans ... Czech hatred of everything German... Pregnant women threatened with rape: eye witness accounts by our special reporters.* The newspaper produced a headline which today seems profoundly absurd but may not have done then.

'PRAGUE THREATENS EUROPE WITH WAR'

Now, in a lock-step, each day deepened the danger while simultaneously bringing the Donington Grand Prix – so eagerly anticipated because it gave a British crowd their only chance to see the mighty German racing cars and drivers – one day nearer. It would be a long journey towards such an occasion of childlike excitements as a motor race; and the race itself played out under international rules which were fair to all and accepted by all. The drivers were sportsmen and regarded themselves as such.

This age of innocence had not many days to run.

Sunday, 18 September

Shirer, still in Prague, wrote that "the Czechs are stiffening as it becomes evident that Chamberlain is ready to support Hitler's demands for taking over Sudetenland and indeed, in effect, Czechoslovakia. Milo Hodza, the Premier, broadcast to the world today and uttered a definite 'no' to the proposition of a plebiscite. 'It is unacceptable. It will solve nothing,' he said. Hodza, unlike most Slovaks, struck me as being very high-strung and nervous when I saw him at Broadcasting House after he finished talking. He showed visibly the strain of the last days. Is he talking strong, but weakening, I wonder. At midnight Murrow phoned from London with the news. The British and French have decided they will not fight for Czechoslovakia and are asking Prague to surrender unconditionally to Hitler."

Chamberlain would fly to Godesberg on Thursday to meet Hitler.

Neubauer was in the fields outside Baden-Baden, a spa town some 60 kilometres from Stuttgart, picking mushrooms.

Monday, 19 September

Shirer, back in Berlin, wrote that "the Nazis, and quite rightly too, are jubliant over what they consider Hitler's greatest triumph to date."

The Auto Union cars left Zwickau in a convoy of lorries, with mechanics Kratel and Tautenhahn on board.

Tuesday, 20 September

Shirer caught the night train for Godesberg, which left Friedrichstrasse station at 10.30.[10] He did a talk to New York from the platform, interviewing various correspondents before they boarded, then "out of the corner of my eye I saw the train moving. My finishing sentence was not smooth but I made the train."

Wednesday, 21 September

The *Volkischer Beobachter* spoke of Czech attacks on the German Reich and the Czech mob's blood lust but even here the juxtaposition lived because the same issue of the newspaper, far from the hysteria and invention of Czechs *attacking* Germany, carried a brief item that Auto Union had named its four drivers for Donington. They were Nuvolari, Hasse, Müller and Kautz.

As a distant echo *The Sporting Life* in Britain wrote that the "latest information regarding the International Donington Grand Prix is that entries have now closed with a total of 21 – nine British, eight German, two French and two Italian. Since the previous list was published, the Ecurie Bleue has nominated two 12-cylinder unsupercharged Delahayes, one of which is the new, and particularly fast, single-seater to be handled by Rene Dreyfus. Alfa-Corse has entered two 16-cylinder Alfa-Romeos, which made a first appearance in the Italian Grand Prix at Monza. They will be driven by Giuseppe Farina and Clemente Biondetti. The other additional entries are Arthur Dobson (ERA) and Robin Hanson (Alta). In view of the carburation troubles which caused the retirement of so many of the German cars in the Italian Grand Prix, where Auto Union scored their first success of the season over Mercedes, the Auto Union organisation has decided to leave nothing to chance. The team in consequence will arrive today and tomorrow, Saturday and Monday being devoted to tuning the carburetters to fit local conditions." The item ended: "The engagement was announced yesterday of Dick Seaman, a member of the Mercedes team, to Fraulein Erica Popp, daughter of the managing director of BMW."

Neubauer spent part of the day boating.

Thursday, 22 September

Chamberlain flew to Cologne and was driven to the Petersberg Hotel, Bad Godesberg, overlooking the Rhine. Ordinarily it would have been a place offering a vista of great settled beauty with, perhaps, the first wisps of autumnal mist hovering insubstantially over the great river and the long, laden barges pushing forward through it low in the water. Instead Chamberlain was fighting his corner. He said that he had agreement from his own government and the governments of France and Czechoslovakia that the Sudeten Germans be allowed the right of self-determination. It was what Hitler had wanted and Chamberlain had now given it to him.

The shape of Europe – and large tracts beyond the Continent – in the latter part of the 20th century and, arguably, beyond the Millennium, were to be decided by Hitler's response.

This wasn't enough any more.

The claims of Poland and Hungary over parts of Czechoslovakia must be dealt with. From where Chamberlain sat, the view over the river meant nothing. Instead he must have seen vultures circling over little Czechoslovakia ready to tear it to pieces.

Sebastian, his brother Wilhelm, Professor Eberan-Eberhorst and Hasse flew from Leipzig to Croydon in a Ju52 "but heavy clouds darkened the political sky. We were worried by the English Prime Minister's journey to Germany and by different radio commentaries. The few Englishmen who were with us looked worried but kept their opinions to themselves. We were in no good mood."[11]

Friday, 23 September

The Auto Union team had reached Donington and all four drivers practised. *The Sporting Life* reported that "at the moment only one car has arrived – the others are due on Monday – so that Nuvolari, Müller, Hasse and Kautz all took turns at the wheel. During the day the quartet put in some 70 laps at high speed, and did not even have to change a tyre. Practice was watched by Herr Eberhorst, the technical director. Rudolf Caracciola, who has been unwell, is expected on Tuesday, but if he is unfit his place will be taken by Baumer, well known for his Continental exploits with Austins." The *Life* added that the five Mercedes-Benz racing cars, including a practice car, were due to arrive at Dover during the evening.

Alfred Neubauer and his chauffeur began the long journey from Stuttgart to London by road. They would go to Kehl, a tiny place on the German side of the Rhine, and cross the broad bridge there to Strasbourg on the French side then continue along the contorting main road through the Vosges mountains and on to Paris, where rooms had been booked for them in the Hotel Tabourin. Hermann Lang and his wife would be making their way along the same route to the same hotel the next day and, Lang would write in his memoirs, that they were looking forward to seeing Neubauer there.[12]

Tomorrow, refreshed, they would drive on to Calais, catch a ferry to Dover and proceed to the Rubens Hotel beside Buckingham Palace, which would serve as accommodation and team headquarters. On the Tuesday they would attend a grand luncheon for Dick Seaman at the RAC Club, Pall Mall – a comfortable stroll from the hotel – in honour of his German Grand Prix victory at the Nürburgring and travel to Donington immediately after the luncheon.

Neubauer and the chauffeur crossed the bridge, passed through Strasbourg without incident and set off into the mountains towards the town of Nancy which was about a third of the way to Paris. After Strasbourg, Neubauer saw "marching soldiers, motorised columns and guns everywhere."[13] Some of the villages were already deserted. They passed through Nancy and on the next 'leg' to the smaller town of Toul, some 20 kilometres further on, the countdown was hardening. Neubauer's chauffeur tried to overtake a heavy French lorry whose driver clearly recognised the German car with its German number plates. If the chauffeur moved to the right the lorry blocked that; if he moved to the left the lorry blocked that, too. This lasted for about 15 kilometres until Neubauer spotted a "gap" and ordered the chauffeur to accelerate hard and get through it. He did – "just" – but, as they were in the act of passing, a woman leant out of the lorry's cabin and "threw a cabbage which bounced off the roof into the ditch."[14]

Along the way Neubauer found somewhere which could – and would – send a telegram. Neubauer dispatched a message to Lang at Stuttgart advising him to change his route and go through Belgium instead but the Langs did not receive it. Neubauer reached the hotel in Paris but, far from welcoming him, found the Swiss manager "anxious to get rid of us."

The manager said: "It looks like war, messieurs. I advise you to move on as soon as you can." Neubauer would depart the following morning for Calais, pausing only to write a note to Lang.

That evening Henderson noted that "the deadlock ... seemed complete. Hitler, having secured one position, was already advancing on the next."[15] Hitler invited Chamberlain to a meeting at 10.30pm but refused to modify his demands. As a 'concession' Hitler shifted his deadline for moving troops into the Sudetenland by a week, from the Monday (26 September) to Saturday, 1 October.

The new date was the day of the Donington Grand Prix.

Saturday, 24 September

In the early hours of the morning, Shirer settled down to make his diary entry: "War seems very near after this strange day." He saw that Hitler had double-crossed Chamberlain. The Prime Minister came to Godesberg ready to "turn over" the Sudetenland under the supervision of a proper international commission but Hitler demanded to swallow the Sudetenland whole. Chamberlain – wearing a funereal pin-striped suit, his narrow, pinched face hollowed into great weariness – undertook to put this to his Cabinet. About the 1 October deadline Hitler would not move.

The lock-step had become a countdown.

Chamberlain prepared to leave for Cologne airport and the flight back to London. The Langs drove to Kehl. They had often crossed there before but now the bridge did not have its familiar feel of peacetime slumber. For years a concrete gun post had stood in the middle of it at the line of the frontier but unmanned and obviously out of use because steel shutters were firmly drawn over the openings. This Saturday the shutters had gone and a gun barrel pointed towards Kehl. However, far from showing any hostility the French customs officers "sat about as usual with cigarettes dangling as I handed in my papers. Customs clearance seemed normal."[16]

Chamberlain's plane took off for London.

The Langs drove into Strasbourg and were stopped at a crossroads by a traffic policeman. They waited and waited because, it appeared, the policeman was giving priority to everyone else and ignoring them.

Eventually they were waved through and Lang could barely believe it when, as he moved past the policeman he heard him say, (presumably in Alsation-German patois which Lang could understand) "good luck for your next race."

They went to Strasbourg's railway station because a nearby bank exchanged money. The whole area "teemed with people. Large numbers of men with suitcases and bundles or boxes streamed towards the entrance, accompanied by women and children." Lang murmured to his wife that this looked like a full-scale mobilisation. He overheard a telephone conversation between a bank employee and (apparently) his wife – in the patois – in which he asked her to bring warm underclothes and socks because he had to report to the railway station within half an hour. "France has mobilised against Germany," the employee added. As Lang returned to his car a "well-dressed, elderly" man brushed against him and asked where he was going. Lang explained: England via Paris. In essence the man said *I wouldn't do that, I'd go straight back to Germany* and melted into the crowd. Lang talked it over with his wife and they decided to continue.[17]

Outside Strasbourg they became "involved in a whole stream of cars and horse-drawn vehicles. All were packed out with bags, cases and bundles, and perambulators, and full up to bursting point with people. Next to the drivers, bedding had been pushed in, so they could hardly move. This exodus looked almost like a panic."

By Sarrbourg, halfway between Strasbourg and Nancy, even Lang's wife – a courageous women, he insisted – was getting nervous and every village from there on "presented the same picture: men hurrying to the station with their cases, women and children running alongside, crying, and other groups standing about arguing and reading the fresh call-up notices on the walls."[18]

The Langs toiled on towards Paris.

Chamberlain would be landing at Heston any moment now.

At Brooklands, the huge saucer of a circuit near London, a race meeting was going on to celebrate the jubilee of the Dunlop tyre. The correspondent for *The Motor* magazine sensed a "most odd and slightly sinister atmosphere." The paddock was its usual bustling, busy place but there was "an undercurrent of uneasiness reminiscent of the meeting in 1914 on the eve of the Great War. Everywhere little knots of people were asking each other the latest news, and many heads were shaken with a grave air." The public address announcements weren't just about racing. A naval officer in the crowd was asked to return to his ship. France had called up another 900,000 men.

After Nancy, the procession of refugees thinned so that the Langs were able to make something like normal progress. Lang fervently hoped Neubauer would be at the hotel because "his wise counsel was invaluable and he knew the answer to all peculiar situations." When they finally arrived the manager handed Lang the note which Neubauer had left for him.

My dear Lang,
Under present circumstances I have left for London. In a telegram to you
at Stuttgart I suggested you should travel via Belgium instead of France.
If it has not reached you, and you have got to the hotel, do what you can
to get to London.[19]

Lang discussed the overall situation with the manager, who he found "pessimistic." The manager insisted that the politicial situation had deteriorated to the "very critical" with Germany threatening to simply swallow the Sudetenland and the Czechs hadn't agreed to anything. Lang expressed his opinion that Chamberlain's visit to Godesberg had "substantially settled matters," but the manager remained insistent: "war is coming." Lang took his car to the garage he habitually used for safekeeping overnight, then he and his wife remained in the hotel throughout the evening. Ordinarily they'd be out taking the air and seeing the sights. The evening of the 24th wasn't for that.[20]

Sunday, 25 September

The Langs rose early to be clear of Paris before the city fully woke and the potential for trouble that that awakening might bring. On the journey up to Calais the road threaded through towns and over railway lines. "When we had to stop at level crossings, crowds gathered and commented in tones which, from their facial expressions, we gathered to be friendly. Whenever the crossing gates went up I put in a racing start."

At Calais, Lang went to the customs shed but the officers there sent him away. He waited a while and returned but realised they still weren't interested. He tried to control himself and repeated, *don't be aggressive.* He and his wife were able to board a ferry by chance: the men loading one assumed he had clearance and waved him on. He found Dover "calm as always," and the customs officers there as courteous as ever, too.[21] He drove to London and the Rubens Hotel where Neubauer greeted him and recounted "a few of the less pleasant incidents" of Neubauer's own journey across France. Neubauer explained that it was these which convinced him not to wait in Paris.

Lang noticed how subdued the Londoners seemed to be. In Hyde Park, around the corner from the hotel, he watched people digging huge anti-aircraft trenches. He saw soldiers manning anti-aircraft gun sites and erecting searchlights and noted "whole columns of lorries" drawing up at "Buckingham Palace to discharge loads of sandbags for the protection of the Royal Palace."[22]

Overall he sensed these Londoners had a very real feeling of imminent war; and that can only have been compounded by events at 10 Downing Street, so near to the Palace and the Rubens Hotel. The British Cabinet decided it could not accept the terms Hitler had offered or urge the terms on the Czechs.

Von Brauchitsch would remember "we were all groping in the dark. Many Englishmen did appreciate their premier's love of peace but they disapproved of his hesitation and retreat which, in their opinion, made Hitler even bolder. In this unpleasant situation the meeting with my old friend Rudi Cent was really helpful to me. He was so reassuring in this hectic atmosphere. He took me by the arm and pulled me into a little adjoining room."

Von Brauchitsch then records this dialogue:

Cent: "Here we can talk undisturbed, and you can be frank without being in danger. At any rate, there is one thing you have to be aware of – if you Germans continue this way then it will be the end of your nice motor racing."

Von Brauchitsch: "Whether you believe it or not, dear Rudi, nobody in Germany can imagine that Hitler will really begin a war."

Cent: "That's precisely it. We abroad see clearly what is going on in Germany and we cannot understand at all why a nation says 'yes' to such terror – and that's what you're all doing together!"

Von Brauchitsch: "It's all very well for you to talk, but the Nazis say, *Who is not with us is against us*. This has been their principle since they took over and so they suppress every criticism. And now the wheels are spinning! I want to drive races and nothing else. Let us wait and see what your government will brew up and negotiate with ours. Maybe we will all go to Nottingham tomorrow despite everything. Maybe I will 'dance' my car round the Donington corners again: you know how much I love this race track. Afterwards we will go to the Oktoberfest in Munich and have beer and 'Brathendl' [chicken]. That will be the beginning of my holidays – with all the pleasures of life."[23]

Donington was six days away.

Monday, 26 September

The feeling of imminence increased. People going to work in London saw sandbags being unloaded outside office buildings and handbills being pasted on walls giving the distribution points for gas masks, while the digging of the trenches in Hyde Park continued. Plans to evacuate London's 600,000 children were being put into operation: parties of invalids and the very young began to arrive at the main railway stations.

The British Government told the French Government it would have full support if France became involved in a war with Germany, although Chamberlain did send Sir Horace Wilson to Berlin with a personal letter to Hitler asking him to negotiate rather than resort to force.

Seaman and Erica flew from Munich to Croydon, where Mrs Seaman met them and must have been disappointed that Erica's father had not taken the flight, depriving her of the opportunity to argue against the marriage with him. Evidently the "political tension"[24] precluded him from making the journey. Erica nursed a heavy cold but came because she was adamant she would not miss a RAC luncheon in Seaman's honour, and, surely, could not bear to be parted from Seaman.

The couple went to stay with Mrs Seaman at her London home, No.3 Ennismore Gardens, Kensington, in a square which remains a stately, dignified and timeless place. Six-storey white stone buildings with porticos overlook the square, their balconies wreathed in wrought-iron railings. Visibly, all of it is, and was, sustained by solid money. The gardens in the middle of the square are surrounded by railings, too, and are forbidden to all but residents. You can picture the 1930s in all this exquisite expression of upper middle class English life, humble maids flitting behind deep velvet curtains serving afternoon tea from china which chimed in the stillness.

Erica remembered[25] that Fleet Street, inevitably excited by such a story at such a time, sent photographers to capture "the famous English racing driver and his German bride-to-be." One picture was of them arm-in-arm in what could well have been the gardens. Erica would confess many years later that "Mrs Seaman was *not* pleased and spent a long time trying to persuade Dick to break off our engagement. He refused."

Far from discussing this problem with his mother, Charlie Martin remembers that "Dick was pretty quiet about that sort of thing. Perhaps it was a sign of the times in that people weren't so outgoing then, it was more stiff upper lip. I met his mother briefly, for tea or something like that. She was a Victorian kind of woman, straight down the line, stiff, everything done according to the rules: an imposing woman, if I can put it that way. Her voice was hard." (Martin estimated the house in Ennismore Gardens would have been worth "a fortune. I'm pretty sure I can remember a butler there.")

Mrs Seaman succeeded in convincing her son that in the present political situation the best place for Erica was at home with her parents. Seaman decided to fly back with her to Munich after next day's RAC luncheon and then return to England, not necessarily for the race at Donington but to be called up for military service. When Erica heard of the plan she refused absolutely and said she would not be parted from Seaman "under any circumstances."

While the couple settled uneasily into the austere atmosphere at No.3 Ennismore Gardens, the Auto Union drivers did four hours of practice at Donington, contenting themselves with familiarisation although all but Nuvolari had been at the circuit before. No significant lap times were attempted.

News came through that Caracciola, as anticipated, would be a non-starter. "My foot and my leg hurt so much that I didn't want to participate in the race at Donington. Besides, it seemed unlikely that the German teams would be welcome there."[26]

At 5 o'clock that afternoon Wilson, accompanied by Ambassador Henderson, met Hitler in the Chancellory, a meeting which Henderson described as "stormy and unsatisfactory." Hitler could only be persuaded "with difficulty" to listen to Chamberlain's letter being read out, shouted that it was no use talking any more and at one point moved towards the door as if to leave. He returned and said that if the Czechs had not agreed to the Godesberg Memorandum by 2pm on Wednesday he would mobilise.

That evening Hitler spoke at Berlin's Sportspalast. Shirer wrote: "Shouting and shrieking in the worst state of excitement I've ever seen him in, he stated he would have his Sudetenland by October 1. I broadcast the scene from a seat in the balcony just above Hitler. He's still got that nervous tic. All during his speech he kept cocking his shoulder, and the opposite leg from the knee down would bounce up."

Hitler said (the reactions in italics are those reported by the *Volkischer Beobachter*): "I am now going in front of my people as its first soldier. And behind me – the whole world may know this – marches one people, a people that is different from 1918. We have no interest in oppressing other peoples. We want to find our own salvation. The others are to do it their own way! We do not want war with France. We do not want anything from France. Nothing at all! The Sudetenland is the last territorial claim I have to make in Europe, but it is a claim that I will not give up. So help me God I will fulfil it."

Breathlessly the listeners have followed the Fuehrer's words, now enthusiasm breaks out like a storm tide.

"In 1918 Central Europe was torn up and newly shaped by some mad so-called statesmen. Central Europe was smashed to pieces and so-called new states were formed."

Boos pierce the air for several minutes.

"It is this process that Czecho-Slovakia owes its existence to."

With renewed and tumultuous shouting, the anger of the thousands breaks out again.

"This Czech state began with one big lie. The father of this lie was called Benes." *Several minutes of boos again.*

October 1 was now five days away.

Tuesday, 27 September

At 1 o'clock in the morning Sebastian was called to the telephone. "Dr Feuereissen ordered me to pack up all the material and return home immediately. The things which happened in the next five hours border on a minor miracle."[1] Within that comparatively short space of time, it would seem, the Auto Union mechanics went to Donington and had loaded everything ready to go.

Berliners woke to a scream of a headline in The Germania newspaper: THE FUEHRER'S ULTIMATE WARNING TO PRAGUE.

The helpless and inevitable juxtaposition between this and what the British motoring press were carrying is one more chasm in this month of chasms. Racing enthusiasts among early London commuters who bought the new issue of *The Motor* from bookstalls heard a much more muted scream, ALL EYES ON DONINGTON. Basic information was set out below this headline:

Admission To the park: 5s. Cars (which can be parked alongside the circuit at almost any point) 2s 6d. Paddock admission: 5s Grandstand (overlooking the start): reserved seats only. Details from Mr. F. Craner, Coppice House, Donington Park, near Derby. Central block £1, side blocks 15s (both inclusive of admission charges). Buses from Derby to the course.

By Train from London An excursion ticket at 13s return is available on the 8.25 LMS express from St Pancras to Derby, where buses will be waiting (1s 6d return). The train leaves Derby at 7.44pm and reaches London again at 10.7pm.

Describing the nature of the circuit, *The Motor* said: "The immense advantage of Donington from the spectators' point of view is that one can either stay overlooking the start for the whole race, keeping a lap score and watching the pit work (always dramatic when the Continentals do it) or one can wander about from place to place perfectly freely and never more than a few yards from the road.

"The stand at the Hairpin is a favourite spot overlooking the spectacular dive down the twisting hill to the corner and the exit from the bend uphill under the stone arch. The stand at the Paddock on Starkey Straight gives a magnificent view of the cars flat out, doing somewhere about 160 mph. Melbourne Corner is another fine view-point for braking, cornering and acceleration, and Holly Wood, with its fast curve through the trees, is probably the most shattering sight on the course. All these points can be visited by a few minutes' walking, and then never out of sight of the race."

At 5 o'clock that morning, while the first of the Berlin workers were buying *Germania* and the first of the London commuters were buying *The Motor*, Fred Craner was woken by the sound of mechanics working feverishly. Craner had temporary accommodation in Coppice Farm, which was separated from its barns by the circuit – the circuit sliced between them. In winter these barns were full of hay and straw for cattle but, cleared in the summer for racing cars, they became temporary garages. From his window Craner could see both Auto Union and Mercedes mechanics packing their equipment and preparing to load their cars on to their lorries. Clearly they were leaving.

After Hitler's speech at the Sportspalast, "urgent telegrams" had been sent to Donington Hall, where the mechanics of both teams were staying.[2] The source of these telegrams is unrecorded. Perhaps the German Foreign Ministry in Berlin, properly fearful for its nationals who could be trapped in the enemy's lair, sent them. Who in Germany could be sure how Britain and the British would react to Hitler's speech? Clearly someone decided the teams and cars should leave Donington as quickly as was practical, travel to

Harwich – where they could catch a boat for the Hook of Holland, thus avoiding France – and drive back to the safety of Germany. Hence at 5am the feverish activity which woke Fred Craner.

By 7.30am Mercedes were ready, a prodigious feat in only an hour and a half because it involved 27 personnel carefully loading the five racing cars and tons of spares on to ten vehicles. The lorries, which bore the legend *Mercedes-Benz Racing Troopers* on their flanks, were described by *Motor Sport* as "magnificently appointed, have wonderful exhaust notes and are truly quick." They set off from the circuit in convoy along the tight, dipping A453 towards the A6, a national North-South artery, and turned on to it at Sawley Crossroads. The convoy headed south.

As Mercedes were leaving, Donington's officials called a hasty meeting at breakfast time and reached a firm decision that, despite the departure of the Germans, "all the arrangements for the race were to be carried out."

The A6, fringed by trees whose leaves were poised to turn, undulated into the heartland of England. The convoy would pass through two solid stone villages, Kegworth – with its church of St Andrew on the hill, its houses dating from 1698[3] – and Hathern towards Loughborough, then Leicester, then Market Harborough where it could begin to work its way cross-country to Harwich.

Auto Union set off from the circuit in convoy some hours later, no doubt because, using rail to transport the racing cars, they had to take them to Castle Donington station and load them first but there are suggestions that the team took one of the cars with the road convoy. Their lorries bore the legend *Auto Union Racing Service* and were evidently as impressive as those of Mercedes. This second and much smaller convoy passed along the A453 to Sawley Crossroads and headed south, too.

Sebastian recounts that "the majority of our team went on the Midland express train to London. The others went with the lorries to the coast."

In round figures, Harwich lay some 150 miles from Donington and a land convoy moved in precisely the same way as a naval convoy, at the speed of the slowest. Assuming the convoys averaged 20 mph on the single-lane main roads (and 20 mph may be an ambitious estimate) the journey would take almost eight hours. When stops for food and fuel were added, Mercedes wouldn't reach Harwich until early evening and Auto Union those few hours later.

From the meagre evidence which survives the team members did not believe they were in danger, although we may surmise that the Mercedes people were apprehensive as their convoy crawled into Loughborough. If trouble was coming it was more likely to come in the towns than the villages. Nothing happened. The convoy crawled through Loughborough and on towards Leicester eleven miles away. The convoy reached Leicester at about 11am, the A6 taking it into the city centre because, like virtually every other town in Britain, Leicester had no by-pass.

The countdown tightened.

The Motor reported that "as soon as the teams were on their way, the team chiefs telephoned to their respective headquarters at Stuttgart and Zwickau for instructions. Both these concerns telephoned Major Huhnlein, Korpsführer of motor sport, in Berlin. He replied that the cars were to stay and race. Dr Feuereissen, of the Auto Union team, and Neubauer, of the Mercedes team, then got in touch with the police, who stopped both convoys on the road near Leicester and gave them orders to return [to Donington]."

The statement that, *as soon as both teams were on their way, the team chiefs telephoned for instructions* is very strange, particularly in context. Without making a caricature of a whole nation, you can venture that a German characteristic is, before acting, to await instructions and when they arrive follow them pedantically. That must have been accentuated at that time.

We know Hitler took a keen interest in what the teams achieved, with all the weight that that had to bring. We know that the race victories were a matter of profound national prestige to a regime already profoundly obsessed with national prestige. We know that, of all places on Earth for two German teams to have found themselves, England was among the most sensitive.

Why, then, did the teams not telephone for instructions *before* they were on their way? As the extent of Hitler's "shouting and shrieking" at the Sportspalast echoed into Britain, did a sense of alarm mount among the small German community camped so deep in the enemy's lair? Did the community panic and decide to make a run for it at first light? More probably, the Wednesday night telegrams were a precautionary measure by the Foreign Ministry in Berlin or the Embassy in London, and *further* instructions were sought as the morning unfolded.

Every person caught up in the situation knew that they risked Hitler's wrath if they made any wrong move amidst such sensitivity. The real nature of Hitlerism would not be laid bare for a further seven years – when a monstrously savage war had been fought and lost – but already no German, including those in the convoy now entering Leicester and those in the convoy a long way back up the A6, could mistake its essential hardness. This is why the final instruction – to return to Donington – was a political one taken by Huhnlein, no doubt cleared at the highest level and perhaps with Hitler himself.

Some reports suggest that the London offices of Mercedes and Auto Union were pivotal contacts between Berlin and the teams; others suggest Feuereissen and Neubauer were pivotal. What true part Neubauer played remains problematical because he had not yet been to Donington: he was still in London with the Mercedes drivers preparing to attend the luncheon at the RAC Club. Perhaps Neubauer had made his way from the Rubens Hotel to the Mercedes head office in Grosvenor Road to co-ordinate from there before going on to the RAC. We simply do not know.

The method of stopping the convoys – telephoning the Leicester police and RAC calls boxes along the A6 – was simple and effective. Because, as we have seen, the A6 went directly though Leicester the police there could hardly miss a convoy of ten German vehicles. All the police needed to do was flag it down. And there were RAC call boxes dotted along all main roads. They had telephones inside them which members could use in emergencies – a key came with membership – but which could also be rung. RAC patrolmen habitually stayed near them.

It explains how the police halted the Mercedes convoy in Leicester but it does not explain how the Auto Union convoy which set off later was not halted until Market Harborough, 14 miles further on.

This seemingly trivial matter does have an importance because it illustrates the difficulty of re-construction, of making the silences speak. In his autobiography, for example, Neubauer makes no mention at all of the convoys leaving and returning this Tuesday. In direct contrast, *The Leicester Mercury* newspaper carried a report which is worth reproducing in full, not least because it gives the sort of human details so absent elsewhere.

"A party of Germans – members of the Mercedes Benz motor racing squad – was stopped by the police in Leicester this morning as they were hurrying to get back to Germany. The Auto Union team, with their mechanics and equipment, were similarly stopped at Market Harborough. Now, with reassurances from Herr Huhnlein, the leader of the German motor sport, following phone calls to Germany, the teams have returned to Donington Park, where they will compete in the Donington Grand Prix on Saturday – the day of the expiration of Hitler's ultimatum to Czechoslovakia.

The Mercedes company consists of about ten lorries, with five racing cars and thousands of pounds worth of equipment, and 27 mechanics, in the charge of Herr Arnold Wychodil, a slight, fair-haired, bespectacled Sudeten German. Following Hitler's speech last night, urgent telegrams were sent to the two German teams who were staying at Donington Hall, and this morning everything was ready for a dash to London and so across the Continent to their headquarters in Germany.

The two firms concerned, however, made a quick change of decision, and all police stations on the route from Donington to London were asked to detain the teams.

Thus it came about that the Mercedes convoy was drawn up at the roadside in Colton-street and Church-street adjoining the Leicester police headquarters from 11 o'clock until just after 12.30. The Auto Union men, stopped at Market Harboro', sought assurance from the firm's London office, and were soon Donington-bound once again.

The Mercedes decision was delayed until the result of 'phone calls to Germany became known. The tone of conversations were optimistic, and Herr Wychodil told a reporter: 'Herr Huhnlein, the Korps Fuehrer, a personal friend of Herr Hitler, has decided, and it is his wish, that we go back to Donington to race on Saturday.'

Herr Wychodil left Czechoslovakia three years ago because, he said, he could make no headway there on account of his German blood. He was the only member of the party who could speak English, although several of the hundreds of people who watched the party tried unsuccessfully to converse with the Germans. The crowd who watched the proceedings interestedly seemed in a very friendly mood, and several women were laughingly collecting autographs of members of the party.

Herr Wychodil remarked on this to a *Leicester Mercury* reporter, and said that in France there had been demonstrations against them, but in England, 'No, no; there is none of that; the people are so friendly and good.'

The men in the party – which does not include the actual drivers, who are in London – were very confident that England would not be involved in a war, although all of them very stoutly supported Hitler's policy against the Czechs.

One of them voiced the feelings of the group, and said, 'England will declare war only if France is attacked and France will not be attacked. Hitler's only objective is the liberation of the Germans in Czechoslovakia.'

None of the party had any thought of their being interned in England, but they were apprehensive of what might happen to them when they passed through France or Belgium on the return journey.

Eight Auto Union mechanics had one racing car in their charge when stopped at Harborough.

I saw them later having lunch at a Harborough hotel (telephones a *Leicester Mercury* reporter).

Only one of them could speak English and he, like his companions, seemed a little bewildered by the rapid change of events. He would not hear of war.

'We don't want to fight,' he said. 'We want to race. We came over from Germany on Friday, and we were returning there when our chief sent a message telling us to go back to Donington. That makes me think there will be a race and no war."

Market Harborough is grouped round The Square, "a most pleasing triangular piece of townscape with the steeple of the fine church forming the focal point."[4] The surrounding buildings are clean, sandy-coloured stone giving the town a mellow, almost autumnal, feel. The A6 narrowed as it reached The Square and somewhere around there a police sergeant flagged the convoy down, explained to the one who spoke English that their manager [Feuereissen] was instructing them to go back to Donington. The team-members went to the Peacock Hotel, which gazed towards The Square from a side street. It had been a coaching inn and, behind its bay windows, was staid and solid, all beams and narrow corridors. They would telephone London to confirm the new instructions and then they'd have lunch.

Simultaneously at Leicester the Mercedes team milled around outside the police station while one of them telephoned inside. The convoy had been neatly drawn up at the kerbside nose-to-tail and now four of the team, including Wychodil, posed for a photograph: a man with a moustache and a cheese-cutter cap wore an overcoat; next to him a man – also in an overcoat – sported a light-coloured homburg hat and smoked a cigarette; then a heavy man in what might have been a white mackintosh, open at the front, his hands dug into the pockets of a waistcoat, thumbs splayed; then Wychodil, bespectacled, wearing a jacket and pullover. All four had collars and ties and, by appearance, might have been plump and rather successful businessmen. Three smiled for the camera. Only Wychodil looked preoccupied.

At 12.15 – while the friendly English crowd were thronging Colton Street and Church Street trying to engage in banter with their friendly German guests – in Berlin Sir Horace Wilson, who had spent the night at the British Embassy and received a further message from Chamberlain for Hitler, was driven down Wilhelmstrasse to the Chancellory. The new message guaranteed that, if Germany refrained from using force, the Czech undertakings would be carried out.

Wilson asked if, "in the light of the Prime Minister's statement, he could take any message back to London." Hitler replied that the Czech Government must either accept or reject the German memorandum. Twice, three times Hitler shouted *"Ich werde die Tschechen zerschlagen,"* which Schmidt, his interpreter, accurately translated as "I will smash-sh-sh the Czechs."[5] Hitler said that if France and England were to strike at Germany "let them do so. It is a matter of complete indifference to me."

Tom Wheatcroft rode to Donington on his motorbike. "In 1935 a new police station had been built in Leicester – a big, wide building – with a new road. An archway led to the station yard and the convoy had been taken under the arch. We tried to get in to see them but you weren't allowed – from where we were we could see the lorries and vans, but from a distance. I remember everybody saying *'oooh, they're going to go back to Donington'.*" Wheatcroft also heard somebody say Auto Union were at Market Harborough and he set off for there.

At 12.30, the new instructions confirmed, the Mercedes convoy crawled back out of Leicester on the A6, headed north for Donington again.

The eight Auto Union mechanics in the Peacock Hotel prepared to eat the lunch they had ordered. They would head north to Donington again when they'd finished it. There was no hurry now, and single-lane roads defeated haste, anyway. Wheatcroft came up on his motorbike and thought "how marvellous to be able to actually see the convoy. As far as I know, there were five vehicles and somebody on guard at the gateway [beside the hotel]. Over the years since, I've often been there for a meal and I've thought *ah, they used to be just here …*"

The Auto Union team members arrived in London on the express train but "having arrived we were surprised to hear that everything would be in order again and we could go back to Derby."[6]

The first of the 90 guests began to arrive at the RAC Club in Pall Mall for what, inevitably, would be a strange and strained occasion full of undercurrents. The RAC was terribly English in precisely the way London gentlemen's clubs were, stately, becalmed, measured, held by tradition and full of its own certainties. Lang would confess that "the nervous tension could be felt."[7] He, Neubauer, von Brauchitsch, Baumer and Uhlenhaut were, as guests of honour, given a genuine welcome. The reporter for *The Light Car* wrote that "a pretty bad dose of war fever had gripped the country on that morning yet there, in our very midst, were Germans who, through several years of association, had become firm friends." Caracciola, of course, couldn't attend because he wasn't in the country.

In *The Motor* 'Grande Vitesse' conceded that the atmosphere was a bit difficult but "this was a unique occasion, when you come to think of it. Here we all were, everybody who is anybody in motorsport (and myself) chatting away with funereal faces about gas masks and ARP [Air Raid Precautions] and such-like nonsense, all more or less calmly regarding the prospect of having a first class war with Germany – and in walk the German team.

"I am bound to admit that the feeling was certainly not one of concealed hostility, which would have been supremely ridiculous, but I fancy most people felt here we were on the verge of war with Germany and here we had a bunch of as decent a lot of chaps as one could wish to meet. The embarrassment was ours, I think. Anyway, the tension eased off, the Germans taking things with an air of complete calm and good humour, and were met with a really warm and sincere welcome which found its voice in plenty of applause at the appropriate moments.

"We assembled with the rather sombre news that the Auto Union team (who were unable to be at the lunch) and the Mercedes mechanics, with all the cars, were making good speed back towards home from Donington under urgent orders. We were met with the slightly more reassuring news that just after they had lit out for home telegrams came ordering them to remain and the teams were stopped near Leicester and had returned to get on with the practising. At the same time I gathered that a definite announcement about the race would be made later in the week, depending on the course of events. Anyway, the Germans were very cheerful and when asked what they were going to do said 'why, we're going up to Donington, of course.'

"The luncheon itself was a great success, with Lt-Colonel J. Sealy-Clarke (Chairman of the RAC) presiding with his usual urbane gentility and putting everybody at his ease. There were about 90 guests to do honour to Seaman's victory."

The spacious dining room was arranged in the traditional way for accommodating a lot of people. Three long tables stretched along the room with a top table butted on to them across it. The seating arrangement at this top table seems significant, with Sealy-Clarke having Mrs Seaman on his left, Dick Seaman on his right and Erica next to Dick – placing her well clear of Mrs Seaman.

"Colonel Sealy-Clarke said just the right things about the guests, Dick Seaman and his very charming fiancée, Fraulein Erica Popp, who was there, looking very happy," 'Grande Vitesse' continued. "Dick replied in just the right strain (which was not easy, politics being what they were). Fraulein Popp and Seaman came in for unlimited hand-shakings and congratulations."[8]

Lang would remember Seaman explaining that "quite a few" of the guests couldn't attend because they had been called up the previous day. "If *it* starts and you're still here," Seaman reassured, "you won't have such a bad time. We are sportsmen."

At 1pm, as the guests sat down to eat the countdown kept quickening. Hitler issued a "most secret" directive ordering seven divisions to move forward to their jumping-off points on the Czech frontier shortly after Wilson left the Chancellery.[9]

The Light Car reflected how, at least within the RAC Club, the tension eased. "Seaman and his charming fiancée, Miss Erica Popp, regarded the scene tranquilly, and the Germans had a ready smile and a warm handshake for everybody. Walter Baumer carried on an animated conversation with Earl Howe, von Brauchitsch with Sir 'Algy' Guinness, and Herr Neubauer was engaged in earnest discussion with Bira, sudden arm actions indicating that they were probably comparing cornering tactics. I met Dick's fiancée, Miss Erica. Although obviously aware of the cloud that hung over the gathering, she was determined not to spoil the enjoyment of the moment, and she looked radiantly happy."

Sealy-Clarke rose and said "I wish to emphasise the fact that our German friends are with us. We welcome them and we wish them to come as often as possible." He proposed Seaman's health and reminded the audience that he was the second British winner of a major grand prix, following the late Sir Henry Segrave in the French race of 1923.

Seaman rose to reply. He wore a dark suit, white collar and tie, looked rather suave and didn't appear nervous. He began by expressing his deep honour at having such an occasion in his honour here and explained that nothing in his career had brought "greater joy" than the Nürburgring victory, although he added the caveat that it had been "at the expense of my friend" Manfred von Brauchitsch.

He broadened into a theme. "At the end of 1936, when I joined the Mercedes team, I thought I knew all there was to know about motor racing, but I soon found out that I did not. I am often asked what it is like to drive a Mercedes. Well, you have to be very careful with the accelerator and think about the corners much farther away than in the case of cars with lesser power. Again I have been asked why I drive a German car. I love motor racing, and when after my successful season in 1936 I was invited to join the Mercedes team I naturally accepted. If there had been a British Grand Prix team it would have been different. There is no such team now."[10] Seaman deplored this, then ventured a joke. "Handling a Mercedes has provided me with great enjoyment *and* great soreness, the latter being noticeable when you're flung out..."

When Seaman said that there was a common international bond between enthusiasts in grand prix racing he was given a great cheer. He sat down and Sealy-Clarke rose to read out a letter from Caracciola's wife, Alice, apologising for their absence and explaining it was because of her husband's burnt foot. Sealy-Clarke then presented Seaman with a pair of cuff links as a memento of the lunch.

The Autocar, taking an overview, felt "it was, of course, most unfortunate that a function which could have done so much to promote international friendliness should have been overshadowed by the political situation. It is some evidence of the essential sanity still remaining to humanity that expression of friendliness on both sides were made by English and German drivers.'

As the guests left the RAC building most of them must have bought newspapers and found the news much worse."

Later editions of the *Evening Standard* carried a brief account of the lunch lost under other headlines: HITLER SUPPRESSES THE PEACE OFFER and RECKLESS, FANATICAL MOOD.

Neubauer felt it was time for a "heart-to-heart" talk with Feuereissen. "What do we do? Go back home or stay?"

"I spoke to the Embassy on the telephone this morning," Feuereissen said. "They seem to think it will all die down. They suggest we go through with our programme."

"That's all very well, but if anything does happen we'll be cut off up there in Nottingham" – where the Mercedes team hotel was.

Feuereissen pondered that. "I tell you what. I'll stay here in London and keep in touch with the Embassy. You go on to Nottingham and, if the situation should get worse, I'll telephone you."

"All right. And I'll keep an eye on your boys as well as my own."[11]

That afternoon, while a steady stream of German nationals, mostly women, went to the German Embassy in London for advice, Sir Horace Wilson flew back from Berlin.

Neubauer, Uhlenhaut and the Mercedes drivers – Seaman took Erica – went from the RAC Club to a reception at the German Embassy and then caught the train to Nottingham, where they were to stay at the Black Boy in the city centre.

At 5.10pm the London office of Mercedes wired Untertürkheim asking them to book calls to Naumann, who was a conduit for information between the team and headquarters, at the Black Boy – with its Bavarian balcony[12] – at 7 o'clock the next day and on Thursday so that he could report the day's events.

Von Brauchitsch would remember "everybody was talking about war. On my arrival in the hotel I could already sense the dangerous tension. The hotel staff were courteous but, equally, reserved and cold. Every single bellboy seemed to be eager to demonstrate to us his antipathy to Hitler. English papers were crammed with the news. *Hitler threatens Prague! Hitler gives a short ultimatum!*"[13]

Erica found the mood at the Black Boy "so depressing. Dick and I were not depressed, of course – we were about to get married – but the others on the team who were also anti-Nazi knew what was coming and they were very, very sad characters. They all advised me to stay in England with Dick, but we had already made that decision. War or no war, Dick wasn't going to let me out of his sight!"[14]

Lang says "we did not feel quite right, although the staff and the other hotel inhabitants were most pleasant."

Meanwhile Ludwig Sebastian recounts that "that very evening, dinner united us" – the Auto Union team – "in Derby." Sebastian noted, however, that the political tension was rising again.[15]

Craner confirmed to the Press and the BBC that Mercedes and Auto Union would be taking part in the Grand Prix and that preparations were under way for the practice session on the morrow, but the Donington offices were being "bombarded" by telephone calls and telegram asking what was happening. Emergency staff had to be summoned to handle the bombardment.

The convoys reached Donington and were laboriously unloaded again. Craner told newspaper enquiries that the teams and drivers had been officially ordered to stay and compete, and the teams "were now at the circuit again."

The countdown quickened. In Berlin in late afternoon Henderson watched as "a mechanised division rumbled through the streets and up the Wilhelmstrasse past the Chancellor's window and those of the Embassy. For three hours Hitler stood at his window and watched it pass. The Germans love military display, but not a single individual in the streets applauded its passage. The picture which it represented was almost that of a hostile army passing through a conquered city."[16]

Shirer also observed this. "I went out to the corner of the Linden where the column was turning down Wilhelmstrasse, expecting to see a tremendous demonstration… The hour was undoubtedly chosen today to catch the hundreds of thousands of Berliners pouring out of their offices at the end of the day's work. But they ducked into the subways, refused to look on, and the handful that did stood at the kerb in utter silence unable to find a word of cheer for the flower of their youth going away to the glorious war… A policeman came up the Wilhelmstrasse from the direction of the Chancellery and shouted to the few of us standing at the kerb that the *Führer* was on his balcony reviewing the troops. Few moved. I went down to have a look. Hitler stood there, and there weren't two hundred people in the street or the great square of the Wilhelmplatz. Hitler looked grim, then angry, and soon went inside, leaving his troops to parade by unreviewed."[17]

In London, many Germans found their way to Liverpool Street station to catch the 8.15 or 8.50pm trains for Harwich and the overnight boat to the Hook. A station official said that a lot of the passengers were women and they looked worried.

A German Embassy official, however, insisted that "in the absence of official instructions from Berlin we are unable to do very much. Nobody has been advised to leave London. We are calm at the Embassy, feeling that there is no need for the alarm that exists in some quarters."

At 8pm, as the worried Germans milled on the platform waiting to board the Harwich train, the British fleet was mobilised.

At 10pm Admiral Raeder, who almost certainly knew of the mobilisation, met Hitler and appealed for him not to go to war. Hitler had to balance "at this moment" a shifting current of factors: "Prague was defiant, Paris rapidly mobilising, London stiffening, his own people apathetic, his leading generals dead against him and that his ultimatum on the Godesberg proposals expired at 2pm the next day."[18]

At 10.30 Hitler telegraphed to Chamberlain and, without modifying his demands, hinted that the Prime Minister might try "one final effort" to make the Czechs see reason.[19]

Henderson had been told by phone from the Foreign Office in London that "yet another communication" was coming to Hitler and made arrangements to go to the Ministry of Foreign Affairs next to the Chancellory at 11pm. Henderson handed over the communication – which had been agreed with the French and pressed the Czechs to accept the "immediate transfer" of the Sudeten territories starting on 1 October – for immediate translation so it could be submitted to Hitler. Henderson went to bed knowing that "if nothing new intervened" Germany would be mobilised the next day.[20]

Wednesday, 28 September

Henderson was woken at 7am by a telephone call from Francois-Poncet, who said that at 4am he had received instructions from Paris to "make a similar communication" to the one Henderson had delivered the night before and that in some respects the French went even further than the British. Francois-Poncet had been asked to see Hitler in person and had "already asked for an audience."[1] The countdown had tightened. When Henderson replaced the receiver after talking to Francois-Poncet, seven hours remained.

It would become known as Black Wednesday.

The *Volkischer Beobachter* set the tone and tempo. THIS IS HOW BENES IS INSULTING THE ENGLISH PEOPLE. A BIASED RADIO SPEECH BY CHAMBERLAIN. PLUNDERING OF SUDETENLAND CONTINUES. 20 YEARS OF CZECH TERROR

A "sense of gloom hung over Berlin" as it did over Prague, Paris and London.[2] Berlin's four million inhabitants were rising and beginning to go about their business, the underground stations already busy, nervous eyes scanning the newspaper headlines. Behind the austere stone facade of this Prussian city with its boulevards, its mighty monuments, its cathedrals and royal palace; behind the leafy suburban villas of the south and the communist tenament districts of the north with their cramped courtyards there lay this dawn something more than gloom. Nowhere was the sense of tension greater than at the Reich Chancellery, where in the course of the next hour or two Hitler had to decide on peace or war.[3]

Heavy rain shrouded Nottingham, the temperature was falling sharply and Neubauer – who had not yet left the Black Boy for Donington – concluded that practice would be "out of the question." He observed the two "love birds," Seaman and Erica, sitting "in a corner of the hotel lounge holding hands and looking far from happy. I was feeling anything but cheerful and when Hermann Lang came in to say there was nothing but military-march music to be heard on the German radio, I realised the situation was not improving."[4]

Von Brauchitsch would write: "I can still remember very well this Wednesday, 23 September [it must have been this 28th]. With the rain pouring outside, we were sitting next to each other around a table in the hotel lobby like hens on a perch – not knowing whether the race would go ahead or not – and hanging our heads. Dr Feuereissen stayed in London acting as an intermediary at the German Embassy. 'At the front', Neubauer had taken command of both racing teams."[5]

At 10am Francois-Poncet rang Henderson again and said he "feared the worst" because his request to see Hitler had been unanswered. Henderson said he'd come over in half an hour: the French Embassy was a two or three minute walk from the British Embassy. Then Henderson rang Goering and explained that Francois-Poncet didn't want just another meeting but bore "fresh proposals" upon which peace or war depended.

Henderson started to explain the proposals but Goering interrupted: "You need not say a word more. I am going immediately to see the *Führer*."

Henderson went over to the French Embassy, and, while he and Francois-Poncet discussed the situation, word came that Hitler would see Francois-Poncet in the Chancellery at 11.15.[6]

At Donington rumours that Germany was preparing to mobilise gathered strength.

Hitler was known for his fingerspitzengefuhl, instinctive feel. Whatever else this man was or was not, he was a consummate politician with an intuitive grasp of men and moments. Some historians suggest that the complete absence of public enthusiasm for the mechanised convoy passing down Wilhelmstrasse the day before made a profound impression on Hitler. The German people were not ready for war. Beyond that, all is conjecture – and conjecture with a man like Hitler is very, very dangerous. There is, however, no conjecture about Mussolini and his motives. Italy was completely unprepared.

In this day of move and counter-move, with each minute a minute nearer the abyss of 2 o'clock, the British Ambassador to Rome, Lord Perth, asked Mussolini if he would not consider mediating. Instantly Mussolini saw this escape route and, at 11am, rang his ambassador in Berlin, Bernardo Attolico, telling him to tell Hitler that he, Mussolini, was prepared to mediate. Mussolini's final word, before he hung up, was *hurry*.

Francois-Poncet met Hitler at 11.40am but in the middle of this meeting was informed that Attolico had arrived. Attolico was breathless and hatless, "his face flushed with excitement."[7] Hitler left the room to speak to him.

"I have an urgent message for you from the Duce!" Attolico, who had a naturally hoarse voice, shouted from some distance off and said Mussolini begged Hitler not to mobilise.[8] Instantly, Hitler saw *this* escape route and said: "Tell the Duce that I accept his proposal." Hitler returned to the meeting with Francois-Poncet and said he would reply to the French proposals during the afternoon.

The Motor speculated that "Herr Neubauer and Dr Feuereissen had no doubt had a long and anxious conference and in the absence of any instructions, and with the menacing tone of the morning papers, had decided that they should be ready for as rapid a retreat as possible. Both teams ... tried to get in touch with Germany by radio, telegram and telephone, but Germany was silent and no communication could be made." Germany was not silent in the strict sense: with a limited number of telephone lines between the two countries bearing the full traffic of an international crisis the teams might have had to wait days for a connection.

Throughout Britain at 12 noon, perhaps fuelled by radio news bulletins, the rumours that Germany was mobilising grew stronger still, and nobody – including the two motor racing teams – knew Hitler had accepted Mussolini's offer of mediation but everyone knew the 2pm deadline was just under two hours away.

Feureissen rang Neubauer at the Black Boy and said: "We have been instructed to leave at once."[9] This pitched Neubauer into what he would describe as a "chaotic" hour of activity. He made enquiries about sailings from Harwich to either the Hook of Holland or the more southern port of Bergen op Zoom. Any attempt to return to Germany via France was completely out of the question now. He made reservations on one of the boats – probably the 9pm for Bergen – after no doubt poring over road maps to calculate the best route to Harwich for the convoy and how long it would take.

At 12.15pm Hitler met Henderson and said "at the request of my great friend and ally, Signor Mussolini, I have postponed mobilising my troops for twenty-four hours."[10]

The countdown slowed, but not much.

Neubauer wanted "all the drivers to be ready to move off at short notice." He contacted the mechanics at Donington.

At Donington the Mercedes racing cars were pushed by mechanics from the low 'garages' – the rudimentary feel of these garages is captured by photographs: a long, gently-sloping tiled roof with little windows set into it at regular intervals, and whitewashed brickwork. The cars were pushed through a low gate to the lorries and loaded. Neubauer had a "brief talk" with the chief Mercedes mechanic – presumably by telephone – and "warned him that if any attempt was made on the way to stop the column and confiscate the cars he was to set them on fire."[11] The seven lorries – large, pug-nosed and strong – had *Mercedes-Benz* written in white along their flanks. They lumbered from the garages on to the track heading for the exit, the A453 and Sawley Crossroads again.

The Auto Union team argued amongst themselves about what to do until 12.30pm although Sebastian says "Dr Feuereissen ordered us to go home once and for all." Then the mechanics emptied the fuel out of the racing cars, pumping it from the tanks along a length of piping and simply letting it pour onto the ground while a knot of curious bystanders watched. The cars were pushed by four mechanics up metal ramps into trucks which drove to the nearby Castle Donington station and loaded the cars onto wagons. The cars would be taken to Harwich by rail. Everything else Auto Union had brought went into two lorries which would form their convoy. Sebastian says "hastily we loaded the lorries and took them to the station. Every single man worked feverishly, inspired by the single thought of bringing home the precious material and cars in time."

The Motor continued to speculate. "The two commanders [Neubauer and Feuereissen] reluctantly gave orders to march and the cavalcade set out for Harwich, first with the idea of crossing that night, and later with the idea of hanging on overnight to await any development."

Craner, unready to surrender the race, announced that a decision would be made at noon the following day.

At the Black Boy, Neubauer faced "the most difficult moment of all. I was very near to tears as I said goodbye to Dick Seaman, and his eyes were also suspiciously moist. Erica was as white as a sheet."

Neubauer asked Erica, "are you coming with us?" although he anticipated what she would reply.

She shook her head. "No, Herr Neubauer. I'm staying with Dick whatever happens."

The drivers made their farewells. Von Brauchitsch says that "when I shook Rudi [Cent's] hand in the middle of all the confusion to say goodbye, his face which was usually so cheerful showed serious worry and he said: *You see, the National Socialists [Nazis] in your country have long been using sport for political purposes. But let's leave it at that. You drivers don't see clearly. You all have to bow when the Foreign Ministry commands. Have a good journey home, remember me to Munich and the Oktoberfest – and stay an optimist! See you soon, dear Manfred!*"[12]

Craner explained to the Press that the Germans had left to be near the coast "in case anything happens. Apparently they heard that there was mobilisation in Germany and they are returning for that reason. The Mercedes left this morning and the Auto Union lorries left Donington at 2."

The Autocar, its deadline imminent, caught the confusion nicely. "It became increasingly difficult to maintain communication with Donington owing to trunk lines all over the country being blocked with crisis-time calls. The news that the French drivers [Dreyfus and Raph] would not compete came through."

Laury Schell, who ran the Ecurie Bleue Delahayes with his wife, was in hospital recovering from head injuries he'd received when he'd crashed en route for England, and several mechanics had been called up for military service.

"Then," *The Autocar* added, "news that the Germans had gone. It was hard to believe that Craner would still hold the race."

At 2.55, as the convoys crawled south, Chamberlain rose to address the House of Commons. The *Derby Evening Telegraph* spread headlines full across the front page. PREMIER TELLS HOUSE OF CRISIS MOVES. "WE FACE A SITUATION WITHOUT PARALLEL SINCE DAYS OF 1914." DRAMATIC SCENE IN THE COMMONS. Much further down, a single-column headline in tiers said GERMAN GRAND PRIX DRIVERS LEAVE COURSE.

Chamberlain spoke long because he had a great deal to speak about. At 4.15 he was passed a piece of paper and he paused, glanced at it and smiled.[13] "I have now been informed by Herr Hitler that he invites me to meet him in Munich tomorrow morning. He has also invited Signor Mussolini and Monsieur Daladier." War had been averted. The feeling, as someone noted, was a curious sense of anti-climax.

By then the Mercedes convoy must have been halfway to Harwich although the Auto Union cars remained in freight wagons at Castle Donington. These wagons had wooden sides and were truly international because they bore the inscription *Societe Belgo-Anglaise des Ferry-Boats Milano*.

Arthur Tyler, working in the family laundry and dry cleaning business at Loughborough, took the afternoon off – "I used to have Wednesday as a half-day because we worked Saturdays. I went over to Donington on my motorbike to see the cars practicing. It was a drizzly, damp sort of day and when I got there everything was dead quiet, nothing happening. They'd been recalled. You could feel the clouds of war hanging over.

"For the family business we were just on the point of starting to build what was to become our present site – the steelwork for it was just up. *I thought oh dear, we've made a mistake, we're not going to want any of that with the clouds hanging over*. That Wednesday afternoon was a particularly strange experience, the emptiness full of foreboding. Very full. I knew the German teams had left for a reason and I thought I knew what the reason must be. *The next thing war will be declared.*"

Among the motor racing community, the news of a Four-Power meeting at Munich on the following day created a frantic attempt to save the Grand Prix, Craner no doubt prominent. He insisted the race would take place and "this decision was reached at a meeting of the Derby and District Motor Club." It conflicted with what he had said so soon before – a decision at midday on the morrow – but everything had changed.

Telegrams and phone calls sang here and there: to the Auto Union and

Mercedes offices in London, to the Germany Embassy, to Howe as BRDC President and Scannell as BRDC Secretary (who, *The Autocar* pointed out, often contacts foreign drivers). The attempt was given urgency because neither convoy had reached Harwich and the Auto Unions cars remained at Castle Donington. The attempt failed.

Seaman and Erica "returned to London and went to dinner at Luigi's to celebrate. Saved by the bell!"[14]

Of the journey to Harwich, Lang would remember that "things looked critical on our way. In and around the towns, anti-aircraft batteries and searchlights were in place, and air-raid shelters were being dug everywhere. A few people behaved menacingly towards us but we reached Harwich without trouble. There we heard that only one ship was going to the Hook of Holland." At Harwich, Lang and the others were "astounded to see the masses of Germans at the port, mostly women who had worked in English households as governesses. There were also many workers who had helped with the assembly of German products in England."[15]

Neubauer remembered that they arrived at 17 hours (5pm) and would remember Harwich "swarming with people, German nursemaids and cooks, students and tourists. All our cars and mechanics were safely on board, and it looked as if I would get the drivers off safely in the morning. I watched the boat disappear in the darkness and walked back to the hotel. On my way I bought an evening paper and read the headline: HITLER, MUSSOLINI, CHAMBERLAIN AND DALADIER TO MEET TOMORROW AT MUNICH. The crisis was over..."[16]

Why Neubauer says that he and the drivers did not board the boat is another mini-mystery, not least because the German Embassy and Hermann Lang insist they did. At 10pm the Embassy confirmed the teams had returned home on the late boat, and Lang would remember the "congestion on the ship was terrific. Our cars had just been cleared by customs and made ready for loading when the wireless bulletin came through that was to change the present world situation in one fell swoop.

"The leading men of Italy, France and England were to go to Munich for talks. In spite of the tremendous relief for us and the British, we did not even consider turning back again. We did not deliberate for long, all of us wanted to get home. The other travellers evidently thought the same and made use of the opportunity to see their homeland again. The trip lasted through the night, and for the first time after the many days of excitement, we slept really well." Lang's reference to the Hook of Holland is yet another mini-mystery because Neubauer referred to *Harrich* [sic] – *Bergen*.

Sebastian records how "that very night we were in the harbour and put to sea in fine weather at 11pm."

The Sporting Life ruminated on the day and it remains a period piece of innocence. This is easy to understand because the global savagery between 1939 and 1945 was frankly unimaginable. Under a sub-heading: SHOULD KNOW US BETTER, the unsigned journalist wrote: "Many reasons have been given for the sudden departure of the teams in view of the brighter crisis news, but I understand that the chief one was the reluctance of the drivers to compete. They feared that, in view of the tense conditions prevailing, they would not be very popular, although assured by all concerned that British sportsmen would greet them as sportsmen."

After 1939 and the war which Hitler wrought, it would never be possible to write such words again. Whatever innocence remained in humanity, Hitler killed it.

Thursday, 29 September

The boat bearing the Auto Union team arrived at the Hook of Holland at 5am. They took the train into Germany and "we all felt a clear tension, especially as the daily papers reported that the political crisis had been overcome."[1] Von Brauchitsch wrote that "never before have I seen so few cars during our journey. Germany seemed deserted."

War had been averted but the runnning sore of the Sudetenland remained. Many headlined screamed at Berliners. The *Germania* proclaimed DR GOEBBELS SPEAKING IN THE LUSTGARDEN TO HALF A MILLION PEOPLE: "WE WANT PEACE AND OUR RIGHT." The *Volkisher Beobachter* proclaimed THE NATION WANTS LIBERTY FOR SUDETEN GERMANS. STANDING SOLIDLY BEHIND OUR FUHRER FOR OUR RIGHT. DEMONSTRATIONS OF LOYALTY ALL OVER THE REICH.

On page 15 the newspaper devoted five lines to Donington. The item was printed in bold in the left upper corner of the page. "The car race for the Grand Prix of Donington, which was to take place on Saturday, has been cancelled. The teams of the Mercedes-Benz-Werke and of the Auto Union are already on their journeys home."

The Autocar accepted that the morning news – both teams had sailed, "leaving a few mechanics and equipment to follow on the next boat" – meant "all hope of German participation in the race was finally and regretfully abandoned."

When the convoys had disembarked at the Hook and were crawling across towards Germany, Lang would remember "we found Holland also ready for defence. Barricades were up, and the Dutch forces were on manoeuvres. We were surprised by the war-like measures as we drove through. Many of the big trees lining the roads were surrounded by belts of high explosive coupled together with fuse. In many places the roads were dug up and barricades erected. Near the German frontier, work was proceedingly feverishly on a tank trap. Upon entering Germany we also expected considerable military preparation. However, nothing like it was to be seen, nor did we observe any traps. The customs people dealt with our car papers quite calmly and we got home in good spirits."[2]

A day of meetings very great and very small. While Mussolini travelled to Munich by train from Rome, Daladier flew from Paris and Chamberlain flew from London to settle the future of humanity, the Derby and District Motor Club met at 12 noon to settle the future of the motor race. They decided it would take place "to avoid disappointing our many supporters." Thirty minutes later the freight wagons carrying the Auto Unions were eased out of Castle Donington station for Harwich.

At 1.30 the 'Big Four' settled at Munich to a demanding and most ungentlemanly timetable, talks, lunch at 2.45, talks resumed at 4.30, dinner at 8.20, talks resumed at 10pm.

The offices of *The Autocar* were flooded with telephone inquiries and "at half-past five we were informed that the race would definitely be held without the foreign drivers, so that presumably the British drivers would be eligible for the big prizes as well as their own special awards." *The Sporting Life* noted that "with the withdrawal of the eight German cars and the two Delahayes, the entry now consists of nine British cars – six ERAs, an Alta, an MG and a Riley. Earl Howe will be a non-starter as he has joined his ship at Portsmouth. His car will probably be handled by another driver."

Meanwhile, the 'Big Four' concentrated on the rest of humanity.

The members of the Auto Union team who had journeyed by boat and rail arrived at Zwickau.

Friday, 30 September

Shortly after 1am Hitler, Chamberlain, Mussolini and Daladier signed the Munich Agreement which allowed German troops to begin occupying the Sudetenland on 1 October. The Czech representatives had not even been allowed into the meeting but were made to wait outside while their country was being sacrificed on other people's altars.

Again magazines with early-week deadlines were trapped. *The Light Car* said: "As we go to press with these pages everyone is asking whether or not the Donington Grand Prix will be held. That question, unfortunately, cannot be answered at the time of writing. All that can be said with certainty is that the organizers will not cancel the race unless circumstances leave no possible alternative. For that reason, we publish on these pages full details of the event, as we hope to see it on Saturday."

The weekly *Harborough Mail* carried a resumé of events which is so vivid in its content – and captures the near-panic which had descended on everyday life so well – that it demands to be reproduced extensively. It appeared on an inside page: even the threat of war did not persuade the newspaper to drop its traditional front page of advertisements. It appeared under a tiny headline, HARBOROUGH'S BIG A.R.P MOVE.

"Market Harborough has in one big jump brought itself up-to-date in A.R.P. organisation.

Nearly 10,000 gas masks have been distributed and by when this paper appears every family should have received their supply.

This afternoon 500 children were due to arrive at Market Harborough station from London.

Yesterday the Council announced that public warning signals in the event of an air raid will come from the syren [sic] at the gas works. An experimental test was made this afternoon.

The crisis affected market day trade in Harborough on Tuesday. In the cattle market, around the stalls and in the shops, the one question was 'Will there be a war?' Many people grew all the more anxious during the afternoon when it was known that gas masks had not arrived.

Members of the German Auto Union car racing team returning from Donington on their way back home, were stopped by a police sergeant in Market Harborough on Tuesday, and informed that their manager had sent instructions for them to go back to Donington. After having lunch at the Peacock Hotel, the young Germans returned to Donington only to receive a further message later in the day that they were to go back to Germany after all. They set off on Wednesday morning.

The gas masks arrived on Wednesday morning and were taken to the largest factories in the town where employees were waiting to assemble them. During the day posters were put out informing the people where they were to go to get their supply. By 6pm queues were forming outside the distributing stations and the volunteers were still busy last evening.

Air-raid wardens are still urgently required and attention is called to the advertisement in another column.

A supply of sixty hand-bells is required for the wardens and people who have any bells in their possession will be helping if they hand them over to the A.R.P. organisers.

Workmen have been busy since Wednesday morning digging trenches in Roman Way and the Recreation Ground, Logan-street, Market Harborough. Trenches are also to be dug in the Welland Park-road and Little Bowden districts of the town.

Kerb-stones have been painted in black and white in Market Harborough streets.

Harborough's water supply has been taken into account. The town fortunately receives its supply from several individual sources."

During the morning Chamberlain met Hitler again and then flew back to London where he held up the piece of paper signed by himself and Hitler which, he promised, guaranteed "peace in our time". The image remains one of the most enduring of the 20th century because, within a year, it would become one of the most tragic. It was greeted, however, with something approaching hysterical relief.

Connell was having lunch at Donington Hall with a "German chap called Berg. I had met him in Sweden when I'd done the ice Grand Prix – he'd been driving in it. He wasn't due to drive at Donington so I suppose he was probably there with someone else. We were sitting there listening to the radio listening to Chamberlain arrive back flourishing his piece of paper and Berg said *ah, now we are friends*." They'd been friends since Sweden, of course, and Berg was either being ironic or stressing that friendship was officially approved now.

John Dugdale recalls "driving north up Sloane Street in London as the traffic stopped for Neville Chamberlain to cross east when he was coming back from the airport [en route to Downing Street]. I and my colleague, another assistant editor of *The Autocar*, were full of disdain. That week we got out a pamphlet sarcastically titled 'Peace in Our Time?'"

Fred Craner surely wasn't hysterical and fully intended to turn the relief to his advantage. The two German teams might be lured back to compete if the race had a new date. Why not? The world was at peace and within that peace Craner moved quickly. He got Shields to agree to altering the date and he persuaded the RAC to agree. He telephoned Germany and, as it would seem, spoke to their governing body, the ONS. They explained that it was now too late to do anything about the race – still scheduled for tomorrow – but indicated that they would return if a suitable new date was offered. Craner mentioned Saturday, 22 October. That would be subject to confirmation by the AIACR (*Association Internationale des Automobile Club Reconnus*), but confirmation would surely be a formality.

While Craner bustled on the phone in his offices in Coppice House, one source says that three cars droned round the circuit practicing and another source says two – an ERA and an Alta. Earl Howe was not among them but on the high seas; Maclure hadn't arrived, nor had Billy Cotton who'd returned to London, promising that he would fly back if the race was on.

By deduction, the two or three cars droning round in the emptiness were a permutation of Connell or Dobson in ERAs, Hanson in an Alta or Cuddon-Fletcher in an MG but such a deduction is dangerous because Connell, Cotton and Hanson had reserve drivers and they may or may not have been out there.

Only "twenty souls in all"[1] were in the pits and cumulatively it was, as one of the 20 remarked wistfully, a Donington of Loneliness.

The race was officially postponed at 3.50 because, with the possibility of only six starters, it was beyond saving but by then the uncertainty had overwhelmed the offices of the specialist motoring magazines. Routine work at *The Autocar* "was at a complete standstill owing to continuous incoming telephones asking whether the race was still to be held. Hundreds of calls were received, some from as far away as Cambridge and Bristol." (It was a parochial society then. What London publication now would judge that receiving telephone calls from "as far away as Cambridge and Bristol" was newsworthy enough to print?)

At 4pm *The Motor* heard of the postponement although by then they'd been receiving hundreds of "telephone inquiries asking for information about the race and the possibilty of the German drivers competing. Up to a late hour on Friday we were still receiving inquiries; never has any event involved so many requests for information. And disappointment was registered by everyone when they were told of the position. A whole year they had waited to see these cars, only to be frustrated at the last minute."

There's an echo of the Tuesday and the RAC boxes along the A6 because 'Grande Vitesse' of *The Motor* was en route from London to Donington – to cover the race on the morrow – when news of the postponement came through. *The Motor* decided to test the AA's ability to intercept motorists using their patrolmen and their call boxes (just like the RAC). The magazine gave the AA full details of the car 'Grande Vitesse' was driving and, within an hour, he was stopped – near Leicester, as it happened.

Chapter 6

Crisis

GERMAN TROOPS ENTERED the Sudetenland on Saturday, 1 October and the eyewitness accounts, the photographs, and the moving film of it retain a shocking sense of homecoming and violation at the same moment. There are plump Germanic women, arms upraised in the Nazi salute, weeping with the release of salvation and, in the background, Czechs weeping silently.

On the Monday, while the House of Commons debated the Munich agreement, Craner invited a reporter from *The Light Car* to a meeting with himself and Captain A.W. Phillips of the RAC who "made it clear" that the Derby and District Motor Club had the RAC's wholehearted support for the new date. Phillips added that he felt it was unlikely the *AIACR* would raise any objection.

Craner made a formal statement: "The Donington International Grand Prix will be run on October 22, starting at 12 noon. People who have purchased tickets will be given the opportunity of having their money refunded or of having fresh tickets for the new date. The race will be run under the existing regulations and, of course, with the entry list already published. Thanks to the recovery of Laury Schell it is more than likely that the Delahayes will run, so that the race will be even better than it would have been on October 1. Needless to say, the German teams of Mercedes and Auto Union will be there. I would like to thank publicly all my staff, who worked so hard during a period of extreme pressure, and the BBC who have given us such valuable help by announcing to the public what was happening at Donington."

Two days later Erica Popp's mother arrived in London. Seaman's formidable mother welcomed her politely – Erica was, after all, staying at No. 3 Ennismore Gardens – but resolutely refused to discuss the couple's engagement, never mind recognise it, until Erica's father arrived. The time "passed largely in the entertainment of Frau Popp." A crisis, however, was at hand. It came "when the young couple wished to sign the lease of a flat in

London. As Mrs Seaman had control of Dick's finances in England, her consent was needed before the lease could be signed. Mrs Seaman refused to give it because she still held that nothing should be done until she had seen Herr Popp."[1]

As Erica's mother was arriving, Neubauer circulated the Mercedes directors and heads of department at Untertürkheim:

Re Donington Park race on 22.10.1938
We have just received from the organisers of the Donington race an official statement that it will take place on 22.10 at 12 noon. We have re-confirmed the information we gave at the time. These drivers will start:
   Rudolf Caracciola
   Manfred von Brauchitsch
   Hermann Lang
   Richard Seaman
   Reserve driver Walter Baumer

Ut [Untertürkheim], the 5.10.38 Race Department
(signed) Neubauer

On the Saturday there was a race meeting at Crystal Palace which included a challenge between B. Bira and Dobson. Seaman, wearing an overcoat and cap (which suited him) spun a coin for who would have the inside position on the 'grid' and gave the start; but the duel was short-lived. Bira retired with a puncture.

The crisis at No. 3 Ennismore Gardens reached a climax after the weekend. Seaman had been trying to appear as phlegmatic and reassuring as possible while the political crisis ebbed to and fro, but the domestic disapproval of his marriage on top of that seems to have been too much to bear. "With his nerves now giving way, he lost his temper." His mother promptly departed for Pull Court, the family's historic house near Tewkesbury, and refused to discuss the marriage ever again.[2]

Erica confirms this. "Things went from bad to worse with Dick and his mother. We had found a very nice flat just off Belgrave Square which we wanted to rent. Dick had given up his chalet at Ambach and my father was going to give us a brand new one in Grainau for a wedding present, but we needed a London home and this flat seemed just right. However, although Dick's father had left him a considerable sum when he died, he had put it in a Trust Fund to be administered by Mrs Seaman until Dick reached the age of 27. When Dick asked her to sign the lease on the flat she refused. She was still determined to stop our marriage and wasn't going to let Dick have a home of his own. There was a very big row and Mrs Seaman left London for her house in the country, telling Dick she never wanted to see me at Ennismore Gardens again!"[3]

On the Tuesday, Sebastian of Auto Union wrote that "our entire racing convoy rolled back to England again. This time we went by train. We went via Cologne, Aachen, Liege and Brussels to Zeebrugge. From there the ferry took us across the Channel but the wind strength was 9. All of us were seasick except Hermann Kraus. We really were a beaten team!"

On the Thursday the Auto Union cars arrived and next day Lang left Stuttgart, taking the same route as he had done before. He found the roads clear, the soldiers gone and, on the bridge between Kehl and Strasbourg, only a sentry keeping "a peaceful watch. The customs officers were polite and helpful, and the hotel manager in Paris laughed when he saw me again. The picture had changed completely. The mechanics in the Paris garage were pleasant, the car loaded at Calais without trouble and the ship only normally occupied. England appeared to be in good spirits."[4]

On the Saturday, Erica and her mother, accompanied by Seaman, flew from Croydon to Munich. As he locked the door of No. 3 Ennismore Gardens behind him he vowed never to sleep a night there again, and never did, although he'd be returning on the Monday to prepare for Donington.

On the Sunday, the Mercedes convoy reached Dover and the 25 personnel stayed at the Lord Warden Hotel in Beach Street, the only four star hotel in the town. It had 75 rooms and a double cost from 15s to 21s: not cheap in its time. As the convoy crawled north next morning Seaman returned to England. When von Brauchtisch and Baumer flew in is not clear, although *Motor Sport* scolded that "as last year, few enthusiasts troubled to meet the drivers, most of whom arrived by air at Croydon."

On this Sunday Neubauer drove from Stuttgart to London via Paris. Next day he and Dr Porsche visited the Motor Show in Earl's Court, London. *The Sporting Life* reported that "Dr Porsche is Germany's motoring engineering genius. He designed the famous rear-engined Auto Union racing car capable of 200 miles an hour, which will be racing at Donington in Britain's Grand Prix on Saturday. He is also responsible for the 'people's car' – the Volkswagen. They first visited the Auto Union and Mercedes stands. Then they went and looked at Britain's 'Volkswagen' – the new Morris 'eight', the new Standard 'eight' and the two 'baby' Austins. Dr Porsche had no public comment to make and Neubauer preferred to talk about Germany's great chance of winning, for the second year in succession, Britain's chief motor race. To their colleagues, however, they admitted how tremendously impressed they were by Britain's 'economy cars'."

There were other visitors to the Show who dealt in speed. An Englishman, Captain George Eyston, held the World Land Speed Record which he had set on 16 September at Bonneville Flats, Utah. His car *Thunderbolt*, powered by two Rolls-Royce engines, had done 357.497 mph, beating the 350.194 mph of John Cobb set at the same place the day before. Now, at Earl's Court, Eyston met Sir Malcolm Campbell, who held the World Water Speed Record (130.93 mph set on Lake Hallwil, Switzerland). A charming photograph survives of both of them on the Castrol stand listening by telephone to each other's recorded account of their successful attempts. Eyston fully intended to attend the Grand Prix.

At Donington there was unofficial practice, Nuvolari literally leading it. Helplessly he was poised to add to his own myth and legend. The Monza victory had "revitalized" him and he was driving hard, setting fastest time so far – all the Auto Union drivers were in action – and explaining that the time did not satisfy him. He went out again "flying down that beautiful wooded straight, the yellow radiator grille slicing through the keen autumn weather."

He passed under the stone bridge and "from a clump of thick bushes saw a dark shadow emerge." This shadow seemed to dive headlong across the track in a wild, terrified burst to reach the sanctuary of the other side before Nuvolari's car struck it. The shadow was so indistinct, and travelling so fast, that Nuvolari did not know what it was. He may have tried to swerve – one report claimed he did – but even he may have lacked the reflexes for that. He braked instinctively but felt a "sharp jar" – impact – and saw the shadow pitched into the air. What must have been simultaneously, he also felt a stabbing pain because, under the sudden decelleration of the brakes, his chest had been rammed hard against the steering wheel.

He stopped within 200 yards, clambered out and ran back. A "beautiful stag with magnificent antlers lay dead on the track in a pool of blood." The stopping and getting out of the car meant he was overdue back at the pits and the crew assumed he must have had an accident and an ambulance set off, siren wailing. When it arrived, the ambulancemen saw Nuvolari bent over the stag stroking it.

"You cannot take anyone to hospital," Nuvolari said, "not even this unfortunate one. He died on the spot."[5]

Lurani gives the background, saying that Nuvolari was in need of hospital attention because the impact had been so hard he'd fractured a rib. However, after Pau when driving an Alfa-Romeo, he had been badly burned, and he "no longer wished to see doctors, nurses and small rooms smelling of ether, knowing full well that if he got into the ambulance he ran the risk of becoming a prisoner, to be amiably lectured by the profession while Mercedes-Benz were left to win this important race. Instead he asked that the stag should be taken away, begging them to let him have the beautiful head suitably stuffed and mounted."[6]

The *Allgemeine Automobil Zeitung* expressed the incident lyrically and sardonically. "Normally, fallow deer graze peacefully at Donington Park with its wide, green lawns and its old trees. Trippers have their tea in tall, dark rooms or in front of the fireplace of Donington castle, which is dreaming in distinguished silence in the middle of the park. Now, however, engines intruded into this peaceful scene and a fallow deer which threw itself in front of Nuvolari's car enters the catalogue of those who have tried in vain to halt progress…"

Gillies explains that "the deer were all over the park, I suppose five hundred of them. There were very few walls except the boundary walls of the track, the only defence against them running on. I expect the noise of the car startled the deer. I seem to remember Nuvolari was doing about 90 miles an hour when he struck the deer."

Nuvolari said "I didn't expect to collect any prizes before the Grand Prix was over, but perhaps this pre-race prize-giving is a good omen."

The countdown towards the Grand Prix quickened. During the afternoon the Mercedes convoy crawled in and began the laborious process of unloading. The Mercedes drivers, evidently at the Motor Show with Neubauer, were expected to arrive at Donington the next day to get down to serious practise. They'd be staying at the Black Boy. Madame Lucy Schell, head of the *Ecurie Bleu,* notified Craner that her two Delahayes, plus drivers Dreyfus and Raph (whose real name was Raphael Bethnod de la Casas), would reach Dover the following afternoon. Luigi Villoresi and his Maserati were expected at Donington the next day or Wednesday. Huhnlein would visit the Motor Show on Wednesday and then journey to Donington, accompanied by his wife, daughter, von Bayer Ehrenberg (vice-President of the ONS) and other leading German officials.

Next day, the Tuesday, both teams practised although reportedly they weren't trying to set times but prepare the cars instead for first qualifying – although of this von Brauchitsch has a revealing story. "Unfortunately, a little accident happened to me when I drove to the first practice. After having opened the park gate to the racing track for Seaman, I stepped on the running board of his car to let him bring me about a hundred and fifty metres across a meadow to the starting grid. Seaman raced at breakneck speed over the holes and the uneven surface and finally even made a sudden steering wheel movement so that I could not get hold of myself and fell like a missile to the side, somersaulting several times. Apart from some bruises at my hip and my left arm I had broken my left little finger. With this handicap I was not fully fit, of course, and it was not of much use to me that Seaman apologised for his intentional or unintentional devilry."[7]

Craner was enraged that one of the British drivers – never named – sent him an account in £ s d for the time he had wasted at Donington before the original race was postponed, and demanded reimbursement. Whether the driver seriously wanted, and expected, to receive the money is open to doubt. More likely, he knew Craner, knew what effect it was bound to have on Craner and decided to give everyone a belly-laugh as Craner exploded. We do know Craner had an extensive command of Anglo-Saxon...

The Mercedes drivers returned to the Black Boy and that evening "after licensing hours" Lang was "seized by a tremendous thirst." He went into the corridor to find a waiter and "after nearly colliding with him I saw that he was carrying a big tray full of foaming beer glasses. Unable to speak the language, I tried to make clear by means of gestures that I was almost dying of thirst, but he indicated that the beer was for a crowd of young Englishmen in a room adjoining mine. The door of this had been open and they had watched the sign language. In less than no time they surrounded me and demanded to know my wishes. When I had made it clear that I was terribly thirsty and belonged to the Mercedes Benz team, all hell was let loose, and an incomparable Anglo-German alliance was formed."[8]

Gillies Shields remembers that some Italian drivers "stayed with us" – at the Hall, no doubt – and "they had very fast road cars never mind racing cars. They were very fond of my sisters, who were quite pretty. As kids they took us to the pictures, took us off to Derby. They drove so fast, they had no idea of English roads and it was thrilling." Shields also remembers one of these Italians giving his sister Geraldine a mascot, a little tortoise. We know that Tazio Nuvolari always wore just such a mascot which suggests that – perhaps – these October days in 1938 one of the greatest of all drivers took Gillies Shields to Derby so he could go to the pictures...

A large crowd attended first qualifying, from 9.30 to 12.30, then 2.30 to 5.30. There was, perhaps, a sense of pace picking up and gathering impetus from a slow, echoing beginning. Neubauer was in the pit lane wearing his Homburg, collar and tie with a white scarf tucked into his jacket and a stop watch on a chain in his fob pocket. The engineer, Uhlenhaut, bespectacled, wore a bow tie and heavy raincoat with pronounced lapels. He stooped to examine one of his beloved Mercedes, smiled, stood up. Then he chatted to Seaman, who had his goggles loose round his neck.

Von Brauchitsch prepared to get into his car, levering off his coat and handing it to a mechanic. Neubauer, who'd put on a coat, stood nearby. Seaman smoothed his hair using both hands and it was evident then how badly damaged his nose had been: almost as if plasticine had been moulded to it. Three mechanics, wearing cloth caps, pushed von Brauchitsch and he was away out on to the track. Not far away, Lang sat in his cockpit using his hands to illustrate some point or other to the mechanic who leant towards him.

Uhlenhaut himself drove one of the cars after detailed conversation with Neubauer. It had a large letter *T* on its bonnet for *Training car* (an expression which survives to this day in motor racing parlance as the *T-car*, meaning the spare). You could see his hands churning the steering wheel as he was pushed off and twisted the car towards the track.

Neubauer, like a circus master, stood on the rim of the track holding a pole with a flag on the end of it which he used – with a flourish – to direct traffic, signalling his cars out and signalling them back in again.

The speed of the cars was immediately evident as they surged and flooded past the little ERAs. Their balance, poise and adhesion was immediately evident on the long descending sweepers to the old hairpin.

Lang thrilled the crowd[9] with a lap averaging 84.59 mph. The speed was "all the more amazing" because "the lap record last year, set jointly by Bernd Rosemeyer and von Brauchitsch with cars of double the capacity, stands at 85.62 mph. The actual difference between the two speeds is only 13/5 of a second. Two hectic skids occurred during the afternoon at Red Gate Corner, where Seaman finished up on the grass and Walter Baumer, who is taking the place of Caracciola, turned completely round."

Lang	Mercedes	2m 13.2s
Müller	Auto Union	2m 14.0s
von Brauchtisch	Mercedes	2m 14.1s
Seaman	Mercedes	2m 14.1s
Hasse	Auto Union	2m 18.3s
Baumer	Mercedes	2m 20.4s

Nuvolari	Auto Union	2m 20.4s
Maclure	Riley 2-litre	2m 34.2s
Hanson	Alta 1500cc	2m 44.0s

Seaman clearly wasn't happy and at one instant fell into a discussion with Uhlenhaut, his eyes hooded, his facial expression held rigid. Von Brauchitsch was in quite a different mood, chatting to a pretty lady and, when a camera approached, he turned, stuck his tongue out and smiled. Neubauer – coat off now – rested a foot on the wheel of a car, held the flagpole like a walking stick and used a handkerchief to wipe his face.

Huhnlein flew into Croydon and was met by representatives of the German Embassy. He went to the Motor Show and made a "thorough inspection of the exhibits and expressed considerable interest in the Rolls-Royce and the smaller British sports cars."[10]

Meanwhile the *Derby Evening Telegraph* reported that the Duke of Kent would start the race and was expected to fly up although "it is still not known whether his aeroplane will land at Derby airport. Wing-Commander E.H. Fielden, Captain of the King's Flight, landed at Burnaston this week, but left without making any comment. An official at Tollerton Aerodrome, (near Nottingham), told a *Telegraph* representative today that nothing had been heard of the Duke landing there on Saturday, and no visit had been made by Wing-Commander Fielden."

The presence of royalty, and the arrangements of royalty, were regarded as genuinely important. More than that, we may surmise that although the Duke was a patron and active follower of motorsport, after all the political turmoil his presence at Donington was genuinely important symbolically.

At 7.40, Naumann reported to Stuttgart by telephone: "From the 19 drivers, just nine took the opportunity to make themselves familiar with the circuit. Only Mercedes had all the cars there punctually. In the morning, Auto Union did no more than three laps with one training car, Müller at the steering wheel. In the afternoon the Auto Unions also restricted their training. Nuvolari and Hasse did a few laps. We could understand this because, as we heard, Auto Union have been at Donington since last week. They have already done hundreds of laps in training to give their drivers the chance to find out all the difficulties of the 5.2-kilometre circuit.

"These difficulties are even bigger this year than before because there are more bumps and unevenness. They demand the driver shows his full art and concentration. One can only admire today's work by Lang who, after only a few laps, finished with the best time of 2:13.2s = 135.09 kph [83.94 mph], really unbelievable. You can only understand it when you see how well the Mercedes-Benz cars hold to the road. This improvement in road holding could be seen particularly on the 'jump' [the Melbourne Rise]. Last year the cars jumped off the road here but now not even one wheel leaves the ground – thanks, firstly, to the road holding. Von Brauchitsch and Seaman were only one second slower and showed their ability."

Naumann then gave the full list of times.

Villoresi and his Maserati reached Dover in the evening, were being examined by Customs and were expected at Donington the following morning. The countdown ticked on, three days to go.

In its issue of the following morning the *Volkischer Beobachter* reported the qualifying under placid headlines.

WITHOUT CARACCIOLA. LANG FASTEST DURING
FIRST PRACTICE. IN BEAUTIFUL AUTUMN WEATHER.
ONLY 17 DRIVERS AT THE STARTING LINE

Four Auto Unions, four Mercedes-Benz, two Delahayes, six English cars were present on Wednesday while the Maserati to be driven by Luigi Villoresi is missing for the time being. English motor car circles are missing the famous E.R.A. and Riley drivers, who are not there except for Dobson.

There is deep regret over the news that European champion Caracciola will not be able to take part, although he really hoped to – he has too many problems with his foot.

Instead of Caracciola there will be Walter Baumer, an ambitious young driver who is thus given the opportunity to distinguish himself. The Grand Prix of Donington will become a **duel between Auto Union and Mercedes-Benz.**

The two Delahayes with Dreyfus and Raph were not in the first practice. Some English ERA and Riley drivers practised quite diligently but did not approach the times of the German racing cars, since without exception they have machines with much lower performance.

Now, on the Thursday, everyone prepared for the second qualifying, the sessions the same as the day before. The reporter for *Motor Sport* wrote such an evocative and perceptive description that – like the *Leicester Mercury* and *Harborough Mail* – large tracts of it demand to be reproduced verbatim:

"I am writing this in the Opel in which we left London at 6am to attend 'the training' for another of the great Grand Prix Races at Donington, of which the late Crisis so nearly robbed us. It has been rumoured that, throughout the Crisis, three Auto Unions remained in their railway vans at Harwich and never left this country.

"Very definitely, this is real racing, inspiring to an undescribable degree and immensley good for the soul. Though the Auto Unions no longer flex and dither as they did last year, and though the Germans cars no longer leap from the rise after Melbourne Corner, where the bump has been eased off, nevertheless, in speed, sound and acceleration the 3-litre Formula cars make other racing look just stupid.

"As I write, some of the drivers play impromptu football, others clock-golf,[11] on the sun-lit lawn outside Donington Hall, where, as last year, they have all lunched together – all, that is, save Seaman. Seaman appeared to arrive late and to exchange a few words with Neubauer. Early this Thursday morning Uhlenhaut took out the Mercedes training car, labelled with a big

T, and committed much lappery. This car had an extra air-temperature thermometer clamped to the scuttle side. Uhlenhaut wears full kit and will apparently be the team's spare driver.

"Soon the other drivers got down to it, including Nuvolari, who sets up the fastest lap [provisional pole]. After lunch there is less activity, Seaman doing very little and Nuvolari nothing at all. But Lang does one immense lap. Hasse, in black overalls, is very cheery, but Kautz suffers from a cold.

"To walk all round the circuit is a truly wonderful experience. Through the wood beyond Red Gate the cars sound terrific, and their speed down to the hairpin is prodigious, but perhaps the most spectacular point is from Maclean's Corner along the straight bit to Coppice Corner. Here one is able to appreciate very thoroughly the work done by the drivers, all of whom perspire freely after only a short spell in the 'seat of government.'

"Hasse keeps his hands comparatively steady on the wheel on the straight and Seaman slides beautifully into Red Gate. Frequently the cars visit the grass verge at Melbourne and they come out of the woods like bombs, sliding sideways through the gate.

"At the pits we see again the amazingly thorough organisation; every lap timed, copious notes made of every piece of work undertaken and cars continually given flag signals by their respective chiefs. At the depots, one's breath is again taken away by the astoundingly complete equipment. The tyre-store, in charge of Continentals' imposing representative, is a wonderful sight, and Mercedes alone brought more than eleven hundred gallons of special fuel. When the cars are warming up the fumes and noise overcome one surprisingly quickly, so much so that we were unable to stay long enough to complete a note to this effect in the Editorial notebook.

"When off duty Seaman and Brauchitsch wore overcoats, Hasse his black overalls, Kautz a teddy-bear coat and Nuvolari, who sat alone much of the time in a Studebaker saloon, a long overcoat and a big cap with an immense badge therein. Quite an excellent crowd of spectators assembled to see the practice. The Mercs were towed by Mercedes-Benz saloons, the Auto Unions by open Horch tourers – part of the DKW/Wanderer/Horch/Auto Union/Audi combine.

"Once again the keenness of every mechanic was evident, and also the splendid relationship between engineers and mechanics, as when an Auto Union man made the mistake of applying his electric start to Kautz's car while it was in gear – temporary annoyance was natural, but clearly the mechanic bore Feuereissen and Eberhorst no grudge and they were conversing with him a moment later.

"Towards the end of the afternoon, Kautz brought in the Auto Union training car, labelled with a big *T* and Sebastian drove it off to the depot minus its lower gears, much laughter greeting him when he stalled the engine trying to start in top.

"The Auto Unions were cleaner than the Mercs, but the finish of both cars is highly commendable. Both use 7.00in x 19in Continental rear covers and Continental Balloons on the front, size mostly unmarked, but 5.50in x 19in on the Auto Union training car. Mercs were rumoured to be boosted very high but Auto Unions to have had better performance since the Italian G.P. Brauchitsch's car showed flame from the exhausts on the overrun. Oil dropped from the Merc rear axles onto the asbestos lagged under-body exhausts, so that the car smoked in consequence when they came in.

"Lang's Mercedes had a longer tail than the other cars and there appeared to be detail differences in the exhaust systems, small springs supporting the pipe at one point. The cowling of Brauchitsch's car was red, Seaman's green, Lang's blue and Baumer's white. The facias contained a central rev. counter reading to '90' (9,000 rpm) with water thermometer to the left and oil thermometer to the right, both these small dials reading 10 degree – 120 degree.

"As on the Auto Unions, the engines are normally electrically started and the steering wheels detach. Auto Union had some bother in engaging their starters. Mercedes-Benz warm up at a steady 2,200 rpm blipping up to 4,000 rpm.

"At the end of the day Lang's engine was considerably dismantled, and the camshaft driving gears were exposed. The intake manifolding is all metal, with neat clips and no lose connections. The Auto Unions have longer gear and brake levers, both on the off side, and the facia has a large white-dialled rev. counter to the left reading to 8,000 rpm (the full figure is used, which is unusual), and five small dials to the right. When an engine was started on the handle [by a starting handle] it was noticeable how soft is the rear suspension. The body sides curve inwards behind the nose cowling and are far more rigid than last year.

"During the afternoon a deer again strayed onto the course, but this one escaped alive and Brauchitsch merely waved to it. The monoposto Delahaye had Dunlop tyres front shock absorbers set high up inside the nose cowling and coupled to the axle by links, and a reverse catch for the gearbox set by the rear axle, outside the car."

During the afternoon, too, Auto Union made a visible effort to go quicker and quicker and the urgency of that communicated itself to the crowd and the pits. Nuvolari was typically magnanimous about his provisional pole position – the Friday morning session remained. "My only regret is that poor Bernd cannot be here today to go one better."

Nuvolari	2m 11.1s
von Brauchitsch	2m 11.2s
Seaman	2m 12.1s
Lang	2m 12.2s
Müller	2m 12.3s
Baumer	2m 13.4s
Hasse	2m 15.2s
Kautz	2m 18.6s
Cotton	2m 35.2s
Dreyfus	2m 36.2s

Wilkinson had prepared Cotton's car in his – Wilkinson's – garage on Wandsworth Common in London and it had been taken up on their transporter. They stayed in the Hall, which served as an hotel. "I'd have a go round the circuit first – the thing was, I could drive faster than my customers! I'd say to Cotton, *Bill, I can't play with your band but the car is my profession, my life.*" Wilkinson was entered as Cotton's reserve driver for the Grand Prix. "Cotton was a good chap and I liked him very much indeed. A sound chap. His word was his bond. He'd throw big parties and if it was exclusively male the Visitors' Book would be full of crude jokes but if the wives were there it was *the book's shut, gentlemen.* As a driver he had lots of guts. He wasn't very happy about the speed difference between the ERAs and the Germans. He pulled a face and said *the bastards!*"

The flow of information was quite different then to now: across the decades we have moved from starvation to saturation. That is to say, *then* a reporter had to go and find out what he could for himself – and might easily not hear about significant events, depending on chance – while *now* a mass of information from every team is brought to the reporter, who has already seen all the action on close-circuit or public television, anyway. This no doubt explains why *Motor Sport* devoted a page and a half to the day's activities then and described Uhlenhaut taking the cars out early in the morning but not that catastrophe nearly overtook him...

The Sporting Life did. "Engineer Uhlenhaut will not soon forget his experience with two jay walkers on the track here today. They came within inches of killing him and themselves. Uhlenhaut was trying out the 200 mph. Mercedes cars before handing them over to the drivers. As he shot over the brow of the hill near the replenishment pits at some 120 mph [the Melbourne Rise] an ambulance man strolled across the road. Uhlenhaut swerved, skidded, and by a magnificent effort just missed him. An hour later exactly the same thing happened again – this time the jay walker was an RAC guide. I have rarely heard such a flow of German expletives. Chief Engineer Neubauer was even more furious than Uhlenhaut. Neubauer was afraid for the engineer and his precious car." The German drivers were complaining about the circuit's bumps. "This road track is very similar to an ordinary English country lane, and the Germans naturally prefer their amazingly smooth, dead straight motor roads."

After the session ended Captain Bemrose, President of the Derby and District Motor Club, had the drivers to tea at the Hall. No doubt the *Motor Sport* reporter attended it and as he made his way there he was suddenly moved to write: "Donington is truly a great spot at which to stage a great motor race. Wandering over the wide expanse of grass-grown paddock, studded with gnarled trees, the Hall forming an imposing background, it was difficult to believe that we had just seen Nuvolari screaming towards us at 160 mph, tail sliding out so that the Auto Union's nose pointed directly at us, four wheels flapping wildly to retain control..."

After taking tea with Captain Bemrose, the Mercedes drivers returned to the Black Boy and at 7.15 Naumann reported to Untertürkheim:

NUVOLARI BREAKS LAP RECORD.
MANF. VON BRAUCHITSCH IS VERY NEAR!
"The last Grand Prix of the year will be a real battle. This has emerged from the second day of training. It was nice, sunny autumn weather and we saw 17 of the 19 entrants in training. Right at the beginning Nuvolari surprised everyone – and quite a lot of people were present – with a time of 2m 11 1/5s. He went under the time of the official record of the year before with only a 3-litre car. Manfred von Brauchitsch likes the circuit very much but he was not satisfied with his own time. He got quicker and quicker every lap. At first he bettered 2m 13s, then 2m 12.2s, and with the next lap he did 2m 11.2s but stopped. Therefore he was second fastest by only 1/5 of a second.

"Mercedes now has three cars on the front row. Baumer, the fourth Mercedes driver, really surprised people with what he could get out of the car. Taking into consideration that he only had very few opportunities with the new car and he didn't know the circuit, it must be recognised that his time was very good. He is on the second row. Hasse did not take part at all, and Kautz didn't do any good times.

"For information. Tomorrow we will not train except Lang, whose car had compressor damage today. Otherwise, if his car had been all right, he would probably have done a faster time than Nuvolari. He will do a few laps because in the meantime his car has been repaired."

The British (and French) drivers were quite prepared to say publicly what was so evident: they had no chance against the German cars. There were, however, incentives: the Team Trophy which the three ERA drivers would win if they finished and all the German cars did not; £100 and the President's Trophy for the first British driver home; Maclure and Cuddon-Fletcher would fight out a private duel for a prize of £250, awarded by the British Motor Race Organisers' Association for the driver with most points during the season. Maclure had 99, Cudden-Fletcher 97. They'd receive three for starting and 12 more for finishing.

That Thursday evening, while the drivers nursed their ambitions and wondered about the final qualifying session in the morning, Rolls-Royce were hard at work for Auto Union, who "needed new parts for their intricate carburettors. These are of a special secret design, and cost £200 each to make." Lacking time to have the parts transported from Germany, the team approached H. Hives, the Works Director of Rolls-Royce, to make them. He agreed immediately. At midnight, technicians in the secret experimental department at the company's Derby factory had completed the "four new carburettor diffusers necessary to the efficient running of the cars. It was a difficult job, involving the drilling of a number of holes that had to be exactly 13-thousandths of an inch in diameter – work more intricate than that of the finest watchmaker."[12]

The *Derby Evening Telegraph* also carried a news item about this. "Practising earlier in the week, the team had been fighting a stiff battle with their national rivals Mercedes, and had experienced trouble because they were unable to adjust their carburettors satisfactorily. The newspaper wrote of the "fine precision work" done by Rolls-Royce engineers and reported that Hives said the company had helped other drivers in similar difficulties and "the gesture was one which he felt sure would be reciprocated if necessary."

On the Friday the *Volkischer Beobacher* took undisguised in pleasure in printing what was so evident.

GERMAN RACING CARS GREATLY SUPERIOR

The postponement of the original race has drawn the English public's attention to this one. Many tickets are already sold. The first practice began on Wednesday but was unofficial and without registration of times. Drivers took the opportunity to adapt their machines to the special conditions. Because of all their experience, Mercedes-Benz and Auto-Union did this quite quickly, but the English drivers and the French particularly had more trouble. Already on Thursday morning you could see that **the German drivers and cars are greatly superior to the foreigners.**

In the afternoon practice Brauchitsch was ahead of Müller, Lang and Seaman. Astonishingly Baumer could keep up with them although, because of Caracciola's foot injury, it is the first meeting he has been in from the start. Hasse, Kautz and Nuvolari hardly had the chance to practise in the afternoon because some minor changes were being made to their cars.

The Duke of Kent, brother of the English King, intends to honour the race with his presence. This is not only a proof of the sportsmanlike attitude of the English Royal Family but also an especially friendly gesture towards the German drivers, who came from Germany to England as the best messengers of peace in order to build the stable bridge of friendship between sportsmen.

Before leaving for Donington, von Brauchitsch went from the Black Boy to No. 3 North Circus Street, the home of a certain Mr Harry Nurse, masseur. He'd been there before and *The Nottingham Journal,* hearing about it, sent a reporter along. Nurse explained that von Brauchitsch had "met with a slight accident" to his left hand practising earlier in the week and it had swollen a little – no doubt the incident with Seaman on the way to the pits during first day of practice. As his arms were massaged, von Brauchitsch occasionally murmured "goot".

The reporter essayed an interview. "Are you going to win tomorrow?"

"I will," von Brauchitsch replied firmly.

"Do you like Nottingham?"

"I do – and Donington, oh, I think it is beautiful."

"Will you beat Nuvolari and the Auto Union car?"

Von Brauchitsch smiled. "Yes."

The reporter showed von Brauchtisch a newspaper photograph of Nuvolari.
"He is my good friend." Then von Brauchtisch spoke of his love of watching football, although he wasn't a player and couldn't do any spectating while he was in England because he was a full-time racing driver. He regretted that he wouldn't be able to attend the England v Rest of Europe match, in which there were expected to be German players, at Highbury, London on Wednesday.

The reporter noted that von Brauchitsch smiled throughout the interview and "as we took leave of each other with a handshake and an exchange of 'good-morning' and *Auf Wiedersehen* I wished 'good luck' to a great sportsman."

The notion that this Friday only Lang would do a few laps – to make sure his car was in proper working order – does not seem to have survived into reality, although Naumann will provide conflicting evidence in a moment.

Motor racing people are by nature helplessly competitive (or they'd be doing something else) and we can imagine the pace of what might have been a becalmed Friday morning gathering. *The Sporting Life* insisted that all the Mercedes drivers, volubly urged on by Neubauer, went out and attacked Nuvolari's new record while Nuvolari went out to defend pole by trying to break the record again himself. None succeeded until near the end when Lang, "engine screaming at the phenomenal speed of 7,800 rpm" did 2m 11.0s, an average speed of 85.88 mph, for pole.

The Maserati had finally arrived, "coming from Bologna in a most imposing Fiat van,"[13] and was fastest after the eight German cars. Sebastian, the Auto Union mechanic, described practice as "very intense," so intense that the cars had to be modified because "the numerous bumps on the course led to the cars jumping through the air like panthers. Nuvolari drove the fastest lap of the last day and H.P. Müller recorded very good times, too so we had legitimate hopes for the day of the race. I examined my car [Nuvolari's] very carefully and found it to be perfectly in order."[14] The grid:

Lang	Nuvolari	von Brauchitsch	Seaman
(Mercedes)	(Auto Union)	(Mercedes)	(Mercedes)
2:11.0	2:11.2	2:11.4	2:12.2

Müller	Baumer	Hasse
(Auto Union)	(Mercedes)	(Auto Union)
2:12.6	2:13.8	2:15.4

Kautz	Villoresi	Dobson	Dreyfus
(Auto Union)	(Maserati)	(ERA)	(Delahaye)
2:18.6	2:21.1	2:24.6	2:25.4

Connell	Cotton	Cuddon-Fletcher
(ERA)	(ERA)	(MG)
2:27.2	2:28.6	2:29.8

Maclure	Hanson	Raph
(Riley)	(Alta)	(Delahaye)
2:30.4	2:32.2	2:36.4

Connell "didn't know any of the German drivers and I didn't try to speak to them. They were very much separate and their cars were all up at the farm buildings. I think I probably met von Brauchitsch. I do remember a chap called Charles Brackenbury, who used to do a lot of motor racing. He was a very odd character, hell of a drinker. I remember a film of when he put a joke thing – a sort of smoke bomb – on Neubauer's car and pointed a cine camera at the car: Neubauer got in and switched the ignition on and the whole thing vanished in smoke! I knew the French drivers a bit although Dreyfus was more American than French and he went to live in America afterwards. The atmosphere between the British drivers was always terribly good. One would do anything to help another driver – if they needed a part for their car and you happened to have it, you'd give it to them. There was always a lot of competition in the actual driving but not anything else. A wonderful spirit."

'Casque' in *The Autocar* applied the human touch. "The personal side of the race is great fun. That excellent little man, Nuvolari, always wears a small gold tortoise, given him by Gabriele d'Annunzio, and inscribed *To the fastest man in the world; the slowest animal in the world.* Hasse, who was a long-distance trials specialist, is supposed to have the largest appetite and needs the most sleep of any present-day driver (which is saying something in view of Dick Seaman's record for both these, especially the consumption of small sausages). Hasse is also captain of the local fire brigade of his home town. Kautz was up at Cambridge before he took to racing and, apart from ski-ing and mountain climbing, was to have made his name in literary circles; while, Bigalke, the Auto Union spare driver, is actually a doctor, so his medical progress takes second place to his racing career."

The Motor's 'Grande Vitesse' wrote that "Christian Kautz (Auto Union), dubbed 'Valentino,' is only 24, was at Cambridge and a very earnest student until motor racing seemed more exciting. Hobbies: Alpine climbing and ski-ing.

"Ulrich Bigalke, Auto Union reserve man, hasn't driven much yet, but he's a busy chap just the same. He looks after travelling arrangements, hotel reservations, time-keeps, takes films, runs-in the cars, practises and makes himself generally useful to the team. Has a doctor's degree and a pocketful of patents. In Italy the ladies call him 'Vesuvio'. My, my."

What chance had Cotton – of whom the official programme said "known to millions of radio listeners as a dance band leader of the first flight" – against this might? What chance Cotton's co-driver Wilkinson? What chance Maclure who "builds and tunes his own cars"? And Connell, "a motor engineer from Watford"? Or Hanson, "usually associated with a one and a half litre Maserati" which he'd driven "without any notable success"? Or Dobson, who *The Autocar* insisted had a youthful face "despite a moustache" and whose "hair is usually untidy and school-boyish"? Or the man referred to by his initial rather than first name – A. Cuddon-Fletcher – "tireless, scarcely ever misses a meeting up and down the country"?[15]

At 3.30 Naumann reported from the Black Boy: "Friday morning was not used for much training by the drivers but the sensation of the whole session was Hermann Lang because he managed what all the experts thought was impossible – he undercut the lap record of the 6-litre cars from last year and displaced Nuvolari's time of yesterday. Lang did 2m 11s, the best time of the whole training.

"Mercedes-Benz today tried out tyres and fuel consumption. Von Brauchitsch did not train at all while Seaman and Baumer only used the training car. Auto Union did very little. Nuvolari and Müller tried out their cars on full tanks. The last two participants have arrived, so the 19 are present."

Naumann added a postscript reminding Untertürkheim to make sure someone "please" make sure certain radio stations received the news. Yesterday the radio stations had been carrying news of Nuvolari's triumph – "now give that of Lang!"

At 5.30 Alfred Neubauer phoned a technical break-down of the three day's training. "The cars of von Brauchitsch, Seaman and Baumer ran without any fault. The transmission was right. The fuel consumption was 118–131 litres per 100 km. The oil consumption was not constant, with Baumer's car using 2.9 litres to von Brauchitsch's 7.2. The drivers became accustomed to the cars and the track very quickly and Baumer's starting lap was remarkable. The difficulties were with Lang's car. The compressor had the same defects as it did at Monza. As this car used an awful lot of oil – 12 litres per 100 kilometres – the compressor had to be changed. The funny thing is that Lang, with this weakest engine, did the best time.

"The training car covered 144 laps of 5 km and the race is 80. In Monza it covered 350 kilometres without any problems so that altogether it ran 1,070 kilometres before the engine gave up. We will have to find out why. Brake wear minimal, only the equivalent of 2 mm for the whole race. Overall, everything in order."

At 5.45 Naumann asked Untertürkheim to place calls to him the following day at 6pm and 7pm at the Black Boy so he could relay news of the race.

Before we leave these days of qualifying, there is a story so delicious it cannot be omitted, although the exact details are imprecise and the two accounts I have – one from Tich Allen, the other from Arthur Tyler – do not agree in every detail. On one of the qualifying days, Huhnlein arrived in a chauffeur-driven Mercedes at the gate at Coppice Farm. He was wearing his military uniform. He demanded the gate be opened so he could proceed along the inner road to the pit area to watch the cars. The gatekeeper had strict instructions from Craner that nobody was to be allowed in unless they had a pass or proper documentation. Huhnlein was so important as a senior member of the German Reich he must have felt he required neither. The gatekeeper remained adamant and Craner was sent for. "I don't care who you are," Craner said, "if you haven't got authority you can't come in." Eventually the German Embassy gave authorisation and Huhnlein went in but, as Tyler says, "until that came along Fred Craner was Fred Craner and he was the boss of the show, full stop."

That night the Germans were guests of Bertram Brown, the manager of the Nottingham Empire, where they met Billy Cotton and the Norwich and Ipswich soccer teams. Norwich were to play Chesterfield and Ipswich to play Notts County on the morrow. Perhaps von Brauchitsch had a long chat with them. Perhaps not.

Chapter 7

High noon

THE *VOLKISCHER BEOBACHTER* carried a headline which somehow caught the mood of the day in its directness and simplicity.

WHO WINS AT DONINGTON?

Beneath, a sub-heading announced

ALL EIGHT GERMAN CARS ON THE FRONT ROW.

The question of who will win causes a stir among people in England. Their favourite, their darling, is of course Seaman in a Mercedes-Benz, who counts among the leading drivers since he won the Grand Prix of Germany, and he already knows the difficult circuit.

But the situation is not as simple as that. On the last day of practice yesterday Lang took pole position and broke Nuvolari's record.

Von Brauchitsch is not among the favourites to win because he fell, hurting his left hand and thigh. Many a driver would have abandoned any idea of starting the race, but not Manfred, who is grimly determined to take up the fight.

Korpsführer Huhnlein will attend the race accompanied by strong interest from the British press. He is on a visit to London to hold negotiations on sport in the coming year. The race starts at 12pm.

Long before dawn, convoys left London for Donington: the Mercedes engineering staff at Grosvenor Road in a special bus, staff of the German Embassy in open Mercedes and BMWs. The dawn was fine but a thin, ethereal mist hovered over the parkland. It would melt into mellow, autumnal sunshine making the perfect day.

When Tazio Nuvolari awoke in his hotel room in Derby and arose, he put on – if his biographer Lurani is to be believed – his "lucky corset, which he had improvised for himself using tight bandages and nothing else." Then, presumably, he and the rest of the Auto Union team took breakfast at their leisure and prepared for the short journey to Donington.

Hamilton-James, who had been a time-keeper in 1937, would act as a marshal on this occasion. "We weren't paid anything, not a farthing. You had to make your own way to Donington and you had to make it back. From our house it was about 14 miles. A friend collected me and took me by car. We were expected to be there as soon after breakfast as we could and we had a meeting in the pit area as soon as we arrived. The chief marshal went round each person and said 'right, you will be a marshal at Red Gate' or whatever it was. I think there were ten marshals, one at each awkward corner. After this meeting you had to walk to your allocated corner carrying three flags: red, which was to stop everything, yellow to say *slow down*, green to say *the track is now clear*. You had to bring your own food – sandwiches."

Towards 10am the crowd began to arrive at the circuit's nine entrances in serious numbers although a steady flow had been seeping in since early morning when the mist still hung. Now, this inflow of vehicles became so heavy that the police were forced to divert the ordinary main road traffic travelling between Birmingham and Nottingham on to minor roads. Nor was all the behaviour of motorists trapped in the lumbering queues impeccable. Reports of the time speak about cutting-in, mad careering down the right-hand side of the road and the constant screeching of brakes as these drivers pulled up to escape collisions with oncoming traffic. A lorry driver had to take drastic avoiding action in an S-bend near Ashby to avoid a head-on collision. Elsewhere a driver did something extremely naughty. Cutting in, he'd banged another vehicle whose owner pulled off to examing the damage – and the driver immediately took his place. Dented wings and bumpers were common.

Cars routinely over-heated in those days, particularly if they were shuffling forward, and their steam created an autumnal mist of its own. Nor did over-heated cars help the smooth traffic flow...

Rob Walker (who after the war would run his own grand prix team, featuring Stirling Moss, no less) remembers the journey vividly because "I had a terrible banger. I used to be buying bangers one after another. My mother would give me a good car and I'd find it was too slow and I'd *go down one*: I'd buy a bigger, faster car but not of such good quality. And so on. And in this car I'd got pretty close to the bottom. It was a Talbot coupé and I think it cost about £10 or £12 – that was expensive. I bought one for half a crown [that's 12$\frac{1}{2}$p!] a Morgan three-wheeler and it wasn't very good, I bought another for £3 and that was excellent. Went on for years.

"I was at Cambridge and the drive up took, I think, something like two hours. One of our favourite tricks was that, if there was a big queue of cars, you'd let the one in front go on quite a long way and then you'd accelerate as fast as you could up to it, jam on your brakes. Behind you all the other cars would do the same and you'd heard squeak-squeak-squeak as they braked then *bang*! You know the ripple effect and how the braking increases as it travels back – and, of course, about the tenth car couldn't make the braking..."

Murray Walker was in the paddock, and overall he remembers being impressed by the "publicity material by the Germans, who were gigantically switched on and they handed you all sorts of photographs. They were give-away things. You know people do brass rubbings in churches – well, they gave you papier mache that you could put a piece of paper over and rub with a pencil and you got these beautiful pictures of the drivers and the cars. They had badges and brochures – things which did not exist in our world. Nuvolari had his little gold tortoise and Auto Union produced a limited run of those. I got given one, presumably through Joe Woodhouse. I wish I'd still got it..."

An 8-year-old, Robert Heelis, had gone with his father. "We parked our car at the side [of the circuit] and stood on the Melbourne Rise. I shall never forget it," he told the *Derby Evening Telegraph* in October 1998, the 60th anniversary of the race.

"The Mercedes team was billeted at Coppice Farm near Coppice Corner. I remember my father and I went over to the farm before the race to look at the cars and there were two German storm troopers on the gate in grey uniforms and pill box hats. They wouldn't let us in, so we went back after lunch when they were not around and went into the farmyard. I have some photographs of the cars and the team manager, Alfred Neubauer."

At 10.10 the Duke of Kent left RAF Northolt in a blue and red Airspeed Envoy flown by Wing-Commander Fielden. It arrived at Leicester Airport, Braunstone, at 10.45. As he descended from the plane accompanied by his equerry, Major Humphrey Butler, and a friend, Sir Stewart Duke-Elber, the Duke smiled warmly at the dignitaries assembled to greet him – the Chief Constable of Leicester, the Chief Constable of Leicestershire and the Chairman of the Council of the Leicestershire Aero Club. It was a time when titles were important and the presence of royalty – any royalty – bestowed an additional importance.

The formalities were quickly enacted and, within a minute of descending, the Duke had taken the wheel of a V12 Lagonda and was driving it towards Donington. (The owner of this car, a London doctor called John Benjafield – a vice-president of the British Racing Drivers' Club who'd won Le Mans in 1927 – had brought it to the airport specially for the Duke and now sat in the passenger seat. Butler and Duke-Elber followed in a second Lagonda.)

The Duke drove up through Charnwood Forest to Donington where, at this moment, the spectators' square, pug-nosed cars chugged in obedient, unhurried columns towards the wooden pay booths on the nine entries to the circuit; and, as they came, the sun filtered through the trees, spreading shadows of the cars onto the narrow roads which they choked as they chugged forward, lock step, to the booths.

The gatemen manning the entrances wore caps and uniforms. They operated a system to hasten entry: the gateman took money from the car drivers and passed it through a hatch to a cashier who handed back both a ticket and whatever change was due. Slowly, like a tide, Donington's seven huge and pastoral car parks were filling. *The Autocar* caught the gathering sense of urgency and anticipation when it described "the enormous procession of cars in the early morning going like blazes along all the roads towards Derby; the enormous congestion of traffic within a few miles of the course, and rows and rows of cars in turnip fields, farmyards, and every sort of improvised car park."

By 11am, an hour to go, many thousands of spectators – one estimate puts the figure at 20,000 – already lined the circuit at the most promising vantage points while, in a delicious (and slightly naughty anecdote) *The Motor* told of how "the paddock was full of Very Knowledgeable People, and all the Experts. Examining the cars were a gentleman and his wife. Presently they pulled up at the cockpit of a Mercedes-Benz. Said the lady: 'The speedometer only reads up to 90.' The gentleman, well known in technical circles, but unaware that racing cars have rev. counters and not speedometers, examined the instrument and replied: 'Ah! when it gets to 0, I expect it is doing the hundred.'"

The Duke of Kent arrived almost unnoticed but the public address system played the National Anthem and the crowd realised royalty must be present. A great cheer echoed round the parkland and thousands rushed to the railings to see Shields and Seaman being presented to the Duke. Then the Duke got into the Lagonda – on the back seat – and Seaman took the wheel, gave him a slow lap of the circuit so that it's main points could be explained. A couple of other saloon cars followed, Huhnlein in one.

The lap completed, Seaman gave the Duke a faster lap...

While the three saloons pretended to be racing cars, M. A. McEvoy, one of the four announcers for the race, welcomed the drivers over the public address in German and Italian.

The Lagonda drew up opposite the pits and a liveried chauffeur bounded towards it to open the doors, but the Duke was already out and opening the front door for Seaman, a breach of etiquette worthy of note then – and now, too. Seaman, wearing a mackintosh and what appeared to be his driving goggles hanging limply round his neck, shook the Duke's hand and they both smiled broadly, understanding why the etiquette had been breached: by this mute gesture of simply opening a door Seaman was being thanked for taking the Duke round.

He led the Duke to be introduced to the drivers but protocol demanded that Huhnlein be met first. Huhnlein, a chunky plumped figure encased in a heavy coat and with binoculars round his neck, shook the Duke's hand, retreated a step, stood stiff and gave the Nazi salute. A British police sergeant on the other side of the track, only marginally slimmer than Huhnlein, captured everything by a studious – and obvious – look of resignation and bemusement at this strange jerk of an arm by this German what's-his-name?

Murray Walker remembers "being very impressed by Huhnlein, who, unusually, was not wearing the 'normal' gear – breeches, brown boots, the military jacket and pill-box hat. They apparently thought that in England they had to wear civilian clothes. They all wore, I think, suits and overcoats – except Huhnlein, who was in tweeds."

Rene Dreyfus, whose Delahaye was on the third row, had already "met Huhnlein many times. I am not Jewish, you know, but half-Jewish – and it seemed the Nazis were always particularly nice to me. It appears ridiculous now but we did not realise what was going on…"

The Duke met Neubauer and Feuereissen, then the drivers. He adopted that precise air of benevolent curiosity which royalty wields, accompanied by a slight stooping towards the subject in question, when he spoke to Cotton who, hatless and wearing spectacles, already looked as full-faced as he would two decades later in the television age as a bandleader and much-loved national institution. Ian Connell remembers that the Duke "went round to all the English drivers and shook hands. It was just like royalty to handle such occasions – he had some little thing to say to each of us. I can't remember what it was."

The Duke also had a word with Craner who wore a sombre suit and waistcoat with its buttons all done up, a stiff collar and tie. He had closely cropped dark hair and a small toothbrush moustache. Small, almost stocky rather than chunky, he stood with his hands clasped rigidly behind his back listening.

At 11.40 mechanics drove the 17 cars from the garages "in slow procession down the course, a sight which set the crowd buzzing with excitement"[1] to their grid positions. The grid itself was a bustle of activity, people working, chatting, gesticulating, waiting.

The Mercedes mechanics (in white) and the Auto Union mechanics (in blue) fussed over their machines, dragged out the electric starters and positioned them.

Deft hands tied the strapping over the Maserati's bonnet.

Four swarthy mechanics were pushing a Delahaye into its place.

Other mechanics, working on cars on the grid, were tightening this and that. Hammers beat wheel-nuts tight. More and more bonnets were being strapped, leather passed through buckles and hauled taut.

Nuvolari wore a tweed jacket with pronounced lapels. A description holds him immortally "with his short, athletic figure, his carefully brushed iron-grey hair, and neat clothes."[2] He wore his usual canary-yellow sweater and blue overall trousers. He smiled a toothy smile, goggles stretched onto his forehead below the red leather helmet, the tortoise hanging above the thin sweater.

Connell was no doubt typical of the Britons. "I didn't always wear overalls, but I did for a Grand Prix. I had white ones, the kind you'd paint the house in. You wore ordinary trousers and a shirt underneath. What I had on my feet varied. That might be plimsolls but some cars got terribly hot on the feet and I'd have on a pair of old black lace-up shoes. The leather soles stopped some of the heat of the pedals coming through.

"I wore a crash helmet and visor. I've needed glasses since I was about 20 and I used to have goggles with lenses in them but that proved highly unsatisfactory because you'd get mud or whatever over them and they were terribly difficult to keep clean. It was much more convenient to wear ordinary glasses with a visor: you could always keep the visor clean by wiping it with your glove. I didn't wear gloves for short races but I did for longer ones. Even in an ERA you had a lot of kick in the steering. The gloves were ordinary leather driving gloves" – such as everyday motorists had.[3]

"How did I approach such a race, knowing it might be dangerous? One just used to love the racing and the whole atmosphere of racing. I don't think it was entirely speed. I don't know quite what it really was: having control of a very fast car, I suppose..."

The Autocar team, headed by their experienced sports editor Sammy Davis, were deployed, John Dugdale among them. Dugdale explains that the regular column Davis wrote – THE SPORT under the pen name 'Casque' (French for helmet) – "had to be read by everybody because Davis knew everybody. I was his number 2. As you are aware, there are always an enormous number of freeloaders at these big races and a great range of passes available. As a journalist there would be a straightforward Press pass, then one for the pit area, then one so you could walk on the track." This was not as death-defying as it sounds. It meant that such as Dugdale could wander among the cars on the grid, which he profited from by taking pictures.

Meanwhile an *Autocar* reporter, C.S. Watkinson, had taken up position at the Hairpin bend – just before the stone bridge – and recorded that "everyone was listening intently to the announcements which came from the loud speakers." Watkinson would be one of the great witnesses of the race and its unfolding drama.

By now some 60,000 people, Captain George Eyston among them, were spread round the ribbon of track through the woodland and parkland. One estimate suggests that 20,000 were in the vicinity of the grid and the pits, some of them very fashionably dressed. One report insisted that the "smart costumes and coats, as well as hats, would have compared favourably with many a special parade of feminine wear."

The drivers got into their cars and covered a warm-up lap. As they reached the grid, three officials – almost scampering – directed them to their places. Once Lang was stationary a mechanic trotted up to his car and put a little choc under the left rear wheel to stop it rolling forwards. Mechanics made last-minute adjustments to the other cars and the Duke smiled benignly on it all.

Ebblewhite positioned himself in front of the grid on the opposite side of the track to the pits. The Duke stood next to him holding a Union Jack on a stick. Behind an agriculteral stockade of wooden palings, the crowd craned and leant and took pictures of them with box cameras.

On a more pragmatic level, the bookmakers were present in force and had Nuvolari as the 2 to 1 favourite, the three Mercedes drivers alongside him on the front row each at 3 to 1.[4]

The photographer, Klemantaski, said "there were two lots of crowds: the people who knew something about it but also, I think, the newspapers had whipped up such a thing about the German cars that there were a whole lot of new people just come to see what all the fuss was about."

A four-minute board was hoisted, the bustle all across the grid continuing.

A three-minute board was hoisted, and still the bustle.

A two-minute board was hoisted, and Seaman – white overalls, green helmet – bedded himself into the cramped cockpit space, a mechanic in a cloth cap holding his steering wheel aloft but ready, so that when Seaman had finished a sequence of taut body-movements – part fidgets, part settling – the wheel was attached.

Müller smiled bleakly towards a roving cine camera – nerves, maybe; Kautz, wearing a white skull cap and flared goggles, seemed lost in the moment, his thoughts visibly elsewhere. His gloved hands briefly touched his steering wheel in a caress, a reassurance, a mannerism. Von Brauchitsch wore a red cap, Lang white, Baumer blue.

Deep within the Delahaye cockpit Raph adjusted the strap of his goggles, adjusted the lenses of the goggles themselves and then buried his hands somewhere under the steering wheel, out of sight. Villoresi seemed regal – a glance to the roving camera showed that – as he adjusted his goggles, touched his steering wheel, adjusted his goggles again; but within his body-movement was a certain arrogance of certainty. *This is what I have chosen to do with my life.*

The British looked terribly British, Dobson with a little moustache and a big visor – not goggles – and what appeared to be a smooth, shining crash helmet. He gazed stoically straight ahead. Maclure – a pinched, boyish face and short, spiky hair – was bare-headed except for his goggles which he pressed into place with a sneak of a smile. He wore no driving gloves.

Cotton was pulling his lucky glove – made from rabbit's fur – on to his right hand. In the pits Wilkinson had his little black cat mascot safe in a pocket. They'd already discussed and agreed on their race strategy. Wilkinson explains that, if Cotton took the first stint, "I'd signal him in after so many laps. The car had to be filled up with petrol and that sort of thing. We worked out how many miles to the gallon – not very many! – and said *well, let's change over on a specified lap.* I'd stand in the pits ready and give him signals for three laps – to make sure he saw, because it's easy to miss one signal." It went *1,* next lap *2,* next lap *3,* then he'd pull in, they'd fill her up, "get the flies off the windscreen and one thing and another, I'd get in and go out."

Nuvolari had been the last to clamber into his cockpit. He was heard to murmur "I keep hearing people say I am too old. I want to assert myself against the young again."

They faced 80 laps, a distance of 250 miles.

A one-minute board was hoisted and all the engines except those of the Mercedes were fired. The engines made a low noise rising to a bellow. With exactly 30 seconds to go the four Mercedes engines – three on the front row, one on the second – were fired. "The portable electric starters whir, the air shakes with the roaring song of the eight German cars, the British cars seem silent in that din. The crowd goes dumb."[5]

From afar, Watkinson suddenly heard "a distant roar of engine waking to life. From the loudspeakers came the warning *there is just half a minute to go*." The mechanics scampered off, carting the starting devices with them.

Ebblewhite nursed a substantial timing device crooked in his left hand. The Duke, next to him, held the Union Jack in his right hand and upward with a sort of flourish: the same shape as a Nazi salute but a different angle and a posture. It was formal, not aggressive in any way. Ebblewhite moved into this final countdown aloud:

"Ten ... nine ... eight ... seven ... six ... five ... four ... three ..."

He cocked his right hand above the Duke's shoulder, ready to give the tap which would be the signal.

"Two ... one."

He tapped the Duke's upper arm and the Duke let the flag fall in a swift scythe of a motion, the flag cleaving the air. Helplessly, instinctively – like any of the crowd – the Duke glanced right towards the rigidity of the grid which he'd just dissolved and the fury which he'd just unleashed.

Lang watched the flag carefully and as he saw it fall "let in the clutch but I did not have enough revs. The engine tried to stall which let several drivers past me. I cursed furiously. *Like a beginner*, I said to myself."[6]

Viewed head-on, a spread of cars exhaled smoke and fumes as they gorged their power on the gentle rise to Red Gate corner, the sharp left. Fleeing from the grid towards this, they came past a string of cameramen who were positioned, like sentries and unprotected, along the front of the pits.

Nuvolari had the power on quickest and already – perhaps twenty metres from the start – was clear "as if catapulted,"[7] angling the Auto Union over to assume the racing line for Red Gate. Sebastian described it as a "wonderful start" – adding that Müller made one, too. By the Dunlop Bridge, some fifty yards after Red Gate, Nuvolari had created a gap to the pursuing pack.

The ERAs revved to 6,500 and as Connell approached that in first gear he was doing 77 miles an hour, then 88 in second, then 110 in third. "Up to about 60 miles an hour you could spin the wheels of an ERA the same as the Auto Unions and Mercedes could spin theirs – although they could keep on spinning, I suppose, to 100. I once asked Dick Seaman what it was like driving a Merc and he replied *like driving on ice with such a lack of grip from the wheels and all that acceleration.*"

Down in his lair at the Hairpin, Watkinson heard a "dramatic cry" over the loudspeakers, *they're off and Nuvolari leads*. He couldn't see anything yet but he strained towards the sound and the fury which, within an instant or two, would be coming at him like rolling thunder.

Nuvolari turned into Red Gate, the pack – led by Müller, von Brauchitsch, Seaman and Lang – jostling and adjusting behind him. Dobson was the first of the British cars, although how far back is difficult to determine. Maclure ran last.

The Duke of Kent moved to a special royal box in the grandstand and was greeted by another thunderous cheer.

Nuvolari led Müller by a hundred yards.

Watkinson recorded "an expectant hush" falling on the crowd "as we waited for the first car to appear from Holly Wood, and soon it came. It was just a silver bullet, speeding its way round the left-hand curve that leads down to where I was standing, and behind it at a short distance were others, radiators-to-tail, all fighting for mastery. It was indeed Nuvolari who was leading. There was a glimpse of a slithering, silver car – at the wheel a lithe little figure, looking almost demoniacal, with red helmet and bright yellow jersey. Behind him came Müller, Brauchitsch, Lang, Seaman and then Baumer, one after another, so that it was difficult to tell Mercedes from Auto Union. I must admit that my heart stood still at the sight of these cars."

The Light Car recorded that "through Holly Wood and down the winding slope that follows they tore, and up the short rise to the awkwardly cambered Hairpin Bend, where Nuvolari was a clear fifty yards ahead with Müller hot on his heels, and the three Mercedes of Brauchitsch, Lang and Seaman just behind. So it remained round the rest of the circuit – through the Stone Bridge, into Coppice Wood with its sharp right-hand, McLean's and Coppice corners, out on to Starkey's Straight (where the leaders screamed along the slightly undulating, slightly curving road at over 150 mph) down the sharp descent to Melbourne Corner, where the circuit doubles back on itself, and so up and past the pits ..."

The Autocar recorded that "the silver speck that was Nuvolari's car flashed over the top of the hill on the far side of the course [Starkey's Straight], shot down to Melbourne at a terrific speed and, handled with wonderful judgement, took that corner in one neat, beautiful swing, so well controlled that it appeared quite slow, then accelerated like a flash up the hill to complete the lap."

Completing it, Nuvolari was several car lengths ahead of Müller giving, overall, a first lap race order of Nuvolari, Müller, von Brauchitsch, Seaman, Lang, Baumer, Hasse and Kautz with Dreyfus the first of the non-German cars, Dobson tight onto him, Villoresi tight onto Dobson, then Connell, Cuddon-Fletcher, Raph, Cotton, Hanson and "finally the indomitable Percy Maclure, hopelessly outclassed with the Riley."[8]

Sebastian wrote that "very excited we watch the race. How long will our drivers be able to withstand the onslaught of the Mercedes-Benz team?"

The order at the front endured through the lap 2, Nuvolari leading by five seconds now although the whole circuit was "singing with sound and the almondy, boot-polish fuel fumes became quite pungent."[9] The order at the back shifted and altered. Villoresi, recovering from his poor start, passed Dreyfus and Dobson, while Cotton had also gained two places and Raph had overtaken Fletcher.

On lap 3 Kautz arrived at Coppice Corner too fast and braked desperately. His wheels locked and plumes of smoke billowed from the front tyres. The Auto Union plunged through the fence and became enmeshed in straw bales. Kautz managed to reverse onto the circuit and struggled as far as Melbourne when the throttle stuck open. He went straight off across grass and, still doing around 40 mph, battered into some banking and flattened a section of wooden pailings beyond. He climbed out unhurt and, visibly disconsolate, walked back to the pits. The fact that he'd had a streaming cold for days and/or tummy trouble couldn't have helped.

'Grande Vitesse' poured out commiserations to Kautz. "That boy gets fearfully worked up before a race, added to which he was ill, having eaten something which went wrong. Last time I saw him was at Rheims, and then before the race [at Donington] he was all a-twitter – and upset on the first corner. I think his crashes were probably due to nothing but excess zeal. From an examination of the bent car it looks as if Chris came down Melbourne slope and changed into a higher gear instead of a lower one, and went a good deal too quickly in consequence. There is also the possibility that the throttle was jamming."

Sebastian wrote that the Kautz crash was "the first blow to shake our confidence."

At the end of that lap 3 Raph brought the Delahaye into the pits with a gale of smoke coming from the engine. He had an oil leak. The bonnet was removed and he went out again.

On lap 4 Baumer slid wide at the Hairpin, scattering earth in all directions while Seaman took von Brauchitsch to be third. Crossing the line, Nuvolari had extended his lead to a quarter of a mile from Müller, who had a 300-yard gap to Seaman, von Brauchitsch close behind.

On lap 5 at the Hairpin, all the Mercedes "scraped the verge, once more scattering earth and grass."[10] Nuvolari was pulling away from Müller, who was pursued by Seaman, von Brauchitsch, Lang, Baumer, Hasse, Villoresi, Dreyfus and Dobson.

On lap 6 Nuvolari lapped Maclure – which, because the race was over 60 laps, emphasised the disparity between the German cars and such as the Rileys. In covering 18 miles Nuvolari had gained *three miles* on Maclure. Connell explains the context. "The German cars, one knew, did 200 miles an hour in normal racing trim [well, not the 3-litre cars]. The top speed of the ERA was about 135 – perhaps 140 if you had the wind behind you! On the straight at the back of the Donington circuit we reached the 135 and, of course, it was downhill at that point. There was a hell of a difference between us and the Germans – not so much in cornering or initial acceleration but in straight line speed."

Villoresi overtook both Baumer and Hasse to run sixth – Baumer, inexperienced, looked "wild" in the corners and was losing time there. Seaman, trying to hold off von Brauchitsch, ran wide at the hairpin and went full onto the grass. The car bucked and dug into the dirt as he grappled with it. Just before it struck straw bales he'd regained control and angled the car on to the track.

Watkinson happened to be standing outside the announcer's box and "ran for my life when Seaman shot off on to the grass verge and careered straight for the ditch. By sheer mastery he got the car round and was back on the course just before he reached the stone bridge."

On lap 7 the order of the front-runners was: Nuvolari, Müller, Seaman, von Brauchitsch, Lang, Villoresi, Hasse, Baumer, and Dreyfus.

On lap 8 Raph pitted again so that oil could be wiped off the exhaust pipe because the fumes were making it difficult for him to breathe. He emerged from the pits again and pressed on but the Delahaye was clearly wounded. Lang overtook von Brauchitsch and hustled on towards Seaman.

On lap 9 the order had steadied to: Nuvolari, Müller, Seaman, Lang, von Brauchitsch, Villoresi, Baumer, Hasse, Dreyfus and Dobson and, a lap later, Raph retired having lost oil pressure completely. The leading positions:

Nuvolari	averaging 81.57 mph
Müller	at 14.6 seconds
Seaman	at 15.8 seconds
Lang	at 22 seconds
von Brauchitsch	at 30 seconds

On lap 12 Maclure's Riley broke a half-shaft on the rise from Melbourne Corner and toured slowly up the side of the track towards the pits while the German cars shrieked past him. As he toured, he might have reflected on how the £250 prize from the British Motor Race Organisers' Association had gone from him now. After Dobson – tenth and lapping at about 76 mph – came Cotton, Connell and Cuddon-Fletcher. Cotton was having a lively race, once almost losing control at Coppice as his little ERA slewed away from him.

On lap 13 Nuvolari lapped Dobson, who had been going hard behind Dreyfus – hard enough that Dreyfus couldn't shake him off. The order at the front remained constant although, in mid-field, Hasse overtook Baumer, the first significant passing move of the race.

On lap 15 Villoresi was sixth, in front of Hasse and Baumer. Wilkinson held out a pit board to Cotton, with all the usual information on it and the figure *1*. A lap later, while Nuvolari lapped Dreyfus, Villoresi forced his red Maserati past von Brauchitsch and Wilkinson held out a pit board to Cotton with the figure *2*.

On lap 17 Cuddon-Fletcher overshot Melbourne Corner and crashed into the banking near the abandoned Auto Union of Kautz. The MG bounced on impact and, when it came to rest, Cuddon-Fletcher sprang from it immediately. Wilkinson held out *3*.

A lap later Müller, Seaman and Lang arrived at Melbourne Corner together. Seaman pulled ahead of Müller and angled his car over to the outside and prepared to turn in to take the racing line for the corner. Lang elbowed a path down the inside and his left front wheel banged Seaman's right rear, pitching Seaman across the track.[11] All three kept on. Cotton (who reportedly had a hand injury, although that doesn't seem to have disturbed the agreed race plan) came in and handed the ERA over to Wilkinson. The car was refuelled, the stop lasting 50 seconds.

Villoresi's race was run. Smoke poured from the Maserati as it slowed round Melbourne Corner then limped up the incline, over the brow and into the pits. "When he blipped the throttle as he coasted in ominous white clouds came from the exhaust. Mechanics hardly needed to take out the plugs to find the cause – a piston."[12]

On lap 20 Müller went into a broadside at Melbourne Corner in front of Seaman but clung on to second place. These front-runners were averaging around 80 mph although an impression was forming that Lang – still fourth – might have speed in reserve. He seemed to be waiting, poised to make a move when he judged the time right. Von Brauchitsch had fallen a long way behind Lang and gave a very different impression – "thoroughly out of form and causing some speculation by carrying on an almost continuous gesticular conversation with his pit."[13] Baumer remained "wild" in the corners. The leading positions:

Nuvolari	averaging 82.07 mph
Müller	at 21.8 seconds
Seaman	at 22.6 seconds
Lang	at 26.8 seconds
von Brauchitsch	at 1m 6 seconds

It was 1 o'clock and all over Germany the radio station *Deutschlandsender* was transmitting a bulletin of the race which began "after 20 laps – a quarter of the total distance – Nuvolari in an Auto Union leads by 300 metres from Müller." The bulletin ended: "We will be coming back at 3.10 with a further report from the Donington race. We expect the race to finish between 3.30 and 3.35."

Wilkinson discovered that the German cars "couldn't use their power in the corners because if they had, they'd have spun. The ERA didn't have so much power, which meant that what it did have you could put straight on to the road. So you could hold them in the corners more or less, but not anywhere else – and, even if you'd tried, the marshals would have put the flags up [*faster car behind, get out of the way*!] You pulled over and let them past anyway, because otherwise it would have been too dangerous. And, on top of that, you played the game. When they were overtaking, with the speed difference, it did create turbulence in the air. You felt it, oh yes. You felt as if you were going *through* something. It happened when the chap had gone by – just after. It was a hole in the air which they had created and you were now in. It didn't worry me, though. But the noise those cars made – you really wanted ear-plugs."

Watkinson recorded that "my outstanding recollections of the first hour were of the Auto Unions cornering steadily as a rock – while the Mercedes, as regularly as clockwork, lifted first the nearside front wheel six inches off the ground and then, as they slid and were corrected, the tail came down with an audible thump on the back springs."

Connell adds a tactical insight. "Donington was a very *convenient* circuit in the sense that you had the Melbourne Corner. I would be coming up the hill *from* it while a Mercedes or Auto Union was going down the hill *into* it and I could see across to where the German car was. I therefore knew when it would have caught and overtaken me – they would always catch up that sort of amount within the next lap. You wouldn't hear them coming because your own exhaust was so noisy. You weren't going to get in the way of someone that much faster than yourself. You weren't dicing! There was a bump at the top of the hill, sometimes I'd be passed there and it was a lovely sight: they'd take off just in front of me. I didn't take off myself. I wasn't going fast enough..."

On lap 23 Dreyfus brought his Delahaye into the pits, spoke a few simple words to the mechanics and "disconsolately took off his helmet. That was that – a broken oil pipe."[14] Nearby, a Mercedes mechanic held out a "large funnel to Seaman, conveying a message which it was impossible to interpret."[15]

On lap 24, amidst the sound and the fury, those who listened closely could hear Nuvolari's engine misfiring slightly. Sebastian caught the moment: "Nuvolari passes the pits. Something is wrong with his engine. We look at each other." Two laps later Nuvolari was visibly losing ground.

One of the enduring, infuriating fascinations of motorsport is that highly stressed machines may fail at any instant, and this gives every race an intrinsic uncertainty. A driver may use all his skill, nerve and speed to create a strong position and have it reduced to nothing by a single errant part. Some of the greatest drives have been constructed around recovering the time lost in such a crisis.

The crowd watched "anxiously" and "yes, no doubt, the leader was slowing. As the neat machine came into its pit there was an almost audible groan of sympathy."[16] In fact the crowd's emotions were drawn two ways because, apart from the sympathy, Nuvolari was given a great yell of acclaim for what he'd been doing.

A plug had burnt out.

It would create not just a great drive but one which has passed into legend.

Sebastian "tore off the bonnet "[17] and a mechanic held it "expectantly"[18] above the engine while this single plug was being changed "quickly" by Sebastian. "Meanwhile my assistant Fritz fills up the petrol tank."[19] Nuvolari sat calmly at the wheel although at one point, it seems, he stood up in the cockpit – perhaps to see how the work was progressing.

Müller went by.

Seaman went by.

Lang went by.

The car had been stationary for 53 seconds and Nuvolari rejoined in fourth place. It was lap 27, and the hunt and chase of legend had begun. Nuvolari needed to regain more than a minute – the plug had reduced his speed and cost time, he'd had to slow further as he pitted, lost the 53 seconds stationary and lost a little more accelerating up to top speed. The pace was intense enough already, the Mercedes and Auto Unions "passing the ERAs in all sorts of impossible places and sending the onlookers into fits by their immense cornering and terrific rush downhill to the Hairpin."[20]

Whenever Nuvolari wanted to overtake a slower car he "waved one hand to the flag marshals, they gave the signal, the other driver pulled over, and Nuvolari went by. The system worked like a charm – but imagine taking one hand off at over 90 mph down the bumpy hill to the Hairpin! I ask you!"[21]

However, the father of one of today's leading British motorsport writers, Nigel Roebuck, vividly remembers Nuvolari beating his fist against the side of the Auto Union in impatience whenever he was held up. The leading positions: Müller with Seaman close enough to press, Lang then Nuvolari – and Seaman lapped Cotton by "neatly slipping past as they shot under the Stone Bridge. Wow!"[22]

On lap 29 Dobson brought his ERA in to refuel and it took 68 seconds.

At 30 laps the leading positions were:

Müller	averaging 80.10 mph
Seaman	at 2.8 seconds
Lang	at 4 seconds
Nuvolari	at 59.4 seconds
von Brauchitsch	at 1m 32.8s

Hanson, whose Alta was so slow he'd only covered 25 laps, pitted for five gallons of petrol and one gallon of oil. He emerged and as he descended the hill out of Holly Wood a con rod broke and "pounded holes in the sump, distributing the nice new oil he had just added on [and before] the left-hand bend."[23] The Alta slithered through this left and Hanson pressed on round the Hairpin. He pulled off on to the grass verge just before the Stone Bridge. Hanson was by no means a top driver and he had altered the race completely, almost destroying it.

Rob Walker was among the spectators witnessing this. "The only protection was a tree which I hid behind occasionally!" Walker hadn't realised that Hanson had blown up, but he would realise very, very soon.

Coming down from Holly Wood, the track resembled an uncoiling snake. The corner where the oil lay was more of a curve, which straightened into the track, dipped a little there before rising to the Hairpin, a hard uphill right. All the way down the right-hand side of the snake ran a wide, slightly hump-shaped grass verge. Down the left-hand side was a narrower strip of grass flanking the curve, then a copse of tall trees with a wooden programme hut nestled at the edge of it, then a broader verge bordered by a ditch, a bank and pailings. This ran along to the Hairpin.

Watkinson heard the "roar of an Auto Union and I looked back towards Holly Wood. I saw Nuvolari."

This heavy metal car and its driver – no crash helmet, no roll bar, no

safety belts – were travelling at 80 mph down the hill towards the oil.
Nuvolari's life was very much in danger.

Nuvolari "sensed something wrong"[24] and steered away from the
biggest patch of oil but he was skating now and "quite unable to take the
corner. Being Nuvolari, he didn't try but allowed the Auto Union to shoot
off the road and tear down the hill on the grass in a series of high-speed
slides."

Nuvolari's thinking: *don't fight the car because that could be dangerous,
let it go where it is going and* then *harness it.*

Like so many instants of great driving, this was also an example of
instantaneous, controlled and logical thinking.

Watkinson watched the car swerve "violently off the course on to the
grass on the right and stagger like some drunken man all the way down to
the bend. Somehow the little Mantuan got round, and after another wild
swerve on to the grass he [stayed on the track and] disappeared into Coppice
Wood."

Throughout, Nuvolari smiled. He must have been very calm and, because
of his experience and speed of reaction, must also have been perfectly aware
of everything which was happening.

An official, positioned at the side of the track, waved a yellow flag
conveying DANGER AHEAD – the other cars were coming round, coming
round, von Brauchitsch already on the descent from Holly Wood. He hit the
oil and "got into a series of wild slides just off the road and back, spun
round twice on the road, arrived sideways at the Hairpin"[25] but somehow
wrestled the Mercedes round. He'd gone off "more or less in Nuvolari's
tracks, but regained the road sooner" before his double rotation, arriving at
the Hairpin "in a terrific broadside."[26]

Then came Hasse, and for him there would be no escape. His Auto Union
veered right and he grappled the steering wheel to correct that, braking
violently at the same time and digging smoke from the rear wheels. The car
was on a carousel ride and spun as – completely out of control – it fled
across to the other side of the track where it just missed a tree and, pointing
backwards, tore down 15 feet of wooden pailings round the programme
kiosk, where Fred Craner's wife was.

"It looked as if he was making for the somewhat flimsily constructed box
which is sometimes used for broadcasting. Observing this impending
calamity, Mrs Craner, who was standing at the door, exclaimed 'I think he is
coming in here' – *and shut the door.*"[27]

Past the kiosk the car slithered on the grassy verge and, still backwards,
thundered into the ditch near a five-bar gate set into the pailings. It sent
the spectators behind it scattering. The impact of the ditch and bank was
so fierce that the car twisted round again and, marooned, faced the right
way.

Once the car was motionless Hasse levered himself urgently out and
scampered clear because other helpless cars could be arriving any second
now. In his haste he put one foot into the ditch and fell headlong. As he rose,

a dozen hands from behind the pailings reached down to try to help him. He was clearly trying to get to safety but, as Walker says, "at the pace these cars were doing, a little fence wouldn't have protected him – or other spectators – much."

The race commentary, echoing round Donington through loudspeakers, had become so excited it was briefly unintelligible.

Then came Seaman with Lang behind, and an ERA behind that. Seaman didn't appear to have seen the yellow flag and scudded off onto the hump of grass ahead and to the right side of the track. He rode the hump but it was so steep that the Mercedes bounced as it regained the track. Then the Mercedes sped across, the rear tyres smoking, and came to rest about ten yards from Hasse's Auto Union – but, crucially, before it reached the ditch. The engine had stalled.

Rob Walker was "sort of peeking out from behind the tree because the cars were travelling so fast and seemed to be going off in all directions. Just skating. Seaman went off right in front of me and stopped. Nuvolari had been fantastic. I'll never forget that performance of his when he hit the oil, got broadside, went broadside for, oh, nearly quarter of a mile. Then he got to the corner at the bottom, notched one gear down and continued in the direction in which he had been facing."

Into the left Lang fishtailed, a rear wheel off the track and gouging a shower of soil. Lang caught the fishtail and dragged the car straight, continued round the Hairpin; and the ERA. continued, too, a square, stubby yet somehow stately vehicle proceeding at its own pace. It hadn't even wobbled on the oil.[28]

Then came Baumer whose Mercedes flicked nearly sideways, his tyres smoking. He caught the flick with two wheels on the grassy hump and drove on towards the Hairpin.

Wilkinson, who'd taken over from Cotton, came "over the brow of the hill at the top and it was downhill very fast. I could see cars flying all over the place so I eased off. I couldn't brake too hard – that would upset my driving. I skidded about when I reached the oil and you had to steer the car hard *like that*" – arms sawing at the wheel. "I could see Hasse's car to one side in the ditch. You didn't think someone might have been badly hurt, not really. You were just thinking about yourself, what's going on, getting out of trouble..."

"Seaman shouted to the crowd not to touch the car and tried to manhandle it himself. An official said it was all right for officials to assist, and Dick shouted for them to push. Eventually he restarted amidst great cheering."[29] Seaman having tried unsuccessfully to push the car himself, using the right rear wheel, then stood while several officials sprinted towards him. He got back in and four of the officials – three at the back, one at the side – shoved the Mercedes across the grass and back on to the track.

Seaman had lost a lap.

Neubauer, in his memoires, claims to have been able to see what happened. "The next in the queue was Dick Seaman. I had my fingers crossed. I could see Erica close her eyes in horror. The car slithered through the oil like an ice-skating star and landed with a thud on the grass beside the track. But I realised to my disgust that his engine had cut out. Racing-cars have no self-starters. The electric starters are kept in the pits. So there was only one thing young Dick Seaman could do: push. No easy task, because the driver is forbidden to accept any help. I saw him switch on the ignition and push the car back on to the track. He jumped back into the cockpit, put the car in fifth gear and steered it down the slight incline of the track. With a bit of a luck two or three of the 12 cylinders would respond. And they did. At the first splutter from the engine he changed quickly to fourth, third, then second gear and opened his throttle. The engine roared into life and he was off."[30]

By the time Seaman was back in the race, Watkinson recorded that "the oil danger had been counteracted by the officials and, once more, we on the Hairpin bend reverted to normal." What the officials did is completely unrecorded.

The order had become: Müller (leading Lang by five seconds), Nuvolari, von Brauchitsch, Baumer, Seaman, Dobson, Connell and Wilkinson. Lang closed up on Müller and might have been toying with him.

Von Brauchitsch feels he was "lucky" to get through the oil but overall "my injuries were handicapping me."

The pit stops began on lap 38. Neubauer had a black and red St George's Cross flag to give signals to his drivers and he used it to bring Lang in for fuel. An official stood motionless, legs apart, holding a red flag held like a matador's cape so that Lang would know where to halt: directly in front of him. As Lang halted, Neubauer trotted up towards him and the refuelling crew moved three or four urgent paces to the car. Lang whipped off his goggles and was handed a clean pair. A front tyre lay nearby – but none of the mechanics went near it. Neubauer fussed and seemed, for an instant, to dip towards Lang and say something to him. As the fuel rig was ready, a protective sheet was held across Lang's head and shoulders for protection in case of any spilt fuel – the tank was right behind him.

The Mercedes had a capacity of 88 gallons and the refuelling pressure system normally delivered five gallons a second. Lang did not take on fresh tyres, presumably because he didn't need them. That's why the front tyre lay neglected. A mechanic rubbed the tiny windscreen clean with a cloth. The car was stationary for 33 seconds, which remains a minor puzzle because the pressure system ought to have filled the tank in under 18 seconds. One report judged that the pit stop took a "comparatively" long time.

Lang set off furiously, getting enough wheel-spin to have smoke pouring from the tyres. "The splash-cover was forgotten in the excitement and Lang flung it clear as he accelerated away."[31] He'd held second place.

The next lap von Brauchitsch pitted and his stop took 29 seconds, costing him fourth place. As the fuel went in he cleaned his windscreen carefully.

Connell pitted and handed his ERA over to his reserve driver Peter Monkhouse, who needed a cushion to enable him to reach the pedals comfortably.[32] At lap 40 – half distance – the leading positions were:

Müller	averaging 80.07 mph
Lang	at 48.4 seconds
Nuvolari	at 58 seconds
Baumer	at 2m 30.2s
von Brauchitsch	at 2m 39.4s

These were followed by Seaman, Dobson, Wilkinson and Monkhouse. Nuvolari now started to go faster and faster, but his own pit stop approached.

On this lap – half distance – the Auto Union flag, the Cross of St Andrews, brought Müller in for fuel and new rear tyres. He was stationary for 40 seconds and, as he moved off, Lang went past. A Mercedes led the race for the first time.

On lap 41 Baumer came in for fuel and had the plugs tested. That cost him 79 seconds. Seaman was in, too, and his stop – fuel only – cost 44 seconds. He was positioned behind Baumer. Neubauer, held by restless movement skirted Seaman's car. A mechanic, whose white uniform appeared almost surgical, walked up and down with his hands clasped behind his back, stopped by the left rear tyre and felt it for wear, walked on. Seaman gestured, *fresh goggles, fresh goggles!* and a mechanic handed him a pair. He hoisted them over the crown of his head and let them rest on his forehead. Neubauer fidgeted. Seaman pulled away – and Baumer was back out, too.

On lap 42 Nuvolari came in, sprang out of the cockpit and circled the car as if he was trying to dissipate some great restless energy. Almost feverishly he rubbed the lenses of his goggles with a bit of cloth. His stop for fuel and four new tyres was completed in 35 seconds, a time considered a genuine feat. Sebastian records how Müller's stop had been fast but Nuvolari's "even faster, although I quickly adjusted his clutch." Nuvolari set off in a cloud of dust. The hunt and the chase were really on.

Nuvolari "rolled his sleeves up and, roaring with laughter, set about motor racing in earnest. He came through the bends with his elbows flashing up and down like pistons, the steering wheel jerking quickly from side to side – and yet all the time the car ran as if on rails, the front wheels always pointing dead on the line of travel."[33] His yellow shirt fluttered and billowed in the wind, his red cap kept darting forward. At the age of 46, and within a month of his 47th birthday, he was truly going to assert himself against the young again.

This was the situation: Lang in the lead, Müller at just over 40 seconds, Nuvolari at 58 seconds (still!), von Brauchitsch at 1 minute 58 seconds, then Seaman and Baumer, but on lap 43 Baumer was travelling slowly up from Melbourne Corner towards the pits, flames visible beneath the bonnet. "As it breasted the rise a dull glow broke out round the engine and the car was on fire properly as it got to the pits."[34]

Baumer "clambered up in the seat. As the car stopped he leapt out, mechanics with fire extinguishers surrounded the car and the blaze."[35] Baumer leapt to the left and two mechanics gripped the car, hauling it to rest. The bonnet was very, very hot – a mechanic tried to open it and as his hand touched the metal it instantly recoiled. Uhlenhaut stood motionless three or four feet away, watching. The mechanics levered the bonnet open and a fire extinguisher was emptied into it. Through the smoke, Neubauer used his flagpole to direct operations, pointing to this and that. As the smoke billowed, Uhlenhaut took several discreet steps backwards, then stood motionless again, hands in his trouser pockets. The car was pushed away, a mechanic leaning in to steer it. Baumer went out to the little area behind his pit and stood amidst heaps of tyres while someone doused his face and forehead with a damp sponge.

Dobson thus inherited Baumer's sixth place – a British car in the top six for the first time. Far, far away at the other end of the race Müller was slowing and Nuvolari gained on him, setting a new fastest lap of 82.72 mph. The leading positions at 50 laps were:

Lang	averaging 78.77 mph
Müller	at 40.6 seconds
Nuvolari	at 58 seconds
von Brauchitsch	at 1m 58s
Seaman	at 2m 48.2s

Nuvolari sustained his attack and when Müller pitted for plugs on lap 53 he was into second place, the gap to Lang at some 39 seconds. "Thereafter, round after round, Nuvolari gained with triumphant ease on Lang."[36] Wilkinson pitted and handed the car back to Cotton.

Barely noticed, as the hunt intensified, was Dobson pitting for more fuel on lap 58. It cost him 61 seconds. Not that that mattered to the real structure of the race; what did matter was that Lang had literally hit trouble.

"I was just about to pass [lap] a car in front when a stone from its rear wheel shattered my aero-screen [windscreen]," Lang would write. "Nothing happened to me, except that I was now exposed to the full onrush of air and everything in it. Only those who have driven at speed without screens will know what I mean. It was hardly bearable. The air pressure on my breathing was affecting me so much that I could hardly hold the wheel." Interestingly, the windscreens were made of bulletproof glass to prevent exactly this.

Nuvolari's prey was wounded.

"Apart from this," Lang continued, "the pits gave me the 'faster' signal all the time. Nuvolari was catching up and they had worked it out that my lead was not sufficient to win."[38]

Lang's plight was obvious, although one reporter – noting how Neubauer signalled a warning every time Lang passed – assumed it was a problem with the brakes. However *The Autocar*'s man glimpsed the windscreen and concluded that "at 160 mph driving must have been very difficult."

Every lap Nuvolari cut the gap, and, on lap 58, set a new fastest time: 82.96 mph. At 60 laps the leading positions were

Lang	averaging 80.01 mph
Nuvolari	at 21 seconds
Müller	at 1m 4.2s
von Brauchitsch	at 1m 59.8s
Seaman	at 2m 26.6s

On lap 63 Nuvolari set another fastest lap by pushing his average up to 83.71 mph and had closed to within 12 seconds.

Sometime, perhaps around now, the Duke of Kent – who had visited parts of the circuit including Coppice Corner – departed. He did so as he had come, largely unnoticed, except to his entourage. Captain Bemrose said that before the Duke left he "told me how much he had enjoyed his visit and how interesting he had found it. He was extremely sorry he was unable to stay to see the finish." Another engagement, perhaps.

On lap 64, along the long straight to Melbourne Corner, Nuvolari came up to Seaman who instantly moved aside, so instantly that Nuvolari didn't have to reduce his speed. Crossing the line, Nuvolari had closed to within ten seconds of Lang who urged himself forward "but it would not work. I was so exhausted that my head swam."[37] On that lap Müller pitted to have his bonnet fixed, losing 38 seconds. The order: Lang, Nuvolari, Müller, von Brauchitsch, Seaman, Dobson, Wilkinson and Connell. That was the sum total of it now; eight survivors.

On lap 65 Nuvolari had closed to six seconds, next lap to three seconds. He could see the wounded prey clearly. That lap Seaman overtook von Brauchitsch and set off after Müller. That lap, too, the hunter was tightening to his prey, closing as if a very great force carried him forward. You could see his arms relaxed at the steering wheel, the hands sensitive and unhurried. You could see his head held rigid, not bending to the undulations of the track. You could sense a master stretching himself but only on his own terms. He looked to have the eternal sleight of hand or possess the rarest attribute, because he could make the fast car go fastest of all *slowly*.

On lap 67, as Lang emerged from Holly Wood, "Nuvolari entered, his car skidding viciously as he hurled it round the curve. Down the hill they sped, round the Hairpin, McLean's, Coppice and on to the straight. They were now only a few yards apart and Lang's fate was sealed. Nuvolari flashed by."[38] Evidently Nuvolari pulled out of Lang's slipstream, pressed the accelerator full down and seared by at 160 mph.

Lang, head still swimming, would explain that "without putting up a struggle I had to let Nuvolari pass. The car was wonderful but the driver below par. There was nothing to be done."

Nuvolari moved away as if the impetus of what he had created wouldn't release him. *The Autocar* captured that. "There was nothing tense about the little man, who was not only relaxed but was looking about him at times in complete comfort."

On lap 69 Seaman passed Müller. Astonishingly Seaman, still that lap down which he had lost on the oil, was not losing any further ground to Nuvolari – comparatively speaking, anyway. It was a moment for a measure of nationalism.

The Motor, suggesting that Seaman "gained a yard here, lost it there," insisted he was "driving better than any German on the circuit."

The Autocar, suggesting that Seaman "gradually gained on Nuvolari," insisted that all the 60,000 spectators urged Seaman on – having forgotten "an entire lap separated the two men." After lap 70 the leading positions were:

Nuvolari	averaging 80.29 mph
Lang	at 17.4s
Seaman	at 2m 21.4s
Müller	at 2m 30.2s
von Brauchitsch	at 2m 59.8s

Still the impetus held Nuvolari and – pumping and pushing, soothing this beautiful car so that it flowed – across the final ten laps he increased his lead over Lang: 41 seconds to 1 minute 1.7 seconds and up to 1 minute 15 seconds, on up through 1 minute 20 to 1 minute 30, and there was nothing Lang could do.

In the other world Wilkinson pitted and handed the ERA to Cotton who overtook Connell and chased Dobson but could, as someone put it, "never get near enough to hurt."

Sebastian watched as Nuvolari began the final lap "which always made me tremble the most. I crossed my fingers for Nuvolari. I looked down the straight to Coppice House. Then I heard the sound of our 12-cylinder car. Nuvolari rushes along the straight, brakes, enters the hairpin [Melbourne] carefully..."

Nuvolari came over the rise from the Melbourne Corner a last time. A man with a chequered flag took a couple of paces on to the track and held it high, dipped it as Nuvolari crossed the line. Another man, in plus-fours, also stood on the edge of the track with a board although he kept it facing up the track towards Nuvolari. What did it say? We don't know. Why did he hold it up? We don't know that either.

Nuvolari crossed the line at 3.10 pm to complete the 80 laps in 3 hours 6 minutes and 22 seconds, an average speed of 80.49 mph. He had scattered and destroyed the chasers utterly. He beat Lang by one minute 38 seconds which, even in the context of a motor race lasting more than the three hours, is a lifetime.

Lang	3 hours 8 minutes 0 seconds (79.79 mph)
Seaman	3 hours 6 minutes 22seconds (79.48 mph)
	A lap down.
Müller	3 hours 7 minutes 9 seconds (79.01 mph)
von Brauchitsch	3 hours 8 minutes 21 seconds
Dobson	3 hours 7 minutes 56 seconds
	Six laps down.
Cotton/Wilkinson	3 hours 8 minutes 14 seconds
Connell/Monkhouse	3 hours 8 minutes 52 seconds

Sebastian and the other Auto Union mechanics "put up their arms! Victory – victory in the last race of the 1938 season."

The time of by-the-minute information was a long way into the future – *Deutschlandsender* were transmitting at 3.10: "You heard from the Donington race after 20 laps, Nuvolari of Auto Union from Müller, Seaman and von Brauchitsch. We hope to be able to give you a detailed report on the race very soon. We shall also broadcast news at 4 o'clock."

Nuvolari stopped, was given a garland, and did a lap of honour.

"Seaman came in third ... and hairpinned round to run up to his pit before cutting his engine. As he did so, the *Deutschland Uber Alles* rang out" – Germans stood giving the stiff-arm Nazi salute – "and our biggest motor racing crowd, now rapidly invading the course, stood most impressively to attention. The *Giovinezza* followed, in honour of the greatest driver of all time – Tazio Nuvolari."[39]

When Nuvolari completed his slowing down lap he stopped at his pit and a uniformed official gestured something – he might have been asking him to move the car! – while a thicket of photographers click-click-clicked. By now flags fluttered over the pits, the Union Jack, the Swastika and the Italian tricolour. The crowd invaded the track and mobbed Nuvolari, hoisting him shoulder-high while now a huge garland was given to him. He smiled broadly – a craggy, toothy grin – and waved a gloved hand.[40]

As the crowd carried him towards the grandstand "despairing scenes were being enacted in the bookmaker's enclosure. Many backers had angrily torn up their tickets when Nuvolari seemed out of the race, and were now kicking themselves."[41]

The crowd took Nuvolari to the grandstand steps which led to the VIP box and set him down. He ascended, goggles still over his head, and Huhnlein's wife presented him with the trophy. Huhnlein, standing behind his wife, could barely conceal his feeling of triumph – it was so evident that people remarked on it. The Nazi salutes were given around Nuvolari – the picture on the cover of this book.

Nuvolari dropped the trophy "through nervousness."

Dobson went up the steps to receive an award as the leading Briton. He, Cotton and Connell in the three ERAs had all finished; thus taking the team award.

Nuvolari was "deeply touched by his welcome but at rather a loss, as he speaks neither English nor German." He seized a bottle of champagne as the crowd carried him, again shoulder high, from the Grandstand.[42]

His first thought now was for something to eat, because all he'd had during the day was a cup of coffee and four sandwiches. He went to the Auto Union's garage at Coppice Farm where, presumably, they had food.

Tom Wheatcroft remembers Nuvolari in the Silkolene Oil marquee in front of the Hall. "He'd won a very large trophy and they sat him on it – like he was sitting on a toilet seat! You know, it's silly little things that stay with you in life."

Later, in coat and cap, Nuvolari was driven to Derby "in a closed Horch by Dr Feuereissen, looking a sad, nervous and very subdued little man."[43] He spoke little on the way back to the hotel except to repeat how delighted he was at the ovation he had received. "England is lucky for me. Three times I have raced here, three times I have won."

At 4.15 Naumann telephoned Untertürkheim from Donington Hall. No doubt he went there to book a call and be able to speak at length when the connection came through. Naumann was doing this because Dr Wilhelm Kissel, had requested him to. Kissel would be as, or more anxious, than everyone else to know the story of the race and what had happened within it. Naumann gave the result (and, if you want to be pedantic, placing Connell at seven laps behind, not six). Laboriously he dictated which positions the cars held on laps 1, 2, 5, 7, 14, 18, 23, 25, 26, 27, 30, 31, 38, 40, 43, 50, 60, 67, 69 and 70. Surely he wouldn't have reported the comments of *Motor Sport*'s reporter who felt that the Mercedes "seemed to give their drivers a dirty ride, spewing oil from the engines onto the bodywork" although the reporter did add "the Auto Unions had quite dirty tails."

There remained the problem of actually getting out of the circuit. *The Light Car*'s reporter said "we might have been there now had not some of the spectators removed the railings here and there so that cars could be driven on to the course itself. As it was, we did not arrive at the Royal, Ashby-de-la-Zouch (about a dozen miles away) until close on 6pm. Ted Hutton (our host) had prepared for an invasion – which was a good thing. He stopped serving teas about 6.45pm and at 7pm you could go into dinner. Slick." The reporter ruminated that "people are asking what will happen if next year's race attracts 100,000. Fred Craner is one of them. We shall see! The Germans, by the way, definitely intend coming next year. The race is fixed for September 30."

An hour and a half after the race, one report describes two lines of traffic still converging on Ashby-de-la-Zouch. Presumably this means the cars occupied the on-coming carriageway, too, by force of numbers. Traffic manners had not improved since the morning and three girls sitting in the front of a large open-top sports car suddenly cut out from the queue they were in, went onto the grass on the far side of the road and cut back across again to avoid a bus. However one driver was seen helping another, who'd broken down, by drawing petrol from his own tank with a glass and pouring it into the tank of the other.

John Dugdale of *The Autocar* journeyed to the hotel in Derby because "I was developing a more personal style of journalism and I was interested in people. It was a way of broadening my scope. I interviewed a lot of the German drivers."

What Dugdale wrote is worth reproducing in full.

"Nuvolari these days is positively dapper, with his short athletic figure, his carefully brushed iron-grey hair, and neat clothes. In racing kit he is a most picturesque person, wearing last Saturday a red leather helmet, his usual canary sweater and blue overall trousers. In these dashing clothes and seated grimly at the wheel of his silver streamlined Auto Union, he made the most perfect subject for colour photography or for a painting.

"As he speaks hardly any English, a little French and a whole lot of Italian, Christian Kautz, the Swiss driver of the Auto Union team, acted as our interpreter. The first thing I asked Nuvolari was his opinion of Donington. After searching for some time he found an adjective to his liking which Kautz translated as 'acrobatic!'

"If the great Nuvolari, the master of short, winding circuits, thinks Donington is 'acrobatic' it *must* be hard on a driver, and, in fact, there has been a deputation to the organisers by the Germans to shorten the race for next year. When Neubauer and Uhlenhaut were suggesting a shorter race Fred Craner seemed willing to accept their advice. They also proposed a small race for one and a half litres before the Grand Prix, the idea in their minds being, no doubt, to have the smaller cars off the circuit when the big cars performed.

"Next I tackled Nuvolari about the oil-skidding incident. He smiled slightly on recollection and explained that he was taken right off the road well on to the grass, but he did not fight the car too much, or broadside unduly and so risk turning completely round. Instead he let the car take more or less its own course and continue on the grass back on to the road.

"Some consider Nuvolari's success with the rear-engined Auto Union all the more remarkable in view of his long experience with orthodox racing cars. Last year, at any rate, Nuvolari's brief appearance with Auto Unions was not promising. I asked him whether there was much difference in driving technique. His reply to that was that the driver had to be rather more careful with a rear-engined car, had to concentrate even more and could take fewer liberties.

"This is, in fact, noticeable on comparative observation of Mercedes and Auto-Unions on a corner. I noticed it particulary at McLean's where the Mercedes drivers sat easily back, their cars obviously beautifully light on the steering, utterly responsive. The Auto Union drivers were inclined to lean forward more anxiously and had harder work with the wheel. Compared with previous years, however, their task is easier. Rosemeyer used to receive a terrible jagging from the short steering connections.

Delius' hands were often bleeding at the end of a race, but after last Saturday Müller showed me his hands and they were perfect. Seaman, on the other hand, had a nasty blister from changing gear.

"About maximum speed Nuvolari was reticent, preferring to refer the matter to the Auto Union Chief Engineer, Eberan von Eberhost, as he was not sure how many revs corresponded to the speed. I understand, however, that Auto Union reached about 160 and Mercedes about 155 mph. Auto Union were also faster on acceleration. Anyway, in spite of lower maximum speed, it was shown in practice that the 1938 3-litre GP cars can lap Donington as fast as the 1937 6-litres. They can also lap the Nürburgring as fast as last year's cars. This must be due largely to improved road-holding, and perhaps, with slightly less power to play with, the driver's task on acceleration is easier."

Three hours after the race, traffic still clogged Ashby-de-la-Zouch where hotels and cafes were packed. One hotel restaurant was so full that the doors had to be locked and people waited in a queue outside for tables to become vacant. Nobody had ever seen anything like that in Ashby-de-la-Zouch before.

That evening the Derby and District Motor Club gave a dinner in honour of the German teams at the Friary Hotel, Derby. The Friary, an elegant Georgian mansion standing in its own grounds near the city centre, had been built as a private house in 1732 and ranked with nearby Chatsworth House among the country's most important homes. It had a very grand lounge and the motor club used it as their headquarters.

Feuereissen, Neubauer, Dreyfus and Shields were among those present and, inevitably, there were speeches, each couched in predictable, civilised language as befitted (and still befits) such occasions.

Captain Bemrose asked the guests to drink the health of "the greatest little man who ever sat at the wheel of a racing car" and congratulated everyone for making the race a success. He expressed particular pleasure that the Huhnleins had attended and extended an invitation to "all concerned" for 1939.

Nuvolari spoke in Italian which Neubauer translated into German and then J.A. Woodhouse – the Auto Union liaison officer and a competent interpreter – into English. Nuvolari said how happy he was at "the reception and hospitality extended to him in England."

Feuereissen expressed his admiration of the race's "wonderful organisation" and added: "You can almost safely say that we shall be here again next year."

Dugdale wrote that Nuvolari "was persuaded to make a speech. In short, clipped Italian phrases he said that he seemed to be lucky on English soil, as almost whenever he had come here he had won, twice at Belfast and now at Donington. In fact, he was a specialist in collecting trophies and Mercedes-Benz would thus have to excuse him on this occasion. Anyway, Mercedes-Benz had won quite enough and ought to be content. Perhaps if they made some new cars they would have more luck! This was naturally greeted with roars of laughter, especially from Neubauer, who practically fell out of his chair in convulsion." (*The Motor* reported that "eventually Nuvolari was prevailed upon to make a speech. After a few correct phrases he added 'and now all Herr Neubauer has to do this winter is to make a Mercedes which will go properly.' At which Neubauer nearly fell off his chair with laughter.")

Seaman also spoke, echoing Nuvolari by suggesting Mercedes-Benz should build new cars for the following season. Seaman was greeted with loud applause from all round the room, to which Uhlenhaut leant across and said to Seaman "somehow we always have the best parties when we lose.'"

Mrs Bemrose presented awards to the drivers who finished.

At 9pm, while the party was still on, Naumann was in the Black Boy and telephoned his race report to Untertürkheim. It ran to almost three typed pages of foolscap. "Five German cars 'won' the Donington Grand Prix. It was beautiful weather and the Duke of Kent, the brother of the King, started it punctually at 12 o'clock. The race was 416 kilometres long. There was a cool wind and the flags were blowing in it…"

Naumann concluded with a note. "Re Doctor Kissel. I met his wish and telephoned from Donington Hall [at 4.15]. It took me a total of three hours to get back to the hotel and therefore my detailed report is only now ready. I don't know how far the Press is aware of the problem with the windscreen [Lang's]. I told the few journalists I saw about it.

"There is still time for you to call me today if you want," and he added, presumably telling the switchboard operator at Untertürkheim what to say if they reached the Black Boy: "H. Naumann is in the hotel (Grill-Room)."

He'd earned a bite to eat. *Everybody* had.

The *Allgemeine Automobil Zeitung* provided a nice postscript. "When the race was over, the green lawns of Donington Park looked sad, the old butler in the castle had nearly suffered a stroke [because of all the excitement] and the fallow deer began to take up their antler fighting and their other activities again – but after the unholy din of the engines, we don't think their hearing will return to normal for weeks…"

It's a wonderful thing that Ian Connell can't remember where he was staying for the race. Sometimes, you see, he stayed at the Hall itself, sometimes at a hotel near Derby station but mostly at a pub in Ashby-de-la-Zouch. "In those days there was a good social side, particularly there. Why, I don't know. We had tremendous parties in the pub. The landlord used to make a contribution and suddenly the bar would be full of people all drinking. We were there often and we all knew each other terribly well. For instance, if there had been practice in the morning and you arrived at lunchtime you could ask how things had gone and they'd tell you *old so-and-so managed to go through the trees and so-and-so turned himself over in a field.*" Whatever, and despite the tricks of memory, we can postulate that on the evening of 22 October 1938 Connell returned to this hotel in Ashby-de-la-Zouch and, in his own words, had "a bit of a booze-up."

That evening, too, at Untertürkheim the Mercedes publicity machine (or whatever its equivalent was) started sending out information to the Press. "For your information we send you details of all the laps and we hope this will help you if you are writing reviews of the season." It was signed off "Heil Hitler!" – all letters in the Reich were, if you knew what was good for you – and had a scrawled signature of the sender underneath. Presumably they were sending out copies of Naumann's three-page race report which he'd telephoned at 9pm.

The end of race day is conjecture: Donington returned to emptiness when the mechanics had stowed the cars safely away in the garages at Coppice, Naumann taking his time over the meal in the Black Boy, cars bringing the Mercedes personnel back from the party in Derby along the dark leafy lanes of England to the Black Boy, Nuvolari alone in his hotel room and seeking sleep, a few lights on at Untertürkheim as the diligent worked on taking care of public relations – and, as they must have thought, by their efforts safeguarding the future of the company and themselves.

Certainly Earl Howe ought to have watched his speed as he drove away from the circuit. Allen has sometimes "seen him in the local police court for speeding. You didn't *have* to be there in person any more than you do now for an offence like that so probably Howe did because he'd been pinched so many times and been advised it might be better if he appeared. The police were waiting for him, you see – he'd got a type 57S Bugatti and it would be the only one around…"

No Mercedes racing car would run in England for another 15 years, and by then there'd be 30 million dead in between, many of them women and children.

On the Sunday evening after the race the British Racing Drivers' Club gave a cocktail party at the Rembrandt Hotel, Knightsbridge in honour of the racers and a good turnout it was, including Seaman, who sported his Gold Star, von Brauchitsch, Lang, Müller, Dobson, Maclure, Eberhorst, Neubauer, Feuereissen, Earl Howe, Ebblewhite and John Cobb – who, as described earlier, had broken the World Land Speed Record at Bonneville Flats (350.194 mph) on 15 September, only for Eyston to beat it the following day (357.497 mph).

Motor Sport noted Cobb in "earnest conversation with Feuereissen and Eberhorst, and apparently expects soon to see them in Germany. Müller was giving away Auto Union pin-badges, notably to the lovelier of the ladies who were present…"

The Autocar noted that "Nuvolari, unfortunately, had been called back to Italy on business, but most of the remaining drivers were there – von Brauchitsch with his hand, which had been injured, covered in sticking plaster, and Neubauer as full of fun as ever. It was confirmed that the German teams will come again to Donington next year, and the drivers themselves are extremely anxious that some of their British colleagues should go over to Germany to see the record attempts on the new road."

This was a reference to Major Goldie Gardner who "by special invitation of Herr Huhnlein" was to take his MG to a new section of autobahn between Berlin and Halle, just south of a town called Dessau, which "has, practically speaking, been designed for records." Gardner was attacking the 1,100cc record. The traditional venue for such attempts was the Frankfurt-Darmstadt autobahn, of course.

The *Allgemeine Automobil Zeitung* noted that "that was it, the last race of the year. The following afternoon a cocktail party was given by the English Automobile Club in London. We drank properly to the season of racing, its experiences and its successes, and to next season. But before that there will be the winter break. *Thank God*, say the drivers."

The suggestion that Nuvolari returned to Italy on the Monday belies the claim by Lurani in his book *Nuvolari* that "two days" after the race – the Tuesday – Nuvolari was presented with the stuffed and mounted head of the stag he'd killed in practice. In its issue of 25 October, *The Motor* carried a photograph of Nuvolari holding the stag's head but it had obviously been taken at Donington (he's wearing his racing overalls and goggles) and you can't see if the head has been mounted. More likely he posed for this and, once the stuffing and mounting had been completed, the head was sent on to him. Lurani suggests Nuvolari said he would like it "to follow him to other race tracks as a lucky mascot. That imposing head eventually won a place in the Mantuan's study beside the monumental Vanderbilt Cup."[44]

On the Monday a telegram was sent by the German sports ministry to Dr Kissel at Untertürkheim. "Donington was a great German victory and the Mercedes cars and drivers helped towards it. Therefore we congratulate you, Herr Doctor, and not only you but the factory."

On the Tuesday, Neubauer drove to Paris and stayed there overnight, no doubt at the Hotel Tabourin. All things being equal, we may safely surmise that he treated himself to a banquet before, next day, continuing to Stuttgart. He had the Thursday and Friday off and returned to work at 10.30 on the Saturday morning.[45]

Nuvolari's car was put on show at Auto Union in Great Portland Street, London for over a week. Immense and silent, it must have commanded awe. Denis Jenkinson was still at technical college but had been able to attend the race and now, as in 1937, went along to gaze at the car in the showroom. This time he took a camera "borrowed from my elder brother" – he regretted not taking one in 1937 and continued to regret that for the rest of his life.[46]

The Donington Grand Prix of Saturday, 22 October 1938 exercised such fascination that the motoring press were reluctant to release it into history. They wanted to keep on and on writing about it.

The Editor of *The Light Car* broached the subject of whether the Duke of Kent really had started the race. "That is a question several people have asked me. The answer is 'Yes' and 'No'. His Royal Highness collaborated with A.V. Ebblewhite, who indicated the passing of each of the final five seconds before zero hour and then tapped the Duke on the shoulder as a signal to lower the flag. It was perfectly done – within ten yards or so of the box from which I was broadcasting."

Two writers were concerned about the dropped oil and the chaos that it caused.

George Monkhouse wrote that this "incident," and others, "particularly the one at Monaco in 1936, makes one wonder if the marshals should not be equipped with a special 'oil' flag. The yellow flag is at the present time used to warn the drivers that something is wrong, and they merely slow down slightly so that if necessary they can avoid an obstruction such as another car or an ambulance blocking the road. However the position is quite different with oil, in that the driver cannot see anything on the road and therefore, not unnaturally, assumes nothing is wrong."[47]

'Casque' in *The Autocar* complained about Donington's loud speakers – "you can only hear about one word in twenty," which no doubt explains why, when the race commentary ignited after Hanson laid the oil, you couldn't even hear the one in twenty. "This race was one more warning that unless some special signal is evolved to convey that there is oil on the road, one or more drivers will be killed."

'Casque' lamented that "we were faced once more with the ghost of that utterly ridiculous rule compelling a driver to re-start his engine by himself if ever he stops when the car is away from the pits. The Derby people had worded the rule in order that the officials could push the car and so start the engine, but on the Continent Seaman might have been excluded. That has always been just silly because you can't start most of the grand prix cars with a handle single-handed."

Motor Sport reflected that "all sorts of 'ifs' arise in analysing the results. Some say Seaman would have won had he not left the road and stalled. Certainly he drove magnificently, holding Nuvolari at the end. Between 50 and 60 laps however, Seaman lost 15.2 seconds to Nuvolari and between 60 and 70 laps another 15.8 seconds. When fuller figures are available, slide-rule wallahs can grapple with the whole problematical story.

"It was a truly magnificent race and all peace-loving peoples will join with us in hope that we may still be at peace in October 1939, and that Germany, France and Italy will again compete in our only Formula Grand Prix."

Charlie Martin, who didn't compete in the 1938 race, of course, has already said that Rosemeyer was an outgoing chap. Nuvolari? "Very uptight, didn't make friends at all. He certainly didn't suffer fools gladly. In a racing car he got round the corners before he reached them! As he approached a corner he lined the car up at the angle of where the track went after the corner so he was already pointing in the right direction. He used to talk to himself while he was driving – in Italian, of course. Sometimes he'd take both hands off the steering wheel. Why? Maybe it was a way of communicating sheer enjoyment or maybe he was up the backside of the car in front and he was saying *come on you so-and-so, bella! bella!"*

Dreyfus confirms that Nuvolari "used to beat the side of his car – genuinely did. That's not a myth." Overall, Dreyfus judged that Nuvolari was "supreme as a driver and as a man. He could do things no-one else could. Often you'd follow him into a corner and you'd just know he wasn't going to make it – and he did. Caracciola perhaps really believed himself to be the best – and he was a great, great driver – but he was not like Nuvolari: very smooth, very fast and without question the best in the rain. Nuvolari never changed. He remained simple and straight-forward, never arrogant. I think we all – including him – believed he was the best. I have no hesitation in saying that."

A week after the Donington Grand Prix of 1938 news filtered through that the stretch of Halle-Leipzig autobahn wouldn't be ready for Gardner's attempt to set records in an MG. He was in Germany, though, preparing and one report said "the run is to take place on the older road near Frankfort [sic], which gives him about five kilometres' straight run and should, in any case, be enough."

It was. On two runs over a kilometre he averaged 186.6 mph and, like the grand prix drivers, vowed he'd be back. Unlike them he was right and, in May 1939, raised the record to 203.5 mph on the Berlin-Leipzig autobahn at Dessau.

By then von Brauchitsch was in Bavaria "for some relaxation in my house at the Starnberg lake. But, before this, I wanted to meet my Starnberg neighbour Hans Albers in Munich. I knew that he was shooting a film and staying at the Regina Hotel. The porter told me that my friend was in his room and happily I stormed up the stairs. He was in the "Prince's Room" of the hotel. Dressed in a housecoat and holding a script in his hand, he was sitting in a comfortable armchair. "Hey, there you are again," he shouted enthusiastically. "Come in, come right in, young man."

Albers commiserated about von Brauchitsch's race at Donington and complained about the way the Nazis were controlling films – "they trample around" – but added: "Never mind, my dear." He laughed and filled a glass. "Here's to better times! Now tell me about your English theatre!"

Von Brauchitsch explained that "Albers had nothing in common with the National Socialists. His longtime companion Hansi Burg, who was Jewish, was driven out of Germany and had to emigrate to England. From the very beginning, he turned down all offers by the film dictator Goebbels to play a part in a National Socialist propaganda film. He was one of the few great actors you would never meet at one of the splendid film parties."

Albers suggested he and von Brauchitsch spend the evening together, which they did with two budding actresses. Von Brauchitsch concludes: "The bitter hours in England were long forgotten. Even the Scottish whisky would not bring back the memories."

Auto Union racing cars would run again in England again. John Surtees drove a D Type 39 car at Silverstone in the early 1990s ("the engine had been redone and the car wasn't set up for racing but it felt very good and the gearbox impressed me a great deal"); then, as it happened, another ran directly in front of a stately home but that wouldn't be until June 1997. Some said it all felt like yesterday, but not many because not many could remember. And, the way time goes, not everyone remembered the 30 million dead in between, many of them women and children. It was too long ago to sustain grief and the Grim Reaper had taken too many of the witnesses – to that, and to Donington, October 1938.

Chapter 8

The day before yesterday

AFTER DONINGTON, Connell "discovered" that his friend Berg – Connell can't remember his first name, or even if he had known it – "went back to Germany and disappeared. He was very anti-Nazi and when we were talking we knew that he didn't like the Hitler regime. He was probably a Jew, I should think, with a name like that and being anti-Nazi and Jewish in Germany in 1938 wasn't really what you wanted to be."

Seaman and Erica Popp were married at Caxton Hall, London on 7 December. It was a quiet wedding, evidently, followed by a luncheon party in a Kensington Hotel. The honeymoon was spent at the Swiss ski resort of Davos.

"When he got married," Ian Connell says, "there was a coincidence. He was at Davos and we happened to be at Klosters. He was a very good skier – much better than me. I remember we were having drinks after dinner one night and he set off on the funicular up pretty high and skied down by moonlight…"

Seaman had asked Monkhouse to contact his mother to restore relations – he had found it a "bitter necessity to break with his mother on account of his marriage"[1] – and towards the end of December was pleased that his mother hadn't directed her anger at Monkhouse for even trying. On 12 December Seaman had written to Monkhouse saying this was a "good sign" and adding that it "may possibly mean that she is toying with the idea of eventually giving way, and therefore does not want to break off every means of reconciliation. I should not, however, rush her too much, but allow time to help too."

The racing season of 1939 took place, although you can be forgiven for not knowing that. Gazing back you can only see the year darkening towards the abyss which, even today, lingers like something hellish, perhaps never to be rationalised, explained or accommodated. Hitler entered Prague on 15 March two days after giving the government an ultimatum. The tramping

German soldiers were jeered and hissed. Hitler now prepared the familiar escalation again. Poland was next.

There were eight Grand Prix races, from Pau on 2 April to Yugoslavia in Belgrade on 3 September. The Belgian Grand Prix at Spa was on 26 June – a typical Spa race, rain lurking in the brooding trees, then drying. Seaman led and went faster and faster. He plunged off the track just before La Source hairpin and the Mercedes struck a tree a terrible blow. Seaman's right arm was broken and almost certainly he was unconscious. The car burst into flames and before he was extricated Seaman suffered extensive burns. He was taken to hospital and regained consciousness. To Erica he said "I am afraid you must go to the cinema alone after all."[2] Neubauer would remember Seaman saying to her: "Darling, I'm sorry ... I gave you ... such a fright.' I could amost see that shy smile under the bandages. Erica sobbed, the tears streaming down her cheeks. 'I won't be able ... to take you ... to the cinema tonight.'[3] He died in hospital just before midnight.

Caracciola remembered "Erica was beside herself with grief. We took her to the hotel, to her room which was close to ours. Baby wanted to stay with her, but Erica said she wanted to try to sleep. After a few hours we heard a shy knock at the door. It was Erica. My wife took that frail little figure into her arms, held her head to her shoulder, and let Erica cry herself to sleep."

Caracciola added that "the following day we stood around a long, narrow coffin. Could Dick Seaman really have found room in that? Neubauer was deeply moved. He posted himself before the coffin and spoke to Dick. I no longer remember his exact words. I only know that it was a speech that moved us all deeply."

It was a "little memorial service" in the mortuary of the hospital. Chula states that "about 40 persons were present, including all the prominent drivers. Other mourners were representatives of the Belgian authorities, the German Embassy in Belgium and the Royal Automobile Club of Belgium. There was not a single representative of any British authorities or clubs present. An English clergyman who had heard of the tragedy, however, came and offered to say prayers."

His body was brought back to England in a hearse, arranged by his friend Robert Fellowes. It went via Ostend and the ferry to Dover where only the manager of Mercedes-Benz in Britain was present.

The German authorities instructed that Seaman be given full honours – the German Ambassador was "instructed" to call on Seaman's mother while "throughout Germany showroom windows of Mercedes-Benz were cleared of motor cars and had instead a large photograph of Seaman framed in a wreath." Amongst the many floral tributes was a gigantic wreath with the inscription 'from Adolf Hitler'.

Seaman was buried next to his father in Putney Vale Cemetery on Friday, 30 June. Neubauer, Lang and von Brauchitsch flew over. Seaman's mother was present – "And the young widow, Erica Seaman, was there, leaning heavily on her father's arm. I spoke a few words to her when the ceremony was over, little realising how many years would pass before I saw her again." That would be at a drivers' reunion at Stuttgart in 1953.[4]

Dugdale points out that Hitler sent the wreath for the funeral, which only seems full of irony in retrospect. "We were not at war and everybody hoped we would not be. One hoped, one hoped. I think motorsports bring everyone together and I still always think better of a chap if he's fond of motorsport…"

Charlie Martin was "very upset about Dick's death, but we'd been in it for a number of years and we knew there was always that chance. The circuits were dangerous: trees, houses, ordinary roads. It was proper motoring – unlike today when, if you go off, you go into a sort of feather bed."

After the funeral Lang would remember the "four-engine plane took us to Paris from London in only one hour, and a few days later practice started for the Grand Prix of France at Rheims."[5] Müller won it for Auto Union, Caracciola won at the Nürburgring and Lang won the Swiss at Berne. That was August 20. By then Hitler's escalation over Poland cast its shadow. While the racing cars were going round the circuit at Berne, Poland was sending troops to defend its borders. Three days later Germany and Soviet Russia announced they had signed a Non-Aggression Pact, which gave Hitler a free run at Poland – which would be divided with the Soviet Union afterwards. It seemed impossible that Britain and France would *not* honour their obligations to Poland. The shadow had deepened and broadened so that it fell full across Europe and in time would reach to every corner of the Earth.

Next day, preparing for the Donington Grand Prix on 30 September – which again would be the season's final race – the Mercedes racing arm reported to the directors that "we have told the organisers we will run three cars. We have announced two drivers, Hermann Lang and Manfred von Brauchitsch. A third driver and a reserve will be named later. The three cars will be entered as a team" – hoping to win the team prize, as ERA had done in 1938.

Both Mercedes and Auto Union competed in the Yugoslav Grand Prix at Belgrade. It was run on 3 September. "The evening before, we were sitting in our hotel when the news came through that German troops had invaded Poland. We looked at one another in horrified silence."[6]

Murray Walker was in Austria "with my parents, because my father was running the British Army team in the international six-days motorcycle trial. The team had gone out in the expectation of there being a war shortly and the War Office had promised to send a telegram in the event of things being so dire that we all needed to get back immediately. My father received a telegram – which had been somehow delayed by 24 hours. So: if it was only going to be sent in dire circumstances and it had been delayed, things must obviously be extremely grave.

"Huhnlein assured my father that there was not going to be a war and that if there was a war he – Huhnlein – would personally give them a guarantee of safe passage out of the country. My father asked him: 'can you tell me where you are in the government hierarchy?' Huhnlein said 'I am number 10.' And my father said 'well, what happens if number nine up to number one say that we've got to stay?' That's when they upped sticks and didn't actually finish the trial. They left on the last day. There was the question of whether to go to Switzerland – which you could reach quicker, but you faced possible internment – or take a chance and dash to France. And that's what we did."

At noon on 3 September Chamberlain told the House of Commons that "this country is now at war with Germany."

Murray Walker remembers that he and his parents got back from Austria via France, "walked into the house, turned on the radio and Chamberlain was giving his declaration of war."

That afternoon, Nuvolari won the Yugoslav Grand Prix from von Brauchitsch, Müller third. Saturday, 30 September – when the Donington Grand Prix ought to have taken place amidst comradeship, sportsmanship and international understanding – the Luftwaffe had pounded Warsaw and Poland lay shattered, French artillery poured shellfire into the German lines near Saarbrucken, the German government warned that armed ships might be sunk without warning and a great civilian exodus from London was under way. Britain and France had been at war with Germany for 27 days.

Some postscripts.

The regulations for the 1939 race had been published long before this, when the world was still a normal place and it seemed possible the race might proceed normally. The entry form hinted at potential problems, however. It said:

ENTRIES must be received by THE CLUB before noon September 2nd, 1939, at the following rates –

At £15 15s 0d per car, being Fifteen Guineas entrance fee, which includes cost of Third Party Insurance.

Entries will only be accepted after consideration by THE CLUB, which may refuse to accept an entry without stating any reason.

Unless in the opinion of THE CLUB sufficient entries are received, the race will not be held.

The entry fee will be returned in full if an entry is refused or if no race is held, but in no other circumstances.

There remains an almost groteseque irony in this talk of Third Party Insurance when a war had been unleashed which would claim millions of lives. The total depends on which source you go to, because nobody really knows and will never really know. In the face of this incomprehensible enormity, it seems impertinent – as well as adding another dimension to the irony – to wonder if Mercedes paid the entry fees for their three cars and, assuming they did, if, how and when it was returned to them. But, anyway, I've found no record or mention of this.

The regulations, incidentally, contain a sentence which might serve as the epitaph for the whole era:

Crash helmets with detachable peaks are recommended, but are not compulsory.

Donington fell silent. And, again, it was adapted to war, becoming a vast vehicle storage depot. Tom Wheatcroft rescued it from that in the 1970s and set his heart on hosting a Formula One race. The problem was that the British Grand Prix alternated between Silverstone and Brands Hatch until, from 1987, it settled at Silverstone. Effectively it seemed to have blocked him.

Wheatcroft is a very tenacious man and in 1993 he finally got his race. It scarcely mattered that it was called the European Grand Prix, a traditional (and handy) way of adding a race to the calendar. There was something strangely, almost hauntingly appropriate about this day because the weather changed constantly, allowing Ayrton Senna to create a masterpiece in his Marlboro McLaren. At one stage he led by a lap. The track didn't have the same contours, of course, but Melborne Corner was in the field over there, the old Stone Bridge wasn't far away and Starkey's Straight – where Rosemeyer and Nuvolari and Caracciola had reached 170 miles an hour – was still called Starkey's Straight and ran close to where the original had been.

To make exact judgements across a complete chasm of time is inherently dangerous but I'll risk one now. Rosemeyer, Nuvolari and Caracciola would have recognised – and embraced – Senna as one of them.

And while we're on the subject of a vault across time, human beings are great survivors and even after the slaughter from 1939 to 1945 was done, many, many people we have come to know in this book had survived. Erica Popp, for example, went to live in America and remarried twice, an American then a German she had known for many years. She died in Florida in the mid-1990s.

It's curious that aspects of the 1937 and 1938 races linger as if, in this most transient of human activities, they weren't temporal but have achieved a kind of permanence 60 years later.

In February 1997, McLaren launched their new car which, for the third season, would be powered by Mercedes engines. The team also had a new sponsor, a German cigarette company called West who, evidently, had decided for reasons of image to make the launch a very modern extravaganza. A whole hall at Alexandra Palace in north London was hired and entertainment provided by the Spice Girls, at that time in vogue and, one assumes, very, very expensive.

Some 5,000 people were there including, I suppose, dozens of journalists and photographers. It was an occasion of imagery as well as image, the McLaren to be liveried in the famous Mercedes silver. Manfred von

Brauchitsch, now in his nineties, had been flown over to grace the occasion by embracing past and present. He sat at a round table nursing a glass of red wine – "good wine, very light." There was an aura about this white-haired man who still seemed to have a great strength within him.

"It's a very serious business to change the colour," he said through an interpreter, "and I am very pleased it has been done to remind us of the old successes which Mercedes had."

What did he think of a night like this, 5,000 people to look at a racing car?

"In those days there was not such opportunities to lay on something of this scale. It is unique. The big thing was that the first race run in these silver colours was won and in a record time. That's 63 years ago, that's as long as it was. I drove the first Silver Arrow to victory and I am here today to applaud the present-day drivers who will be driving this car. I haven't met them yet but I will later."

Have you seen them on television?

"Naturally. I have seen them all."

How do the drivers of then and now compare?

"It is completely different today. You simply cannot compare a driver from 1910 – that's where I go back to – with one from today. It is two generations that you are jumping and now you have different techniques, modern techniques."

You raced against Nuvolari, Rosemeyer, Caracciola, you saw Fangio, Jim Clark, Ayrton Senna…

"No comparisons possible. There is such a vast time difference…"

June 1997 an Auto Union made the great return, at the annual Goodwood Festival of Speed. This major event, centred around a rising, twisting strip of road through the grounds of Goodwood House in Sussex – truly a stately home – is an opportunity to see cars of yesterday and the day before in motion.

Hans-Joachim Stuck was due to drive the Auto Union – his father Hans had driven one in 1937 and 1938 although, as we have seen, not in the Donington Grands Prix. The Goodwood programme pointed out that the car was a "mountain climb model, complete with dual rear wheels."

After the run he spoke, quietly but sincerely. "I didn't come here to compete against lap times, I came here to show this masterpiece of time, of heritage and so I thought I should look as much like the drivers of those days as possible. To drive in an Auto Union car of the 1930s wearing a full visor and carbon fibre crash helmet would have created the wrong atmosphere, you know. I sat in the car yesterday, but we decided not to go out because of the weather. I drove it on the ramp into the marquee, that was all."

What did it feel like?

"I had a very emotional moment already in 1991 when I drove the Grand Prix car, which is sitting in the museum in Munich, and did a lap of the Avus. This to me was, of course, very emotional because it was the first time

I sat in a race car which my dad had driven. Today the feelings were pretty close, but not as much but the driving here today, that was something hard to describe because the road reminds me of the old race tracks: the straw bales and the trees and the walls, and spectators very close – not in any concrete monument grandstand but standing there close.

"Getting to the car was a funny story, because we came very late here this morning, we had lots of traffic, we had to park a mile away, we came to the paddock and they told us the car had left for the start, so I had to run to the start-finish line and when I came to that John Surtees was sitting in the car ready to drive it – because I hadn't arrived. A marshal saw me and I jumped over the fence and skidded because there was so much mud – I don't know how I survived upright! – and they shouted *have you signed on*? and I said *yes, yes, yes*."

Hans-Joachim Stuck was discovering that time always goes by at the wrong speed.

No doubt his father had, too.

What was it like to drive the car?

"I was using four gears today, although it has five. The car's response to the throttle was amazing. I mean, you musn't confuse it with modern day cars and their electronic engine management systems – but this one, the moment you move your foot on the throttle, booop, the engine responds. And the gearbox – fantastic, you don't have to double-declutch but you have to feel for the gears. No, the car did not feel heavy and compared to the one I drove from the museum this one had a much better set up. It ran straight, it turned in nicely whereas the one I drove on the Avus was very nervous. Here in the right-hand turn I tried to get some oversteer and the car responded very nicely."

What about the driving position?

"You must not forget that in those days the cars did not have power steering and when they were doing races of 500 kilometres at the Nürburgring you couldn't drive with your arms outstretched to the steering wheel, you had to drive like they did" – with their arms crooked and close to the wheel. "It was too heavy to do anything else. Yes, it's heavy. And you think about the Grossglockner, the hairpins there. Incredible." The Grossglockner was the mountain pass in Austria where Hans Stuck was something of a master.

John Watson, a Grand Prix driver between 1973 and 1985, is (if I may put it this way) a connoisseur of all performance cars and has driven both the 1937 and 1938 Mercedes. What were they like?

"In the mid-1930s Mercedes-Benz ran a model which was called the W125. I think from memory it was a 5.6-litre straight-8 two-stage supercharged engine. It was a phenomenally powerful racing car by even today's standards. And when you consider that these cars ran on the sort of wheels and tyres that they did, it becomes mind-blowing. The response of the engine as well as its power is genuinely unbelievable. I have to salute the drivers of that generation because they were truly Titans. At that time, of course, these racing cars were the most sophisticated in the world although, relatively, they were lacking in aerodynamics and the frontal area was quite small. It was, incidentally, the first time I'd driven a car with the throttle pedal where the brake pedal should be – in many pre-war cars the throttle was the central pedal.

"To think about driving those cars at circuits like Spa-Francorchamps, the Nürburgring – Donington, even, because it was lesser in terms of its sheer scale but none the less very demanding – remains just amazing.

"I think it was the speed which impressed me most. In relation to today's cars there was little traction and little braking and of course the cornering speeds were very much lower as well but what you could do was steer them on the throttle. That was very much the driving technique. You'd point the car at the corner and then you'd use the throttle as the real mechanism for turning the car in. There was a balance of steering and throttle control and that was the applicable driving technique of the time for the greatest drivers – Caracciola, Seaman, Lang, Nuvolari in the Auto Union.

"Then the regulation change came [for 1938]. The governing body felt that these things were too fast. They reduced the engine capacity to a mazimum of 3 litres and they altered the basic formula. The W154 was introduced and that was a significant step forward because it was very much a low-line version of the W125. The driver sat lower in the car, the weight distribution was centralised. The engine was a V12, again supercharged, but maybe 150 – 200 horsepower less than the W125. That loss was more than compensated for by the improvement in the car design, the chassis design, the weight distribution and the simple driveability. It meant that you could use the horsepower and torque more easily, and, in conjunction with what I've called the low-line chassis, it did represent a significant change for grand prix engineering. It became the first car to lap the Nürburgring at over 90 miles an hour and it wasn't until 1956 that that lap record was finally broken by Fangio."

We've come full circle. We're back to the test track at Stuttgart and David Coulthard trying the Mercedes from the 1930s.

What about the gear changes?

"Never mind the gear changes – I'm high on fuel! With the engine being in front of you, you get all the fuel smells."

Did you know there was fire, proper fire, coming out of the back?

"No, I saw the smoke but … but it's amazing, it is an absolute animal. I have no desire to drive it more than I have done now, and that was at a very low speed. I can't imagine what it must have been like to go flat out in it. I'd want to be on an airfield to try that."

Was it trying to get away from you?

"Yes. You know, you just touch the power and it lights up. OK, the initial throttle response isn't quite as good as we have nowadays but there's a lot of grunt there, a load of torque. It's not a boy's car, that's for sure."

Were you aware of what gears you were in?

"Oh yes, I'm quite good at counting [!]. I knew what gear I was in. That was the most important thing: keep it in a low cog [gear] and you're likely to keep it under control – but it's a bit confusing with having the brake on the outside. A couple of times I got on to the power and it took off, I went to hit the brake and, of course, I hit the power again. So you've to be a wee bit careful. I don't think I'd commit myself to doing any racing in something like that."

What about the brakes?

"They're not there. Nothing."

Steering?

"The steering is surprisingly positive. It feels like a Mini in terms of the initial response but then the weight comes into play. It is very, very heavy. It is also very physical. Even my left arms knows about it after doing only three laps round the test track. Obviously I was a little bit nervous because it's such an expensive car – seriously powerful, overpowered, underbraked, undertyred…"

Three hours round the old Nürburgring?

"No chance."

Or Donington when it was bumpy?

"I wouldn't do three minutes in this thing anywhere. It's from a different time altogether and I just cannot relate. It's just another world altogether and you have to drive it yourself to appreciate how frightening it is."

The circle was truly completed, however, at Donington Park itself on a chill May day in 1999 when a Mercedes W154 ran again. It was leant by Mercedes as part of the Richard Seaman Memorial Trophy Meeting, organised by the Vintage Sports-Car Club of Great Britain. The car was, strictly, a 1939 car incorporating some modifications from those which had raced here in 1938 but "underneath it is a W154", as the programme insisted and reassured.

Everything had changed and nothing had changed. Over there the Hall still stood, dignified in all its timeless English elegance. Many in the crowd who'd come to bear to witness spoke in soft Midlands accents, and you'd surely have heard the same if you'd listened carefully in those Octobers of 1937 and 1938.

The Mercedes was parked in one of the pits and anyone who cared to could wander in and stand beside it, as dozens did, gazing, murmuring, shaking their heads. Just this once nothing had changed: it was possible now, as it was possible then, to leave something valuable unguarded and know that it would be respected, not damaged. The mechanics wheeled it from this pit and pushed it to the little road which bisects the paddock, pushed it harder there until it fired up and the engine burst into a mighty explosion. Imagine a thousand wolves howling in agony. The dozens grew to a hundred, two hundred, and they smiled in disbelief, their fingers in their ears against the howling; and they coughed as the 'boot polish' fuel choked them, as it had choked their fathers in those two Octobers which were so long ago – and somehow, too, yesterday or the day before. Yes, a Mercedes mechanic confirmed, "it's the same type of fuel, we mix it specially…"

John Surtees did three demonstration laps of the track in this hauntingly beautiful machine, his hands working the enormous wooden steering wheel hard to keep the car straight, the engine crackling and gurgling as he changed down for the first corner, Redgate – now one word, not two. Rosemeyer and von Brauchitsch, and Seaman, and Lang, and Caracciola had passed this way – or very near to it – doing the same thing, leaving the same echoes in their wake; and now they could be heard again.

Completing the third lap, and rounding the left-hander on to the start-finish straight, Surtees had the power on and the car twitching. He caught that. He was enjoying himself and so was everybody else bearing witness.

"It's a car which is just as it was when it raced in the 1938–39 period," Surtees would say, beaming with delight, "although you must remember that it is not a race-prepared car, and you have to allow for the fact that the brakes are not balanced and things like this – but, you know, anything which stands stationary for considerable periods of time will show this, even your road car. It takes a couple of laps for things to bed in. Compared to the more modern racing cars, it's a lot more lively on the road. It does bounce around over the bumps. That's all fairly well controlled: the big thing is it's very difficult to get the power on the road although the power is very, very usable. It doesn't come on with a great big thump, it's typical of super-charged engines that it has a power band that virtually runs from nothing. Stationary it bangs and pops but as soon as you put a little load on it, it runs cleanly and it goes straight through the power range."

The twitch?

"It was deliberate [impish smile]. I floored it and I thought right, we're going to spin the wheels or break away a bit to show how the car can be driven."

And there it was, in that sudden and molten movement: a precise vision of what it had been like, the day before yesterday.

Notes

Chapter 1: From a distance

1. Author interview with John Gillies Shields.
2. op. cit.
3. *Donington Hall* by Penny Olsen (British Midland/Granta Editions)
4. *The Donington Grands Prix* by Dave Fern (Donington International Collection)
5. *The Racing Car* by C. Clutton, C. Posthumus and D. Jenkinson (B.T. Batsford Ltd)
6. *The Racing Car* op. cit.
7. *Speed Was My Life* by Alfred Neubauer (Barrie and Rockliff)
8. *Racing The Silver Arrows* by Chris Nixon (Osprey)
9. *The British Grand Prix 1926–1976* by Doug Nye (Batsford)
10. ibid.
11. *Dick Seaman* by HRH Prince Chula Chakrabongse of Thailand (G.T. Foulis & Co. Ltd)
12. ibid.
13. ibid.
14. Fern op. cit.
15. Chula op.cit.
16. Nixon interview with Rudolph Uhlenhaut, *Autosport*, 14 January 1982
17. *Chronicle of the 20th Century* (Longman)
18. *The German Grand Prix* by Cyril Posthumus (Temple Press Books)
19. ibid.
20. Chula op. cit.
21. ibid.
22. *Racing The Silver Arrows*
23. Alfred Neubauer internal memorandum, Untertürkheim, 17 September 1937
24. Nixon op. cit.

25. *Grand Prix Driver* by Hermann Lang (G.T. Foulis & Co. Ltd)
26. I was presuming this because, although nothing seems to have survived to indicate which hotel, the Mercedes convoy stayed there in 1938 – making it likely they simply repeat-booked from 1937.

Chapter 2: Friends – and enemies
 1. Caracciola op. cit.
 2. Neubauer op. cit.
 3. ibid.
 4. *Racing the Silver Arrows*
 5. Lang op. cit.
 6. ibid.
 7. ibid.
 8. Neubauer op. cit.
 9. *Omnibus of Speed* (Stanley Paul, 1961) in the chapter Seaman: the Daring Young Man on Mercedes-Benz, by Brown Meggs.
10. *Rosemeyer!* by Elly Beinhorn Rosemeyer and Chris Nixon (Transport Bookman Publications, 1986)
11. *The Autocar*

Chapter 3: The master's last win
 1. *The Sporting Life*
 2. Lang op. cit.
 3. Boddy in *Motor Sport*
 4. Lang ibid.
 5. *Hinter Drohnenden Motoren* by Ludwig Sebastian (BKZ Einband 1958)
 6. Boddy op. cit.
 7. Sebastian
 8. *Rosemeyer!* op. cit.
 9. *Speed Was My Life* by Neubauer
10. *Rosemeyer!* op. cit.
11. Neubauer op. cit.
12. Lang op. cit.
13. ibid.
14. Sebastian op. cit.
15. *The Derby Evening Telegraph*
16. I've used the comparison with 1935 because, as far as I can ascertain, no times survive from 1936.
17. *The Autocar*
18. *The Light Car*
19. *The Sporting Life*
20. *The Autocar*
21. Humanising this even further, it's legitimate to speculate that because the roads in Britain in 1937 were the opposite of autobahns Caracciola simply took longer than he had anticipated to reach Donington but *as a racing driver* could not admit as much and fell back on claiming to have

got lost. It's also legitimate to speculate that Caracciola and his wife found somewhere pleasant along the way for an ample and leisurely lunch (British main roads groaned with hostelries), lingered and savoured and knew he wouldn't make it in time and knew he was good enough to make it all up in the next day's session…

22. Boddy op. cit.
23. Playing a practical joke of exactly this nature on Neubauer was by no means a unique happening. See Ian Connell and the 1938 race…
24. All these years later, Powys-Lybbe is gently amused that he is down as an entrant. He has no memory of entering at all – "no recollection and no explanation. What would have been the conceivable use of running an Alfa against the Mercedes and Auto Unions? No point whatever." Interestingly, Powys-Lybbe tried to prove that you could go motor racing without owning a fortune. "I did it by being … economical (chuckle). There wasn't any starting money in England but there was in Ireland. And they paid one's shipping. The suppliers paid one a retaining fee and bigger bonuses as time went on. The fuel was free and the tyres were nearly free. And there was some prize money. It did about balance out against the cost."
25. *The Motor*
26. *Racing Driver's World* by Rudolf Caracciola (Motoraces Book Club/Cassell)
27. Sebastian op. cit.
28. *The Sporting Life*
29. Boddy op. cit.
30. *The Sporting Life*
31. Strangely in the local Press I cannot find any details of a greyhound meeting in the area that night, but we do know that of the era there was a huge amont of it going on all the time, much of it at very minor tracks and it may well be one of these which Auto Union visited.
32. It is simply not worth while translating these into today's values because 60 years of inflation make such an exercise grotesque. 5 shillings is 25p – imagine getting into the British Grand Prix at Silverstone these days for *that*. However, as you'll see in a subsequent chapter, I do make a translation – because a chap called Rob Walker bought a *car* for the equivalent of 12$^{1}/_{2}$p.
33. *The Leicester Mercury*
34. *The Derby Evening Telegraph*
35. Boddy op. cit.
36. *Nottingham Evening Post*
37. This is not so amazing as it sounds to us now. Until, I suppose, the 1960s tiny numbers of police were adequate to handle football crowds of 50,000 and were able to stand with their backs to the crowd watching the play. Moreover parents were content for their kids to go alone to the matches because a football stadium was a safe place to be.
38. *The Motor*

39. ibid.
40. *The Autocar*
41. The Light Car
42. Lang op. cit.
43. *The Light Car*
44. *The Autocar*
45. ibid.
46. Boddy op. cit.
47. Sebastian op. cit.
48. Boddy op. cit.
49. *The Sporting Life*
50. Boddy op. cit.
51. For reasons of authentic flavouring, I've left the fractions exactly as they were presented to the Press in the Official Bulletins during the race.
52. Boddy op. cit.
53. *Nottingham Evening Post*
54. *The Light Car*
55. *The Autocar*
56. Lang op. cit.
57. *The Motor*
58. Lang op. cit.
59. ibid. Sebastian's claim is understandable, and I don't want to be more pedantic than necessary, but the Mercedes mechanics, of course, had already done faster pit stops.
60. *The Derby Evening Telegraph*
61. *The Light Car.*
62. Official Bulletin
63. *Nottingham Evening Post*
64. Official Bulletin
65. ibid.
66. For younger readers (and this will seem little short of incredible) cars – including road cars – were started by a crank handle which the motorist, standing at the front of the car, had to insert into the engine and, using both hands, crank it until the engine fired.
67. Official Bulletin
68. ibid.
69. *The Autocar*
70. The difficulties of recreation are amply illustrated by this incident which decided the race. Wisdom in *The Sporting Chronicle* wrote that "once again the lead changed hands, this time as a result of a front tyre going on Brauchitsch's car" – but Rosemeyer was in the lead and it did not change hands. *The Light Car* reported that "Brauchitsch drew a well-deserved round of applause from the grandstand when his nearside front tyre shed its tread just over the Melbourne brow on the 60th lap. Although travelling enormously fast, he pulled the car up at its pit with hardly a snake. Lucky it happened just there" – rather than on the way

down to Melbourne, as Boddy attests. Nor is Boddy alone. *The Autocar* reported that "von Brauchitsch's Mercedes came into sight, and, travelling at a terrific pace, went down towards Melbourne Corner. As he reached full speed..." Von Brauchitsch himself (interviewed by John Dugdale in *The Autocar*) said "I was just over the hill at my maximum speed and it threw me on to the grass."

To put it bluntly, there is only one mention of which lap this happened on (*The Light Car*) and you can see the conflict above about where it happened. Clearly it did happen between laps 60 and 65 because at lap 60 von Brauchitsch was 20 seconds behind Rosemeyer and five laps later that had become 30 seconds – so something had happened; and that is reinforced by the fact that on lap 60 Caracciola was 1m 20s behind von Brauchitsch and five laps later that had closed to 42 seconds – so yes, something happened: the tyre burst.

71. *The Motor*
72. Which leads to a strange mystery. Boddy wrote: "Five laps later [meaning lap 75] Rosemeyer was in front by a mere 0.8 of a second but Caracciola was nearly 56 seconds away [in third]. Rosemeyer had stopped, you see, quite by routine. The excitement was indescribable. Rear tyres were changed once more amid yells from the mechanics and Rosemeyer lifted his goggles and looked desperately back. But he left ahead of Brauchitsch." The mystery is that Rosemeyer pitted, as we have seen, on lap 62 and there is no record of him pitting again at all. How then did von Brauchitsch suddenly close to 0.8 of a second? The Official Bulletin did not give the positions at lap 75 but *The Sporting Life* did:

Rosemeyer	averaging 82.84mph
von Brauchitsch	at 0.8s
Caracciola	at 56s
Müller	at 3m 30.6s
Hasse	at 7m 55s
Bira	no time

It seems inconceivable that von Brauchitsch could have closed to within that 0.8 – creating a tense, tumultuous final five laps – and yet *The Autocar, The Light Car* and *The Sporting Life* make no mention of it at all. Rather, *The Autocar* wrote: "Von Brauchitsch drove a terrific race. He could just not catch the Auto Union and for the last few rounds gained nothing on his rival." *The Light Car* wrote: "Brauchitsch's unfortunate extra stop when his front tyre peeled made all the difference between a close finish and the other thing; thus, sincere as the spectators were in their admiration of the magnificent driving of the Germans, they cannot be said to have shown hysterical excitement when Rosemeyer took the checkered [sic] flag 37⁴/₅s before the arrival of Brauchitsch." Wisdom wrote: "Mays went out with brake trouble near Melbourne

Corner after a hectic moment when he had completed 51 laps. Otherwise there was little of incident to the end."

73. Sebastian op. cit.
74. Von Brauchitsch op. cit.
75. Boddy in *Motor Sport*
76. The received wisdom is that, and I quote Doug Nye's *The British Grand Prix 1926–1976*: "After the regulation 15 minutes had elapsed [from Rosemeyer crossing the line] the remaining runners were 'flagged off' which meant that 'Bira' – sixth on the road and leading the English-based contingent – was too far behind even to be classified as a finisher!" *The Light Car* pointed out that the Donington regulations said: "A white flag will be displayed at the pits after the fifth car has finished, or not later than 15 mins after the winner has crossed the line, to indicate the finish of the race."

This explains why Bira appears in the results as having covered 78 laps, which on the face of it isn't a total chasm away from Rosemeyer: two laps were six miles. What the result *really* means is that Rosemeyer finished, Bira continued *for another 15 minutes* and at the end of that had still only covered 78 laps. If we compute a Bira lap at two and a half minutes, he *really* finished approximately eight laps (24 miles) behind Rosemeyer.

It also explains why Bira's time is given as 3 hours 13 minutes and 49^3/5 of a second, which again on the face of it puts him within 15 minutes of Rosemeyer's 3 hours 1 minute 2^1/5 seconds. It doesn't of course. It means Bira took 3h 13m 49^3/5s to cover 78 laps – and since he wouldn't be able to cover a further lap before the 15 minutes elapsed, they flagged him off. Ditto Howe, Dobson and Hanson.

None of this alters the fact the organisers decided that Bira, Howe, Dobson and Hanson were classified sixth, seventh, eighth and ninth.

77. *The Sporting Life*
78. Boddy in *Motor Sport*
79. *Rosemeyer!* op. cit. That this happened on the evening after the race must mean that Rosemeyer returned to London and proceeded to Weybridge, where Petre was in hospital. Presumably he'd known she was in hospital – she'd been there before he even arrived in England – so a dinner together was out of the question. It seem strange he didn't tell Elly before.

Chapter 4: Life – and death

1. *The Derby Evening Telegraph*
2. Denis Jenkinson, *Porsche Past and Present* (gb)
3. This is the only mention I have come across of such a drastic suggestion. I don't doubt that Neubauer was alarmed and concerned at the notion of one of his racing cars hitting spectators at well over 100 mph ... but withdraw? We can never know now.
4. Roland King-Farlow was an eminent motor racing official and historian.

5. Lang op. cit.
6. *The Autocar.* The mention of a television van is intriguing because television itself was in its infancy, very few people had sets, and so did the BBC really send a van? (It must have been the BBC because they were the only broadcasters in Britain!) Today the BBC point out that the first OB (outside broadcast) was the Coronation on 12 May 1937, but they're not sure if that was radio or television. The probability is that it was TV since radio commentaries on, at least, Test matches had been going on during the 1930s, and wouldn't they count as outside broadcasts? It means that by Autumn 1938 a television van may well have been despatched to Donington.
7. Chula op. cit.
8. The Emsland, around the River Ems, is near the Dutch border.
9. Rangsdorf, an aerodrome far to the south of Berlin.
10. Bigalke is a mystery. In the 1938 Donington programme his entry is:

LURICH BIGALKE. *The last and least-known member of the Auto Union outfit. Has never yet driven for them.*

In Chapter Six there is a fuller description of him. What seems clear is that Lurich is a simple misprint for Ulrich – *The Motor* styled him Ulrich in 1938, and Nixon refers to him as Ulli, an obvious contraction of Ulrich. However, if he ever made films, or what kind of films, is something I haven't been able to penetrate. All that I have discovered is that he "takes films". *(The Motor)*

11. *The Autocar*
12. *Racing the Silver Arrows*
13. Chula op. cit.
14. Caracciola op. cit.
15. *The Land Speed Record* by Peter J.R. Holthusen (Guild Publishing)
16. *The Rise and Fall of the Third Reich* by William L. Shirer (Pan)
17. Chula op. cit.
18. Shirer op. cit.
19. *The Racing Car* op. cit.
20. *Racing the Silver Arrows*
21. Caracciola op. cit.
22. Shirer op. cit.
23. *Racing the Silver Arrows* op. cit.
24. Chula op. cit.
25. *Racing the Silver Arrows*
26. *The German Grand Prix*
27. *Racing the Silver Arrows*
28. Ken Purdy in the Omnibus of Speed (Stanley Paul), itself a compilation book. Purdy's words had originally appeared in *Time* magazine in 1954.
29. Neubauer in *Speed Was My Life*
30. ibid.
31. ibid.

32. ibid.
33. England had played Germany at football in Berlin in May and some of the England players observed protocol and gave the Nazi salute before the match. It was very controversial then and remained so: some of the players were still agonising over the rights and wrongs decades later.
34. Chula op. cit. I don't dispute this account but I wonder about it. There's a temptation for *us* subconsciously to make caricatures of *them* and read into what they said and did what subconsciously we wanted them to say and do. It may be that Huhnlein, speaking of course in German and himself caught in a hard place, tried to smooth the impact of Seaman winning without descending to the absurdity of pretending Seaman hadn't really won. It may be Huhnlein did descend. Nazis were certainly capable of it and, with Hitler watching from a distance, woe betide those who weren't prepared to descend. It's only a thought which I introduce on behalf of that strange creed (which the British would so soon be fighting to preserve apart from co-incidentally preserving themselves): fair play.
35. Caracciola op. cit.
36. Neubauer op. cit.
37. *Racing the Silver Arrows*
38. Chula op. cit
39. ibid.
40. Shirer op. cit.
41. *Racing the Silver Arrows*
42. Chula op. cit.
43. *Racing the Silver Arrows*

Chapter 5: Each dangerous day

1. *Racing The Silver Arrows*
2. Caracciola op. cit.
3. Chula op. cit. *Dick Seaman Racing Motorist*
4. Nixon: op. cit.
5. Chula op. cit.
6. Nixon op. cit.
7. *Berlin Diary* by William L. Shirer (Hamish Hamilton)
8. ibid.
9. Chula op. cit.
10. A station in central Berlin which, when the Wall went up in 1961, became the only overground rail link between the two halves of the city. The station itself was heavily partitioned and westerners saying their farewells to loved ones who had to remain in the East did so in a room which became known as the Hall of Tears.
11. Sebastian op. cit.
12. Lang op. cit.
13. Neubauer op. cit.
14. ibid

15. *Failure of a Mission* by the Right Hon. Sir Nevile Henderson (Readers Union Limited).
16. Lang op. cit.
17. ibid.
18. ibid.
19. ibid
20. ibid. There are obvious difficulties with the timetables of Neubauer and Lang, which seem to conflict. We know from Neubauer's diary that he left Stuttgart for Paris on Friday 23 September and continued to London the following day. This is at complete variance with Lang, who wrote in his life story that "we left Stuttgart on September 24" – which, if true, means he couldn't have hoped to meet Neubauer in Paris *unless Neubauer intended to remain in Paris for a whole day until Lang arrived.* Perhaps Neubauer did. However, memories are deceptive instruments and, I suspect, Lang is at fault.
21. ibid.
22. ibid.
23. Von Brauchitsch op. cit. Incidentally it is important to understand that Manfred von Brauchitsch's book from which I have taken so many extracts – *Ohne Kampf Kein Sieg (No Victory Without Struggle)* – was written when he had moved to East Germany and was published by the *Verlag der Nation* company there. East Germany was rigidly communist, of course, and exercised state censorship so everything in print was approved. Moreover the East German government insisted upon an unending and almost pathological hatred of anything Nazi. This may explain why the tenor of what von Brauchitsch says is framed in that reference.
24. Chula op. cit.
25. *Racing The Silver Arrows*
26. Caracciola op. cit.

Tuesday, 27 September
1. Sebastian op. cit.
2. *The Leicester Mercury*
3. *The Shell Guide to Britain*
4. ibid
5. Henderson: *Failure of a Mission*
6. Sebastian op. cit.
7. Lang op. cit.
8. *The Motor*
9. *Rise and Fall of the Third Reich*
10. Quoted in Chula's *Dick Seaman*
11. Neubauer op. cit.
12. Nottingham Civic Society
13. Von Brauchitsch op. cit.
14. *Racing the Silver Arrows*

15. Sebastian op. cit.
16. Henderson op. cit.
17. *Berlin Diary*
18. *Rise and Fall of the Third Reich*
19. *Hitler, a Study in Tyranny* by Alan Bullock (Pelican)
20. Henderson op. cit.

Wednesday, 28 September

 1. Henderson op. cit.
 2. Bullock op. cit.
 3. ibid.
 4. Neubauer op. cit.
 5. Von Brauchitsch op. cit.
 6. Henderson op. cit.
 7. Shirer: *Rise and Fall of the Third Reich*
 8. ibid.
 9. Neubauer op. cit. The perils of trying to reconstruct history are amply illustrated by Hermann Lang's account of these days in England in his autobiography.

"As always, we stayed at the Black Boy Hotel. Although the German radio news was calming, the information in the British papers was quite the opposite, and this caused us some disquiet. We did not feel quite right, although the staff and other hotel inhabitants were most pleasant. Next morning Dietrich, the Continental Tyres expert, told us something that made us more than thoughtful. Having risen early, he had seen that gas masks were being distributed to the hotel staff. 'I'm buzzing off,' he added, 'you can race here as much as you like, but I don't want to spend the rest of my life behind barbed wire!' The English papers became more and more explicit. Six hours after the breaking off of diplomatic relations, the guns would speak, so they said. That was hardly long enough for us to get home, and our spirits sank when faced with such news. We did not feel like practising, this being made even worse by the terrible rain. Yet the German news was still calm, and *every evening* [Author's italics] I used to drive out of town to listen to the German news and inform our little group.

"On the second evening, we went to bed early and suddenly there was thunderous knocking at the door. Neubauer was outside, gasping for breath, hardly able to breathe. Then he managed to get it out, 'Lang, things are getting serious, pack immediately, we leave at dawn tomorrow! The private cars will form one column, the lorries another. The Embassy has just told us to leave for home, even if the cars have to be left behind.' Off he went from door to door, to wake up everyone and to repeat his orders because most of us had retired for the night. The mechanics at Castle Donington had also been given instructions by telephone to leave next morning. The leaders of the lorry column had further been secretly instructed to burst the fuel tanks of the lorries and burn the whole outfit if they were stopped. No more sleep for us that night, and at dawn we left for Harwich."

To rationalise all this and reconcile it with the known facts is impossible. That a member of the team – Dietrich – would depart on his own and of his own volition seems highly unlikely. We know that the drivers arrived at the Black Boy on the Tuesday evening and left on the Wednesday morning: one night. Yet somehow Lang remembered driving out of Nottingham *each evening* to listen to the German news. And why would he drive out of Nottingham to listen? His account of Neubauer waking them *on the second evening* is not only at variance with Neubauer's account but all the other evidence, as is his account of leaving at dawn. Lang is dead now and cannot defend himself. On balance I believe what he wrote was a product of the distortion of memory. Because the events were genuinely dramatic he remembered great drama and over time convinced himself it was true.

10. Henderson op. cit.
11. Von Brauchitsch wrote: "Out of mistrust of the English, there was a big can of special petrol on each lorry. Our racing cars could very well have been the first fiery signal for the war. Our racing cars of all cars..."
12. Von Brauchitsch op. cit.
13. *Rise and Fall of the Third Reich*
14. Erica Seaman quoted in *Racing the Silver Arrows*
15. Lang op. cit.
16. Neubauer op. cit.

Thursday, 29 September
1. Sebastian op. cit.
2. Lang op. cit.

Friday, 30 September
1. *The Light Car*

Chapter 6: Crisis
1. Chula
2. ibid.
3. *Racing the Silver Arrows*
4. Lang op. cit.
5. *Nuvolari* by Count Giovanni Lurani (Cassell & Co. Ltd)
6. Ibid.
7. Von Brauchitsch op. cit
8. Lang op. cit.
9. *The Sporting Life*
10. ibid.
11. Connell remembers that he and a friend, Mort Morris Goodall, "once went out and practiced golf" during a grand prix meeting.

12. *The Sporting Life*. M. H. Evans, Head of Corporate Heritage at Rolls-Royce, adds some intriguing dimensions to this story, and some invaluable background.

"Nothing is impossible but I am unaware of Rolls-Royce being asked to remake carburettor parts for the Auto Union.

"The name Hives is absolutely right, although his initials were E.W. – not H. Ernest Hives worked for Rolls even before Rolls met Royce. He returned to Rolls-Royce as a chassis tester in 1908. Having established the brilliant Experimental Department he became General Manager in 1936 and a Director in the following year. It would have almost certainly been he and he alone who would have authorised an oddball exercise such as helping Auto Union – so the main factors seem right.

"Memories remained then of the First World War and Mercedes or Daimler Benz aero engines. I would find the story hard to believe had it been suggested that Hives helped them – but he might have helped Auto Union in the hope they would beat Mercedes. All this is conjecture, however.

"In the early '60s when I first joined the company I shot with Tommy Fisher, then retired, who had been one of the best engine and gearbox men in the 'Experi' department. Back in the 1930s Ernest Hives would send him as the 'R' Engine specialist to support *Miss England* World Water Speed Record attempts. It was Tommy who told me about Chris Staniland and a car he called the 'Multi Union'.

"I queried that at the time but my reading of it was that Tom felt Staniland had given the car that name with tongue-in-cheek. It was, I think, a mongrel in terms of origin and a "one off." Tom told me that Staniland (a test pilot and therefore known to us) had rung Hives and appealed for help. Hives had sent Tom out to Donington to do what he could. Tom showed me a picture of himself with overalls on and head beneath the bonnet. The car was not a Mercedes or Auto-Union but had a radiator grille appropriate to the late 1930s. Tom did say it all came to nothing, but not why. I think carburation was the problem but can no longer be certain."

Interestingly, the issue of *The Motor* which carried the evocative Getting Personal column by 'Grande Vitesse' – 25 October – had a photograph above the column with this caption: "Mountaineers. The field swoops up the banking on the Members' Turn in the first lap of the recent Mountain Championship. In the lead is the winner, Raymond Mays (No. 4, 1,980 cc ERA), who led from start to finish, piled up a good lead and then eased off to win at 80.39 mph from Staniland's Multi Union (seen behind Mays)."

The official company biography of Hives includes this: "When the Rolls-Royce company was but two years old, in 1908, Mr Ernest Walter Hives joined the staff, being then closely associated with the late Sir Henry Royce. By 1912 he was a prominent personality in the Rolls-Royce Experimental Department, subsequently becoming Manager, a position he retained for over twenty years. He was thus intimately connected with development of both Rolls-Royce cars and aero-engines.

"He was responsible for the development of the record-breaking Schneider Trophy engines which were later fitted to Sir Malcolm Campbell's *Blue-bird.*

"In 1936 he became Works General Manager and in the following year he was appointed a Director. This promotion came at a time when aero-engine production was being slowly expanded; with characteristic energy he undertook the building of a new factory at Crewe where Rolls-Royce Merlin was produced in larger numbers than ever before. This boost to production proved to be insufficient to meet the demand for the Merlin engine and a Government factory was then built at Glasgow, the future Lord Hives again being the driving force behind the extremely rapid completion of this enterprise."

13. *Motor Sport*
14. Sebastian
15. Cuddon-Fletcher appears in every reference I have been able to find with no first name, just the initial A. This holds true, incidentally, for the race programme itself. It may be a charming period piece to have a driver in a Grand Prix and no first name, but somehow it irritated me. Ian Connell couldn't help – he couldn't remember him at all! Connell lent me William Boddy's *Motor Sport History of Donington* and sure enough there he was, A. Cuddon-Fletcher. Nigel Roebuck suggested contacting the British Racing Drivers' Club, saying "he must have been a member." Kate Scott of the BRDC looked up their files and found Cuddon-Fletcher, who was elected a member in 1938 – but initial R., not A. Ms Scott pointed out that this could easily have been a typing error (and an easily understandable error) when their extensive archives were re-done some years ago. She promised to ask around, did ask instantly and was recommended to contact historian Doug Nye. She rang him, he *knew* and she rang me back with the glad tidings inside, I suppose, two minutes. It may not be much in terms of the scope of this book or the scale of the Second World War but, ladies and gentlemen, may I present to you at last *Andrew* Cuddon-Fletcher.

Chapter 7: High noon

There are many obvious difficulties with Alfred Neubauer's account of the race. Officials were allowed to push Seaman and could Neubauer really see the Hairpin from the pits?

Equally there are instructive differences in the accounts of Hasse's crash – instructive because they show how easy it was to make mistakes in an era before television and when, perhaps, talking to drivers afterwards was not done. By a time-defeating paradox, we have a perfect picture now of the crash because film of it is available on video.

The Autocar said that Hasse was flung out "as it landed." *The Sporting Life* said that Hasse was "catapulted from his car into the crowd. He landed without a scratch and hastened to the adjacent marquee for refreshment!" *The Motor* said Hasse "tried hard to impress on the officials that something should be done about the oil." *The Light Car* more accurately said that Hasse "missed by a foot a little hut in the old paddock (where Mrs Craner looked up in time to see him hurtling by the window) and crashed into the protecting ditch and bank. A cheer went up when he scrambled out – unhurt." *Motor Sport* said that Hasse "was unhurt and, they say, at once leapt the fencing and shook off the ambulance men." The *Nottingham Evening Post* said that "horrified spectators saw the driver's body hurled out of the cockpit and flung over a bank."

1. *The Motor*
2. *The Autocar*
3. Connell relates a painful tale to illustrate how exposed the clothing of the time left the drivers. "I think it was at Albi [a street circuit in the southern French town]. There was a pretty sharp corner at one point and I was driving in an open shirt and a wasp went down inside it. It was stinging me. So there was I, arriving at this corner to find the person in front losing control of their car and blocking the way. I had to go into the escape road *and* beating my chest with one hand to try and kill the wasp. I stalled the engine doing this. The ambulance came rushing out wondering what the hell I was doing beating my chest! Then they started treating my wasp stings…"
4. *Nottingham Evening Post*
5. *The Motor*
6. Lang
7. *The Motor*
8. *The Autocar*
9. *Motor Sport*
10. *The Autocar*
11. This may have been fine for the German factory cars but everyone else had to be more circumspect about crashing. "As a rule, one took care not to have collisions," Ian Connell says, "because the car usually belonged to one's-self and it was expensive repairing them. Not like nowadays: you blow up an engine and just stick another one in. I don't think I ever hit anyone else and I didn't have an awful lot of accidents. Mind you, I did manage to go down a ravine backwards at Spa…"
12. *The Light Car*
13. *The Autocar*
14. *The Light Car*
15. *The Autocar*
16. ibid.
17. Sebastian op. cit.
18. *Motor Sport*
19. Sebastian op. cit.
20. *Motor Sport*

21. *The Motor*
22. ibid.
23. *The Light Car*
24. ibid.
25. *The Motor*
26. *The Light Car*
27. *The Motor*
28. On this matter of Nuvolari letting the car go where it would, Rob Walker relates a tale about Luigi Chinetti, who had become the sole Ferrari agent in North America. After the war a race for sports cars was held somewhere in the south of France on a circuit using normal roads. Chinetti drove a Ferrari and was "flat out going down one of these heavenly French 'straights' with poplar trees either side. That Ferrari must have done 140 miles an hour, I suppose. A woman pushed a pram with a baby in it across the road directly in front of him. He jammed on his brakes and spun about six times. After the race I asked him how he didn't go off the road and he said: 'when you're spinning, never fight it. Let the car go its own way and it'll stay on its axis.'"

    I mentioned to Walker that there is a certain unanimity about how great Nuvolari was. "Enzo Ferrari always said, whenever he was asked about the best driver, that it was a stupid question because, every decade, things are completely different. But, he said, if you have to press me I'd say that the two best drivers have been Nuvolari and Stirling Moss. The reason I say this is that they could drive any car faster than anybody else."
29. ibid.
30. Neubauer op. cit.
31. *Motor Sport*
32. This is the only example I have ever found of the proper use of the word cushion i.e. something to support your back. Usually in motor sport it means gaining a big advantage over the driver behind you – say, enough to make a pit stop and still lead.
33. *The Motor*
34. *Motor Sport*
35. *The Light Car*
36. *The Autocar*
37. Lang op. cit.
38. *The Sporting Life*
39. *Motor Sport*
40. I'm indebted to Doug Nye for a lovely anecdote about the huge garland given to Nuvolari. In its flora and fauna were roses and evidently some of these fell to the ground. A spectator from Derbyshire picked them up, took them home and planted them. They grew. When the Donington Grand Prix Museum was opened in the early 1970s a lady appeared with some cuttings and explained they were the direct descendants of those on Nuvolari's garland...

In fact as the 60th anniversary of the 1938 race approached, the Museum tried to unravel the whole episode. They contacted the *Derby Evening Telegraph* for help and that newspaper's Bygones column carried a large picture of Nuvolari with a schoolboy wearing a cap gazing in admiration at him. Bygones wrote: "Rumour has it that the young schoolboy picked up a rose which fell from the winner's garland and took it home to his mother. She planted it in their cottage garden and it grew into a healthy plant which climbed up the cottage wall. Donington Park's management have asked Bygones to help trace that young racing fan and the whereabouts of the cottage." Alas, no information – and no former schoolboy – appeared.

Incidentally, the anniversary of Nuvolari's victory was marked by a commemorative luncheon in the Senna-Fangio Conference Centre at the Donington Museum on 22 October 1998. The menu was Italian, from zuppa di zucca con parmigiani E prezzemolo (pumpkin soup with parmsean and parsley) for starters to formaggi Italiani (Italian cheese) to finish – with Italian wine and mineral water to wash it all down, of course. There was a nice touch for the main course: Donington scaloppa di Cervo con funghi E polenta (Loin of Donington venison with mushrooms and polenta).

The mayor of Nuvolari's home town, Mantua, wrote to Tom Wheatcroft thanking him for holding the commemoration and included these words: "A man who conquered the heart of all his fans, even for the remarkable simplicity that remain [in him] despite his unstoppable victorious career and the humbleness that contributed to the Nuvolari mythology taking root – which still exists today amongst new generations [of his fans]."

41. Lurani op. cit.
42. *Motor Sport*
43. ibid.
44. Lurani op. cit.
45. My neighbours, who are German and help enormously in translation (and assorted information), were openly amused at my failure to grasp how Neubauer wrote down time. For example the symbol for half followed by the figure 11 – meaning 10.30, namely half before eleven. They insisted this was logical and made as much sense as writing 10.30.
46. Jenkinson, *Porsche Past and Present* (gb)
47. Monkhouse

Chapter 8: The day before yesterday
1. Chula op. cit.
2. ibid.
3. Neubauer op. cit.
4. ibid.
5. Lang op. cit.
6. Neubauer op. cit.

Bibliography

Beaumont, Charles and William F. Nolan *Omnibus of Speed* Stanley Paul, London 1961

Beihorn, Elly Rosemeyer and Chris Nixon, *Rosemeyer! A new biography* Transport Bookman Publications, Isleworth 1989.

Birabongse, Prince, *Bits and Pieces*, G.T. Foulis and Co, London 1943.

Brauchitsch, Manfred von, *Ohne Kampf kein Sieg*, Verlag der Nation, Berlin.

Bullock, Alan, *Hitler, a study in tyranny*, Pelican, Harmondsworth 1962

Caracciola, Rudolf, *A Racing Driver's World*, Motoraces Book Club, Cassell, London 1963.

Chakrabongse, Prince, *Dick Seaman Racing Motorist*, G.T. Foulis and Co, London 1941.

Clutton, C., Posthumus, C. and Jenkinson, D., *The Racing Car*, B.T. Batsford Ltd, London 1962.

Fern, David, *The Donington Grands Prix*, Donington International Collection 1993.

Frankenberg, Richard von, *Die grossen Fahrer von einst*, Motorbuch Verlag, Stuttgart 1966

Henderson, The Right Hon. Sir Nevile, *Failure of a Mission*, Readers Union Limited, London 1941.

Holthusen, Peter J. R., *The Land Speed Record*, Guild Publishing, London 1986.

Jenkinson, Denis, *Porsche Past and Present*, gb.

Lang, Hermann, *Grand Prix driver*, G.T. Foulis and Co. Ltd 1953.

Lurani, Count Giovanni, *Nuvolari*, Cassell, London 1959.

Monkhouse, George, *Grand Prix Racing*, G. T. Foulis and Co Ltd, London 1950.

Neubauer, Alfred, *Speed Was My Life*, Barrie and Rockcliff, London 1960.

Nixon, Chris, *Racing the Silver Arrows,* Osprey, London, 1986.

Nye, Doug, *The British Grand Prix 1926–1976*, B.T. Batsford Ltd, London 1977.

Sebastian, Ludwig, *Hinter Drohnenden Motoren*, EKZ-Einband 1958.

Shirer, William, *Berlin Diary*, Hamish Hamilton, London 1941.

Shirer, William, *The Rise and Fall of the Third Reich*, Pan, London 1971.

Taruffi, Piero, *Works Driver*, Temple Press Books, London 1964.

Wilkinson, Wilkie with Chris Jones, *'Wilkie', The Motor Racing Legend,* Nelson and Saunders.

Index